Managing within
Networks

Managing within Networks

Adding Value to Public Organizations

Robert Agranoff

Georgetown University Press
Washington, D.C.

As of January 1, 2007, 13-digit ISBN numbers will replace the current 10-digit system.
Paperback: 978-1-58901-154-0
Cloth: 1-58901-154-6

Georgetown University Press, Washington, D.C.

Portions of chapter 6 first appeared in the grant report *Leveraging Networks: A
Guide for Public Managers Working across Organizations,* Washington, D.C.: IBM
Center for the Business of Government, 2003. Reprinted in *Collaboration: Using
Networks and Partnerships,* Lanham, MD: Rowman & Littlefield, 2004.

Library of Congress Cataloging-in-Publication Data

Agranoff, Robert.
  Managing within networks: adding value to public organizations / Robert Agranoff.
    p. cm. — (Public management and change series)
  Includes bibliographical references and index.
  ISBN-13: 978-1-58901-154-0 (alk. paper)
  ISBN-10: 1-58901-154-6 (alk. paper)
    1. Public administration—United States.   2. Interorganizational relations—
United States.   I. Title.

  JK421.A56 2007
  351.73—dc22   2006031171

∞This book is printed on acid-free paper meeting the requirements of the American
National Standard for Permanence in Paper for Printed Library Materials.

14 13 12 11 10 09 08 07   9 8 7 6 5 4 3 2
First printing

Printed in the United States of America

Contents

TABLES AND FIGURES

TABLES

FIGURES

PREFACE

THE TERM "NETWORK" is widely used these days, and we can ordinarily decipher from the context what type of network is meant. We sometimes use a modifier, like "broadcast network" or "network of friends," because in this age of the network there are so many different kinds of networks. Those of us studying the emergent entities that involve public organizations, both governmental and nongovernmental, note that their operatives increasingly engage in cross-organization networks. As a result, these networks deserve to be profiled and understood in the same way that bureaucratic and nonprofit voluntary organizations have been. That is the mission of this work.

I call these networks "public management networks" (PMNs) because they primarily involve officials at the administrator/specialist level in federal government, state government, metropolitan-level government, local government, and nongovernmental organizations (for-profit and nonprofit). These officials exchange information, manage knowledge, and address problems of mutual concern. These public entities come together to deal with problems that they cannot solve alone. They use the network or PMN form of organized entity because it provides the flexibility and stability needed while partners' home organizations, where they spend the majority of their time, remain largely intact and do most of the work. It is important to look into these networks since more and more public organizations are choosing the network form for collaboration.

As the title suggests, the distinguishing feature of this volume is the focused look inside the PMN. Many works talk about the importance of networks; considerably fewer look at how they operate and are managed, the results that their work accrues, or the impact on the public organizations from which they are drawn. Using an inductive qualitative methodology, I look deeply into the fourteen PMNs we study here and provide additional academic and practical information. Whereas there were multiple data sources, the primary one—the basis for most tables and illustrative quotes—was confidential discussions with network participants. The aim is to broaden understanding in order to improve action.

The book is designed for a broad audience of students, practitioners, and academic researchers. For many students, it can provide an introduction to these emergent entities, how they work at the boundaries of organizations, and how nettlesome public problems are approached. The book would be useful in a wide range of courses, including political science, public administration, public policy, urban studies, and intergovernmental relations. To practitioners in transportation, community development, environmental protection, economic development, information systems, communications, and numerous other public policy fields, the book can serve as a guide to their work in PMNs. It will aid them in their understanding of what to expect in practice. For the academic research community, the book develops insights into the internal workings of these organized entities. It is dedicated to the idea that scholars must go beyond theoretical assertions about the importance of networks, and investigate their functioning and results as well.

As one of the first attempts to look at the internal workings of networks, there were some aspects of network management that had to be set aside. Some examples include a full treatment of network power, more extensive process treatment of how agreements are reached, key social network interaction flows, and operational rules of networks that may be analytical parallels of trust. These exclusions will no doubt disappoint some network researchers, inasmuch as these arenas are topics that have been explored elsewhere. The decision to focus on decision type, structure, knowledge management, value-adding, and the role of networks vis-à-vis government precluded other important arenas. Moreover, the grounded theory methodology, adapted and focused by topics within the core literature as in the social sciences, allows only limited emergence of some topics from the data.

Many acknowledgements are due to those involved in the development of this book. At the top of the list are Mark Abramson and John Kamensky of the IBM Endowment for the Business of Government, who commissioned and reviewed some of the early work on this project, and whose grant supported the research travel. Also at the top of the list are Beryl Radin of American University, series editor; and Gail Grella, Georgetown University Press editor, who encouraged this project and provided feedback from start to finish. Michael McGuire read all of the first draft manuscript and provided many conceptual and detailed suggestions, and served as a content/presentation consultant throughout. Mete Yildiz helped with the initial sampling, the ICT knowledge management portions of the study, and participated in part of the field research in Indiana and Iowa. Others who read parts of the manuscript and provided feedback at various stages include Francis Berry, Manuel Villoria, Charles Wise, Christine Reed, and Dale Krane. Several important suggestions also came from the anonymous reviewers commissioned by Georgetown Press. My PMN principal contacts also deserve mention: Joe Coram, Enhanced Data;

Tom Kane, Des Moines Metro; John Bond and Jacqueline Niedes, Indiana Economic Development; Don Koverman, Indiana Rural Council; Tami Fujinaka, Iowa Communications; Beth Danowsky, Iowa Enterprise; Kevin Kane, Iowa Geographic; Rodney Verhoff and Glen Johnson, Lower Platte; Charlotte Narjes, Partnership for Rural Nebraska; Steven Grossman, Small Communities; Anthony Sasson, Darby; Clifford Kumm, USDA/Nebraska; Harold Tull, Kentuckiana Agency; and Jim Hammond and the late Costa Miller, 317 Group. All were helpful during my intrusion into their and their colleagues' spaces, and were giving of their time at all stages of the research. Any errors in interpretation of what they or their colleagues relayed to me are, of course, my responsibility. Finally, a huge thanks goes out to Patricia Withered, faculty assistant at Indiana University, who produced several versions of the manuscript, including preparation of the tables and figures that contained a great deal of text. She deserves the final thanks for making it all work.

Abbreviations

Arc of Indiana	Indiana Association for Retarded Citizens
CARI	Center for Applied Rural Innovation, University of Nebraska
CDBG	Community Development Block Grants
DAS	Department of Administrative Services
DDARS	Indiana FSSA, Division of Developmental Disabilities, Aging, and Rehabilitative Services
DEM	Department of Environmental Management
DHHS	Department of Health and Human Services
DHS	Iowa Department of Human Services
DNR	Iowa Department of Natural Resources
DOC	Indiana Department of Commerce
DPHO	Department of Public Health Operations
EPA	Environmental Protection Agency
FEMA	Federal Emergency Management Agency
FHWA	Federal Highway Administration
FSSA	Indiana Family and Social Services Administration
GIS	geographic information systems
HUD	Housing and Urban Development
ICT	information and communications technology
IDOT	Iowa Department of Transportation
IGM	intergovernmental management
IGR	intergovernmental relations
IIDC	Indiana Institute on Disability and Community
INARF	Indiana Association of Rehabilitation Facilities
INDOT	Indiana Department of Transportation
IG	intergovernmental

IO	information officer
IPTV	Iowa Public Television
ISU	Iowa State University
ITTC	Iowa Telecommunications and Technology Commission
KM	knowledge management
KTYTC	State of Kentucky, Transportation Cabinet
MPO	Metropolitan Planning Organization, under the U.S. Transportation Equity Act
MR/DD	mentally retarded/developmentally disabled
NCRS	Nebraska Conservation Resource Services
NDN	Nebraska Development Network
Nebraska DED	State of Nebraska, Department of Economic Development
NGO	nongovernmental organization
NRD	Natural Resource District
Ohio EPA	State of Ohio, Environmental Protection Agency
OWDA	Ohio Water Development Authority
PMN	public management network
POSDCORB	planning, organizing, staffing, directing, coordinating, reporting, and budgeting
RCAP	Rural Community Action Program
RDC	Research Development Commission
REA	Rural Electrification Administration/USDA
SBA	Small Business Administration
SBDC	Small Business Development Center
SCORE	Service Corps of Retired Executives
STP	strategic transportation plan
SWCD	Soil and Water Conservation District
SWOT	strengths, weaknesses, opportunities, threats
TIP	Transportation Improvement Program
TNC	The Nature Conservancy of Ohio
TTCC	Transportation Technical Coordinating Committee
UMTA/DOT	Urban Mass Transportation Administration/Department of Transportation
USDA/NRCS	U.S. Department of Agriculture/Natural Resources and Conservation Services

USDA/RD	U.S. Department of Agriculture/Rural Development
USDOT	U.S. Department of Transportation
USEDA	U.S. Economic Development Administration, Department of Commerce
USFWS	U.S. Fish and Wildlife Services
USGS	U.S. Geological Survey
USSBA	U.S. Small Business Administration

CHAPTER ONE

· · · · · · · · · · · ·

PUBLIC NETWORKS

The key is to get as many relevant interests that deal with small town water and wastewater to the table. Then we have to mutually explore potential solutions. Sometimes it is patently apparent, when all of the funders and programs are present, but often we have to search for new or adaptable solutions that are complex. They involve adaptable technologies, conflicting regulations, and intractable finance challenges. As a group of water-concerned organizations we then have to manage our way to a potentially positive outcome for the communities we serve.

THIS INITIAL RESPONSE from one of the principal contacts in this study underscores a core issue for those who work together in the public and nongovernmental organization sector. The interorganization network has become an important part of the managerial enterprise, but little is known about the structure of networks or how they are managed. Twenty-first-century management includes network management, and thus its process needs to be studied. This book is designed to introduce some basic concepts of managing within networks that involve federal, state, regional, and local government officials working with nonprofit and for-profit nongovernmental organizations. It looks intensively at fourteen such networks in the central states.

NETWORKS AND THE COLLABORATIVE ENTERPRISE

Today many things are connected through networks. Social networks keep friends, acquaintances, and their support systems together. Broadcasting networks include points of central production and transmission, along with local outlet stations that include their own means of reaching viewers and listeners. Networks of manufacturing supplies encompass many business organizations and involve chains that range from raw materials to component parts to finished products. The Internet links millions of end users by narrowcasting with transmission nodes called servers that travel through satellites, creating the possibility of person-to-person networking. Organizations—public and nonpublic—also network for public purposes, sharing information or matching services, or solving policy problems. Working in these increasingly important public networks has become part of the job of the public manager.

The aim of this book is to reach beyond the usual accounting for the growing significance of public networks. That has been done repeatedly (Agranoff and McGuire 2003a; Berry et al. 2004; Lipnack and Stamps 1993; Milward, Provan, and Else 1993; O'Toole 1997). This work looks more deeply into the how and what of organizing and managing networks, and takes a look at whether this managing makes a difference.

The perspectives to be shared are not those of the academic or consultant observer, but of the managers themselves as they work across the boundaries of their organizations. How do public administrators and nongovernmental organization (NGO) executives and specialists see their boundary-spanning roles? Do they think they manage differently in networks than they do in their home organizations? What results do they believe they accrue from participation in public networks? In what ways do these public networks change the roles of government? These questions are addressed empirically from the perspectives of those involved.

Just as the rise of industrial organization and the separation of ownership and control gave rise to the study and practice of organization management, the era of the network highlights the importance of understanding how people who work within them guide and steer them toward results. Public networks as defined here are collaborative structures that bring together representatives from public agencies and NGOs to address problems of common concern that accrue value to the manager/specialists, their participating organizations, and their networks. Klijn suggests that "networks facilitate interaction, decision-making, cooperation and learning, since they provide the resources to support these activities, such as recognizable interaction patterns, common rules, and organizational forms and sometimes even a common language" (2003a, 32). They are also described as bodies that connect "public policies with their strategic and institutionalized context: the network of public, semi-public, and private actors participating in certain policy fields" (Kickert, Klijn, and Koppenjan 1997, 1). How these tasks are accomplished and their connections are therefore central questions for analysis.

The broadly used term "network" needs to be further defined. We must find a term that fits the activity of cooperation or mutual action without making it so broad that it encompasses every human connection. "Cooperation" refers to jointly working with others, usually to help resolve a problem. It can be occasional or regular, and within, between, or outside of formal organizations. Here the interest is more focused on certain activities by individuals representing organizations working across their boundaries. Agranoff and McGuire have defined such collaborative processes as "the process of facilitating and operating in multiorganizational arrangements to solve problems that cannot be solved, or solved easily, by single organizations" (2003a, 4). In other words, the focus of the networks studied here goes beyond informal and intra-organizational networking among individuals. Here we include interorganizational, in this case intergovernmental, entities that emerge from interactions among formal organizations.

MAJOR THEMES OF THE BOOK

Delving into the concepts, methodology, examples, quotations, tables and data matrices, findings, and conclusions that compose this book should not be undertaken without the big picture in mind. Hopefully the supporting information will be absorbed, but at the same time the thematic overview to be presented will also be maintained. Bearing six points in mind should help academics, students, and practitioners alike maintain a sense of purpose.

First, however much the present may reflect the "era of the network," networks are by no means replacing hierarchies. In the book *The Age of the Network*, Lipnack and Stamps (1994) discuss the evolution of organized activities, from small groups to hierarchical organizations to large bureaucracies and, ultimately, to networks. They refer to the network as the signature form of the information age. But as each new era brings a shift from one dominant worldview to another, they form an overlay over the others. "The age of the network includes rather than replaces its predecessors" (63). Each of the discussants that shared information for this book was a representative of an organization, usually a large bureaucracy. While they related that an increasing amount of time is spent in collaboration and in bodies like public management networks (PMNs), no one expected their organization or agency to be phased out as a result of network activity. Indeed, with the exception of program specialists who spend considerable time making links with other agencies and a small corps of full-time boundary spanners, public administrators continue to do an overwhelming amount of their work within their organizations. As a well-known baseline essay on economic forms of organizing concludes, it is not markets or hierarchies or networks but markets, hierarchies, and networks (Powell 1990).

Second, networks are differentiated. Just as subsequent analysis will present a topography of collaborative vehicles, and therefore answer the perennial question "What is the difference between coordination and _____?" (fill in anything), this study maintains that there are differences between networks. A fourfold typology will be introduced. It does not represent pure types, but predominant modes. The case material will demonstrate some overlap. Also, one or two networks are in the slow process of moving from one category to another. Because these PMNs have different purposes, they operate somewhat differently and their outcomes will differ considerably. For example, it will become clear that while all networks explore and manage knowledge, only one type of network formally reaches actual policy- or program-related decisions. One cannot fairly assess the policy or program results of different kinds of networks that do not work in policy/program areas. It is therefore important to maintain a sense of network purpose.

Third, whereas networks are nonhierarchical and largely self-organizing (Weiner 1990), the process of structuring and operating does not automatically happen. The absence of clear lines of authority and mutual tasking does not mean that a sequence of actions and managerial actions do not ensue (Agranoff and McGuire 2001b; Kickert and Koppenjan 1997). Someone must guide the process, the work needs to be divided, courses of action need to be agreed to, agreements are carried out. Do these sound like management processes? Indeed they do. Just how different is network management from traditional management? If the processes are similar in name are they similar or different in substance? In the information era Drucker says that contrary to Fredrick W. Taylor one hundred years ago, "One does not 'manage' people. The task is to lead people" (2001, 81). The task here is to find out when, if, and how such leadership is different or similar.

Fourth, PMNs and all networks, for that matter, are more than distinctive forms of information-age organizing. To be sure, networks are employed to bridge organizational information gaps and asymmetries. Alter and Hage (1993) pointed out very early in their study of networks that networks not only provide opportunities to gain information as shared sources, but they also provide opportunities to transform information into new learning and adaptation opportunities, to develop additional competencies, and to engage in new joint efforts as a result of the mutual information processing. Therefore an explicit theme is to demonstrate how knowledge—both formal and informal—gleaned from interagency processes is managed and adapted to solutions.

Fifth, networks do make a difference. The PMNs studied here clearly added important value to the public undertaking that undoubtedly would not have otherwise occurred. The question is, do they add value in the same way that single organizations do? To some extent they do, similarly pooling information and making necessary adjustments across boundaries of organizations rather than departments. In other respects, networks add value in very different ways. For example, as O'Toole (1997) suggests, they tackle the wicked policy problems that cut across boundaries of agencies and programs, deal with ambitious policy goals in contexts of dispersed power, face political demands for inclusion and broader influence, and deal with second-order effects (such as unemployment/education and job training), and layers of mandates from federal and state governments. These issues are normally beyond the domain of the single organization and thus are part of the distinctive turf of networks. The degree to which they achieve these values and increase the ability to reach solutions is thus an important network theme.

Sixth, and finally, networks do change the way public managers work, but perhaps not as dramatically as is often assumed. They do push managers into working at the boundaries of the state, not only with other public agencies but with NGOs of all types. PMNs bring to the table profit-oriented enterprises and nonprofit organizations to discuss public issues and many of them carry out public programs by working with public agencies as contractors or grant-ees, or through some other arrangement. To some, this means that the employ-ment of networks, including those of implementation, has led to minimization of the role of governmental actors. They feel that government has lost its capacity to govern, losing such power to self-organizing interorganizational networks (Rhodes 1997) that engage in "co-managing, co-steering, and co-guidance" (Kooiman 1993, 6). To others such as Peters, "Governments continue to play a major, and perhaps still dominant, role in governance, and . . . there has been a substantial influence of networks . . . for some time " (2000, 30). Because this book focuses on the work of the fourteen PMNs, the degree to which managers representing agencies are influenced, are made to change pro-gram decisions, and how they make policy adaptations within networks are im-portant lines of inquiry. In general, this work suggests the importance of collaborative management activities for public managers, but such work re-mains at the margins or boundaries of the public agency, with its legal and related resources.

SOCIAL NETWORKS VERSUS ORGANIZATIONAL NETWORKS

There is a rich tradition of studies on informal networks, or what are some-times called "social networks." While related, they lie largely outside of this study of formal interorganization activity. As Laumann, Galaskiewicz, and Marsden define it, a social network involves "a set of nodes (e.g., persons, or-ganizations) linked by a set of social relationships (e.g., friendship, transfer of funds, overlapping membership) of a specific type" (1978, 45–48). Social net-works in this sense refer to patterns of recurring linkages, either inside or out-side of organizations. As Nohria suggests, "The premise that organizations are networks of recurring relationships applies to organizations at any level of analysis—small and large groups, subunits of organizations, entire organizations, regions, industries, national economies and even the organiza-tion of the world system" (1992, 4). In this respect, Castells suggests that this is the age of the network, where networked social relationships are taking the place of other intermediate organizations:

Yet identity is becoming the main, and sometimes the only, source of meaning in a historical period characterized by widespread destructuring of organizations, delegitimation of institutions, fading away of major social movements, and ephemeral cultural expressions. People increasingly organize their meaning not around what they do but on the basis of what they are, or believe they are. Meanwhile, on the other hand, global networks of instrumental exchanges selectively switch on and off individuals, groups, regions, and even countries, according to their relevance in fulfilling the goals processed in the network, in a relentless flow of strategic decisions. It follows a fundamental split between abstract, universal instrumentalism, and historically rooted particularistic identities. **Our societies are increasingly structured around a bipolar opposition between the Net and the Self.** (1996, 3)

While not every observer would agree that institutions/organizations have become quite so delinked, it is clear that deep understanding of today's social relationships includes multiple networks of relationships within and between social organizations, ranging for some people from local to global in scope.

As a result there is a rich tradition of examining and measuring social networking, including in organization and management (Carrington, Scott, and Wasserman 2005). This movement is based on the notion that "the actions (attitudes and behaviors) of actors in organizations can best be explained in terms of their position in networks of relationships" (Nohria 1992, 6). As Burt (1980) suggests, network analysts normally use network cohesion, equivalence, prominence, range, and brokerage to analyze network position and to explain influences on action. Further, the formation of concentrations of power and alliances tends to occur at certain nodes in networks that Burt calls "structural holes" (1992, 5). Not all network ties are equivalent—some are strong and others are weak (Granovetter 1973). Moreover, if network actors are conceived as relationally or socially constructed, networks can be "constitutive" in the sense that they shape identities and thus their preferences, as well as their action capacities or rules (White 1992). There is a substantial empirical research tradition in this social network arena, such as the work of Burt (2001) on the development and evolution of trust and information, which is beyond the scope of this study. These social network contacts have been carried over into the analysis of transactions in the market. Economic networks have been defined as a group of agents who pursue repeated, enduring exchange relations with one another and, at the same time, lack a legitimate organizational authority to arbitrate and resolve the disputes that may arise during the exchange (Rauch and Hamilton 2001). Again, this area of study is beyond the scope of this book.

The structure and operations of the networks analyzed in this book go beyond social interaction, and include ties that entail the formal or virtual representation and exercise of organizational effort. They involve interorganizational networks, to use a sociological term, and as such are much more formalized than the broader analytic social networks identified above. While the process of social networking can indeed account for a great deal of their operational postures, the networks under study not only have real live interactions but have identifiable structures and actions. They are more than analytic constructs, but have a being and presence that are as unmistakable as that of formal organizations.

They are constituted of formal organizations; organization representatives, in most cases their top level and operational administrators and other specialists, are largely network participants. As applied to the public sector, they are identified as public management networks, those led or managed by government representatives as they employ multiorganizational arrangements for solving problems that, as has been suggested, cannot be achieved, or achieved easily, by single organizations. To follow the definition of O'Toole, "Networks are structures of interdependence involving multiple organizations or parts thereof, where one unit is not merely the formal subordinate of the others in some larger hierarchical arrangement" (1997, 45).

CHARTERED AND NONCHARTERED NETWORKS

As with other types of formalized interorganizational networks, the public management networks under analysis are either chartered or nonchartered in character. Both types of networks share certain characteristics: permanent status, regular formal meetings, a definable communication system, leaders and participants, taskforces or work groups, an identifiable governance structure, identifiable partners, and some form of division of labor/task allocation. Chartered networks are formally established as organized entities, often by intergovernmental agreement, registration as a 501c(3) nonprofit organization, by act or resolution of a state legislature, a governor's executive order, and/or through corporate registration with a state government representative, such as the secretary of state. Nonchartered networks have no such formal-legal status, but their continuing presence and operations, regular meetings, concrete problem-solving actions, websites, newsletters, and the like are testimony to their existence. Indeed, one of the oldest and most active of the study networks is nonchartered. Nonchartered networks are often harder to locate in telephone books or in websites than those that have been formalized, but we will see that those without (chartered) status can prove to be equally viable bodies.

By examining only PMNs with status as formalized bodies, it is clear that a great deal of both the social network type of networking behavior and the more discrete organization-to-organization linkages/coordinative behaviors will be excluded from analysis. Public managers solve problems beyond their boundaries through a variety of means, often without resorting to formal networks. In the larger scheme of public management, these actions also form important components of the managerial task (Agranoff and McGuire 2003a; Kickert and Koppenjan 1997; O'Toole 1997). Formalized networks have been selected as windows into collaborative behavior, with the hope that administrative theory can be realistically constructed by looking at organized entities as one of several means of managing across boundaries. Moreover, they are the emergent form of interorganizational structure in public management. The behaviors researched, analyzed, and conceptualized here may or may not represent the entire network fabric, but they do provide an initial look at the level of the manager at an important organized form of collaborative management.

These PMNs bring the nonprofit and for-profit sectors together with government in a number of policy arenas, including economic development, health care, criminal justice, human services, information systems, rural development, environmental protection, biotechnology, transportation, and education. Their activities are purposeful efforts to bring parts of organizations together in order to access knowledge and technology, and to guide, steer, control, or manage. Moreover, the public and private actors involved do not act separately but in conjunction, operating as metaorganizational bodies. Since the networks under study involve government, our interest is in patterns that emerge from the governance activities of the actors—for example, codiscovery, coregulation, costeering, coproduction, cooperative management, and public-private projects and partnerships.

IN SEARCH OF NETWORK MANAGEMENT

Do public managers operate differently in interorganizational networks than they do in their organizations? Is management in networks different from that of hierarchical organizations? These are assertions from the limited network literature that require exploration. Some observers may answer no, because both entail a type of boundary spanning and "dealing with people" that is common to traditional management functions. Others feel the answer is a definite yes, because of the absence of the normal trappings of standard management—for example, hierarchy, authority, and direction. Speaking about one network studied here, a state official said, "We manage by consensus in the Partnership for Rural Nebraska. . . . In my department I supervise and direct, based on the legal authority vested in my position . . . in the network I am an equal partner." But is there some substitute for legal authority?

This study investigates public managers as they participate in these collaborative undertakings. Experiential lessons about network management are derived from the responses of managers in federal government, state government, local government, and universities, as well as NGO officials as they work together to approach issues that cross the boundaries of their organizations.

THE ART AND CRAFT OF NETWORK MANAGEMENT

How to manage in a network is an important twenty-first-century issue because of networks' prevalence in the managerial enterprise. No single agency or organization at any level of government or the private sector has a monopoly on the mandate, resources, or information to deal with the most vexing of public problems. Moreover, a century of knowledge building in management—public and private—has focused on hierarchy and its derivatives, for example, POSDCORB (Planning, Organizing, Staffing, Directing, Coordinating, Reporting, and Budgeting). Such targeted focus on running the single organization was appropriate during a time when the concept of management as a guidance function within organization management was developed. The importance of organization management is likely to continue, but research also demonstrates a parallel importance of managers working across organizational boundaries. One study of collaborative management in economic development found that about 20 percent of public managers' time is spent in collaborative activity outside of the home government organization (Agranoff and McGuire 2003a). In a number of public policy arenas—for example, environmental protection—an increasing portion of this time is spent in formal networks (Wondolleck and Jaffee 2000; Imperial 2004). As a result, works on both knowledge bases (for example, Agranoff and McGuire 2003a; Kickert, Klijn, and Koppenjan 1997; Bardach 1998; McGuire 2002) and practical books (Lipnak and Stamps 1994; Austin 2000; Chrislip and Larson 1994) on collaborative or network management are finding their way into the field of public management.

FOCUS OF THE STUDY

Not every question regarding network management can be answered in a single study involving fourteen networks. On the other hand, it is important to go beyond mere description of the structure and operation of the networks. The process of management in many of its important aspects appears to be critical, as well as learning about what networks do. We also want to discover how they accomplish, or do not accomplish, what they are expected to do.

DIFFERENCES AMONG NETWORKS

The result of this dual mission is to offer a balanced assessment of the structure and operation of the networks, focusing on exemplary types and how they engage in management. It was discovered in the initial research phase that the fourteen networks performed different functions. As a result it became impossible to treat all networks alike. Chapter 3 demonstrates how the field questions did not perfectly fit each of the fourteen networks because their missions proved to be so different. Not all networks followed the theoretical lines of previous literature, particularly the assumption that networks adjust policy. In fact, some come together primarily to provide information and some go further by also mutually developing capabilities, whereas others additionally provide new programming opportunities for their component organizations. A minority of networks studied do make joint decisions and take policy action.

The distinctions among networks are nevertheless so basic to the analysis that they must be introduced in brief. They are described in table 1.1 as informational, developmental, outreach, and action networks, corresponding to their primary purposes that range from mutual exchange to actually making policy and program adjustments. The typology proved to be useful for comparisons in both the operational and analytical phases of the study.

TABLE 1.1   Types of Networks Studied

Informational	Partners come together exclusively to exchange agency policies and programs, technologies, and potential solutions. Taking any action is entirely up to the agencies on a voluntary basis.
Developmental	Partner information and technical exchange are combined with education and member service that increase member capacity in order to implement solutions within home agencies or organizations.
Outreach	Partners come together to exchange information and technologies, sequence programming, exchange resource opportunities, pool client contacts, and enhance access opportunities that lead to new programming avenues. Implementation of designed programs takes place within an array of public and private agencies.
Action	Partners come together to make interagency adjustments, formally adopt collaborative courses of action, and/or deliver services along with exchanges of information and technologies.

RESEARCH QUESTIONS

The analysis also focuses on a set of questions based on both research findings and observational assertions in previous literature (chapter 2). These relate to the nonhierarchical nature of network management, where information and expertise are substituted for authority structure, through self-organizing processes, held together by mutual obligation that develops over time by reaching consensus-based decisions, and by blending knowledge bases from different technical and organizational arenas. Managers in these PMNs were asked how various tasks and roles in the promotion and operation of these networks are different, if at all, from their other public roles working within bureaucratic organizations.

As a result of this general line of inquiry, the following research questions guided the study:

1. How do public managers organize, convene, and operate in PMNs?
2. What processes replace the standard approaches to management, that is, planning, organizing, staffing, coordinating, and so on, when working in PMNs?
3. How does the role of the public manager as decision maker change when working in a PMN?
4. How is expertise mobilized in PMNs? How is this different from that of bureaucratic organizations?
5. How do information systems and knowledge management support network management and operations?
6. How do networks accomplish their stated and operational purposes?
7. Do networks add value to public undertakings? What kind of value do they add that single organizations cannot or do not provide?
8. What effect do networks involving public agencies have on the boundaries of the state? That is, do PMNs change the role of government?

Answers to these questions should be helpful to public managers and NGO representatives as they operate in networks, as well as add to the network management knowledge base.

ANALYZING WHERE THE REAL WORK IS DONE

Prior experiences in examining how government and NGOs work together (Agranoff and McGuire 2003b; Radin et al. 1996) drove home the importance of flying below the radar, so to speak, to select networks and look at managers who were at the working level, trying to solve intractable problems at the field level. However tempting it might be to look at "blue ribbon" policy networks made up of Washington, D.C., bureaucrats, national NGO executives, and heads of giant corporations heads, the real work of many programs is done in places like Indianapolis, Indiana; Des Moines, Iowa; Lincoln, Nebraska; Columbus, Ohio, and in many of the large and small jurisdictions within these states.

At this level federal and state officials have to coordinate with local governments and NGOs to make things work. For example, it will be demonstrated that the Indiana officials who tried in (1999) to develop and implement a new program for home and community services for the developmentally disabled quickly discovered the need to work with state and federal Medicaid officials, the Indiana Department of Family and Social Services (three divisions), two other state agencies, advocacy organizations, university-based programs, and a host of providers of case management, home service, and small residential services. Almost at the same time, the federal government began to prod states to expand services for people with developmental disabilities out of large institutions, due to a Supreme Court ruling (*Olmstead v. L.C.* 1999). A broad group of state-local actors had to make a variety of programs work effectively, relying heavily on federal funding. This represents an example of the "real work" that networks do.

The problem is that with few exceptions (O'Toole 1996; Agranoff 1986; Thomas 2003; Church and Nakamura 1993), research in this area rarely looks at the less obvious examples. Most policy implementation research is on highly visible programs, for example, emergency management coordination after September 11, 2001; the politics of welfare reform; or the educational performance movement in "No Child Left Behind."

The networks under study are less visible but are real working operations. A summary of each of the fourteen is presented in table 1.2. Each PMN is named in the first column, and in most cases an abbreviated identifier for ease of recognition is introduced. A brief statement regarding the entity's major purpose is presented, followed by its classification according to the fourfold network typology introduced. Next, the official enabling vehicle or authorization mechanism is listed for each of the eleven chartered networks. The three nonchartered networks are identified as a nonformal group. Finally, the primary agencies or partners that make up each network are listed in abbreviated form, demonstrating the variety of components that constitute these multisector NGO and multilevel government agencies. A more complete identification of the networks, including network descriptions and enumeration of the actual partners, is included in appendix A.

Who are the officials that work in these networks? Table 1.3 presents a profile of the affiliations of the persons who are part of the active or working core actors in each network. Each network is broken down by type in the fourfold

(text continues on page 18)

TABLE 1.2 Networks under Investigation

Name of Network	Purpose	Type	Enabling Authority	Primary Agencies
1. Access Indiana/ Enhanced Data Access Review Committee (**Enhanced Data**)	Sets policies for state web portal, reviews, modifies, and approves agency agreements and private use	Action	State government	SA, NGO, Cit, Media
2. Des Moines Area Metropolitan Planning Org. (**Des Moines Metro**)	Transportation planning for metropolitan area	Action	Intergovernmental agreement	CtyGov, CoGov, SA, FA, R/Met
3. Indiana Economic Development Council (**Indiana Economic Development**)	Research consultant for state economic development	Informational	Not-for-profit 501c(3)	SA, Priv, NGO, Un
4. Indiana Rural Development Council (**Indiana Rural Council**)	Forum to address rural issues, establish partnerships, and enable partners to take action	Developmental	Intergovernmental agreement/ Not-for-profit 501c(3)	FA, SA, CoGov, CtyGov, Legis, NGO
5. Iowa Communications Network (**Iowa Communications**)	Operates a statewide, state-administered, fiber optics network	Action	State government	SA, FA, CtyGov, CoGov, Legis, NGO, Cit
6. Iowa Enterprise Network (**Iowa Enterprise**)	Supports home-based and micro-enterprises	Developmental	Not-for-profit 501c(3)	FA, SA, NGO, Priv

continued

TABLE 1.2 (continued)

Name of Network	Purpose	Type	Enabling Authority	Primary Agencies
7. Iowa Geographic Info. Council (**Iowa Geographic**)	Clearinghouse for coordinated systems and data sharing	Developmental	State government	Un, FA, SA, R/Met, CoGov, CtyGov, NGO, Priv
8. Lower Platte River Corridor Alliance (**Lower Platte**)	Supports local efforts at water conservation, comprehensive and coord. land use; promotes cooperation among Nebraska organizations	Informational	Intergovernmental agreement	R/Met, SA, FA, Un
9. Partnership for Rural Nebraska (**Partnership for Rural Nebraska**)	Provides resources and expertise to enhance rural development opportunities	Developmental	Intergovernmental agreement	SA, Un, FA, R/Met
10. Small Communities Environmental Infrastructure Group (**Small Communities**)	Assists small Ohio govts. in their water and wastewater systems	Outreach	Nonformal group	SA, FA, Un, Priv, NGO, R/Met

11. The Darby Partnership (**Darby**)	Shares information and resources to address central Ohio watershed threats	Informational	Nonformal group	FA, SA, CoGov, CtyGov, R/Met, NGO
12. United States Department of Agriculture/Rural Development Nebraska (**USDA Nebraska**)	Outreach and assistance to leverage funds of other programs for public and private development	Outreach	Federal government	FA, NGO, SA, R/Met, Un, CtyGov, Priv
13. Kentuckiana Regional Planning and Development Agency (**Kentuckiana Agency**)	Transportation planning for two-state Louisville metropolitan area	Action	Intergovernmental agreement	CoGov, CtyGov, FA, SA, R/Met
14. Indiana 317 Taskforce/Group (**317 Group**)	Strategies for developmentally disabled community services	Outreach	Nonformal group	NGO, SA, FA, Un, Cit, Priv

Key

FA = federal government agency at regional or state level; SA = state government agency; CoGov = county government; CtyGov = city government; R/Met = regional or metropolitan agency; Un = university, college, or community college; Legis = state legislature/congressional staff; NGO = nongovernmental organization/advocacy group; Priv = for-profit business organization; Cit = citizen representative

TABLE 1.3 Organization Affiliation of PMN Core Participants

PMN	Type[a]	Federal Agency	State Agency	County Govt.	City Govt.	Regional/ Metro.	Univ./ College	State Legis. Congr. Staff	NGO/ Advocacy Org.	Bus./ For Profit	Size of Core[b]	Broader Participants
Enhanced Data	A		7					1	2	1	11	Intelnet Commission of 25 persons
Des Moines Metro	A	2	1	1	6	2		1			13	Policy Committee of 32, and 5 ex-officio members
Indiana Economic Development	I	2	5			5	3	2	7	1	25	Board of 55 state leaders
Indiana Rural Council	D	3	5	1	2		2	1	3	4	21	Board of 28 sector reps.
Iowa Communications	A	2	8				1	1			12	Five-person board of directors not part of activist core; hundreds of agency contacts
Iowa Enterprise	D	3	4			1			1	3	12	Advisory Committee of 22 until 2002

Organization	Type[a]									Total	Description
Iowa Geographic	D	1	2	1	1	2	5	2		14	Board of 25 in 7 sector categories
Lower Platte	I	3	6	1	1	2	1			14	Contact with 350 watershed stakeholders
Partnership for Rural Nebraska	D	3	5	3	5	2				18	Coordinating team of 15 since 2003
Small Communities	O	3	6	1	2	3	1			16	Contact with 113 organization reps.
Darby	I	7	5	3	2	3	4	4	2	30	Mailing list of over 100 organization reps.
USDA/Nebraska	O	4	3	1	1	1	5			15	Working contacts w/ hundreds of local govts. and finance institutions
Kentuckiana Agency	A	4	6	3	4	3	1			21	Policy Committee of 18 and 7 ex-officio members
317 Group	O	2	7	1	1	1	8			20	One citizen rep.; almost 200 provider executives

[a] A = Action; I = Informational; O = Outreach; D = Developmental
[b] Estimate of real activists based on discussions with activists

typology; its component representatives, the total size of its active core, and some general comments about its broader set of contacts, boards, stakeholder contacts, and the like are included. Most important here is the size of each PMN's organizational representative core, which ranges from ten to thirty individuals. The typical PMN core involves federal and state government representatives, NGO officials, and university college personnel officials. The for-profit sector is involved in ten different PMNs, but has a strong presence in two networks. The two transportation agencies have strong local and regional government representation. Only one PMN has a total absence of federal government involvement. Several look very state-government oriented, an unsurprising finding since most are state-based PMNs that involve federal intergovernmental programs. Finally, it is clear that government officials at different levels are the major players in these particular networks.

There is no way of knowing how representative these networks might be, nor is representativeness a primary concern. This work does not make claims of applicability to some larger population. One might say that the universe of PMNs is limited to these fourteen under study. It is clear that most of these networks appear to be, according to participants and observers, "successful" in reaching their aims. Nevertheless, one or two have gone through months of inactivity, only to be revived. Currently only two of the fourteen appear to be struggling to survive, whereas a third is under considerable political pressure but its short-term future is assured. Several have been extremely productive in achieving process and outcome successes on a regular basis; a few are more sporadic in results. Thus the typology as well as other findings represent conclusions that only apply to this group of fourteen. However, the findings are clearly grounded in the fourteen networks. Hopefully, they are sufficiently typical of working-level PMNs to hold up with regard to other such networks.

PURPOSES OF THE STUDY

It is important to study PMNs because they have become essential vehicles of collaborative public management, taking their place alongside: (1) informal administrator-to-administrator links and (2) formalized patterned networking matrices, the latter being administrative equivalents to social networking. All three of these types of transactions have become important for those working on public problems and within public programs: program specialists, program supervisors, program administrators, and executive officers. Moreover, growing interdependence has accelerated a new type of network actor, the interorganizational boundary spanner. This is a person who works within an organization but whose primary and often exclusive duties are engagement of personnel of external organizations. PMNs contain all of these different types of organizational personnel and thus allow us to study how these different public actors operate across their boundaries.

The initial purpose, then, is to provide a deep understanding of network structure and processes. Are they different from those of the organizations that spawn them? For example, there is speculation that problem orientation and commitment to goals brings PMN participants together (Mandell and Steelman 2003), whereas others point to resource dependency/interdependency as a convening force (Klijn and Koppenjan 2000). Another related issue is that of trust (Fountain 1994), which to some is a more essential force than purpose in holding network actors together. These and other issues, particularly those related to how networks are managed, need explication in an era where an increasing amount of time is bound up in network activities.

Another purpose entails sorting out what is new and different about network management and what is not. In the most general or theoretical sense the public administrator must test the assumption that shared governing activity has shifted the roles of the state, implying "a growing awareness of the limitations of traditional governance by the state on its own" (Kooiman 2003, 3). This conclusion about governing in a networked society has obviously led to the research question regarding the changing boundaries of the state. With respect to the process of management, public administration must go beyond the generalization that networks are managed nonhierarchically. What does that mean? Does something or someone take the place of a line administrator? How are differences resolved without a person in line authority? How is work sequenced and tasked? In other words, the field must go beyond the broad assertion that network management is nonhierarchical and say what it is. These are the kinds of issues that will be sorted out, albeit in baseline fashion.

This work also wishes to inform practice. Well over half of the 150 plus discussants repeatedly asked, "Why are you studying us?" Many related that most of their little band of administrators represent the second echelon of administrators, and felt that I should be talking to members of their state governor's cabinet and the undersecretaries in Washington. I patiently tried to explain to them that my interest was not so much in the "big picture," but in how that picture played in Des Moines, Iowa; Clarksville, Indiana; Jefferstown, Kentucky; Chadron, Nebraska; and Shenandoah, Ohio. I told them that the experiences that they shared with me would be helpful in organizing concepts and theoretical propositions that would be of use to other public administrators, NGO officials, elected officials, and those students who would soon be facing a world of networks as well as their hierarchical organization. In short, the knowledge gained from this research would be considerably less useful if it could not be derived from the so-called "real world."

Finally, an aim is to contribute to the knowledge base of network management. It bears repeating that the field must go beyond reflections on experience and speculations to fill in the gaps in understanding PMNs. The field of "management" took a good half-century, from Max Weber, Fredrick Winslow Taylor, Luther Gulick and Lynall Urwick, the Hawthorne studies, and others until Peter Drucker (1974) finally pulled several of these strands together into a comprehensive statement in *Management*. In this work he referred to management as both a discipline, or organized body of knowledge, and a culture or social function embedded in society, carrying with it values, customs, and beliefs in governmental and political systems. The world of PMNs, or at least their recognition, is relatively new. It will take time to build a discipline and culture in the sense that Drucker uses. At this stage there are more questions than answers (Agranoff and McGuire 2001b). Within the limitations of this study, the book hopes to add to public management knowledge by providing answers, or partial answers, to those questions raised earlier.

THE PLAN OF THE BOOK

The chapters that follow explore the research questions and themes introduced in this chapter. The journey is designed to present field-based findings and statements about network management and the surrounding body of knowledge. The story is by no means a complete theory of network management or even of PMNs. It clearly does not cover every facet of management. Its realism, that is, grounding in the world of administrative actors, may well disappoint some, because fewer profound differences from organizational or hierarchical management than some would expect were actually found. It will particularly disappoint those whose armchair observations may have overreached on some conclusions regarding these differences. The findings will hopefully add dimensions of useful managerial knowledge to the scholarly and practitioner community.

Chapter 2 has two basic purposes: laying out the theoretical basis of the study by examining previous literature, both empirical and assertive; and providing a more detailed introduction to the nature of networks. After establishing some basic definitions regarding collaborative management, the chapter focuses on the basics of public sector networks and how they are managed. The theoretical background under examination will be derived in large part from governance, network management, and organizational management, as opposed to that of social and economic networking. This leads to an explanation of the networks under study, their basic makeup, and how these less-visible PMNs represent the kind of collaborative work "in the trenches" that is hard to see but very real. It is this work, representing cross-agency, cross-sector information exchange and problem resolution, that gives rise to the age of the network.

Chapter 3 profiles the study's methodology—grounded theory—and offers the initial findings on how networks differ. As the research approach is explained, it shows how the fourfold PMN typology emerged from the data. Empirically, the first coded data results (with appended methodological presteps) are presented on PMN decision making and action formation as a means of developing the typology. Methodologically, some understanding of the basics of grounded theory is essential to understand the processes under examination.

Chapters 4 and 5 directly introduce the fourteen PMNs by their type. Eight of them are discussed in greater detail. These are designed to provide the basic "character" information regarding how these PMNs are structured, how they operate, and most importantly, how they represent their type of PMN. Chapter 4 features those networks that are informational and developmental, and are not directly or indirectly involved in policy/programming. Chapter 5 features outreach and action networks that are either indirectly or directly involved in the type of program solutions that are normally ascribed to networks.

Chapter 6 begins to explore the research questions on a cross-case basis by exploring the basics of managerial processes. The nonhierarchical, information/knowledge orientated, self-organizing, trust-based, and consensual decision nature of the networks are explained. Standard managerial processes, such as planning, organizing, directing, and other processes are compared with regard to organizations and networks. Finally, the core of power and authority within the PMNs is explained.

Knowledge management by PMNs is the focus of chapter 7. It examines how these information-era entities encourage broad participation, promote their activities, involve organizational colleagues, find and broker extant knowledge, create new information bases, and support their actions. In a sense, these processes are managerial extensions of the more standard processes identified in the previous chapter, and while not necessarily unique to networks they are central functions in PMNs.

Network results or the public value created by the participation in and work of PMNs is the focus of chapter 8. A series of network benefits is established. The various processes and tangible outcome results are explained in regard to the professional/administrator, the home agency, the PMN process, and PMN outcomes. Although costs that balance against the benefits of participation in these networks are not a prime focus of this study, respondents' identification of costs is analyzed. Bearing these costs in mind, each network is evaluated by type, on the basis of some twenty-one activities previously identified.

Chapter 9 examines questions relating to the effect, if any, of PMNs on government and governing. To what degree have managers felt that changes have occurred between jurisdiction and management? Do PMNs change agency decision domains? How does the work of public sector networks change the role of top executives? Line managers? Program specialists? What kind of decisions do networks actually make? Chapter 9 also explores whether the work of networks affects the core or the margins of government decisions.

In conclusion, chapter 10 brings together the findings into a framework regarding their contributions to public network management. This is followed by an identification of emerging arenas for the study of public network management. The book concludes with a discussion of the positioning of network management in public management and its role in governing.

. . . .

CHAPTER TWO

NETWORKS IN PUBLIC MANAGEMENT

Rural development is an area that has no easy problems and no easy solutions. A lot of us are in the mix: governments, associations, agribusiness, small business . . . and then there are the environmental questions. In this state there is a tradition of working together on mutual concerns. That is why there are so many rural partnerships and coalitions.

WHY ARE NETWORKS important for public managers? According to the prevailing knowledge, a convergence of forces, including life in an information society, the existence of multiple organizations that make and implement policy, and the need for a variety of resources to deal with the most difficult government problems all contribute to people working across their organizations. These forces lead to the need for collaboration. The network mode of organization is well suited to facilitate collaboration, thus bringing public managers and NGO officials together to work in PMNs. Most workable grounded theory approaches do not start with a completely blank slate, but with a focus on the conceptual assumptions that frame a field of inquiry. So it is with this study, where previous exploration of public networks frames assumptions and questions. As a result, it is important to examine these findings and assertions. This chapter explores the basic theoretical concerns behind this type of interorganizational network, the PMN. It concludes with an introduction to the common features of these entities.

WHY NETWORKS?

Many reasons are behind the emergence of networks as a form of public management activity. One is the transformation of societies from labor oriented to knowledge oriented, and the need to integrate human capital into collaborative problem identifying, strategic brokering, and problem-solving activities (Drucker 1993; Reich 1991). A second is the change in government roles, shifting from direct operation toward steering, partnering, and contracting (Kooiman 2003). This in turn has led to the emergence of intergovernmental programs that work on the second- and third-order problems, and issues raised by these shifts in governmental operations (Agranoff and McGuire 1998; McGuire 1999; O'Toole 1997; Radin et al. 1996). Related gaps in clear-cut solutions to these problems lead to knowledge collaboration, both outside of governments and intergovernmentally. This brings on the prevalence of various forums of collaborative behavior, such as knowledge exchange, shared resources, coordinated strategies, task forces, coalitions, and many other forms, along with network structures (Campbell and Gould 1999; Mandell and Steelman 2003). Next, organization structures themselves (chapter 6) are becoming more collaborative and more hierarchically flexible (Clegg 1990), thus making their employees more "positioned" to accept interorganization collaboration. Finally, these forces lead to a world of multiple overlapping connections in which managers must meet the challenge of increasing complexity in the midst of uncertainty, and thus are often forced to network collaboratively in order to move from the edge of chaos to reasonable solutions (McMaster 1995; Sherman and Schultz 1998). Together these forces make public agency networks prevalent.

Behind these forces, then, are the interdependencies that have emanated from intergovernmentalization and have led to the rise of the particular form of network studied here, that of PMNs. Again, several forces contribute. First is the rise of welfare states during the twentieth century. This initially bureaucratized, centralized, and managerialized social welfare, but in the long run put programs into the hands of subnational governments and NGOs as copolicymakers and/or implementers (Ashford 1986; Wilson 1975; Flora and Heidenheimer 1981). Second, this interdependence in turn led to a familiar concern for intergovernmental relations (IGR), the focus on patterns of regularized governmental contacts among a variety of jurisdiction levels and public officials (Wright 1988). Third, managers working between governments and NGOs had to learn to operate within this system to solve the everyday problems in making programs work, a process that has come to be known as intergovernmental management (IGM) (Agranoff 1986; Wright and Krane 1998). Fourth and finally, these intergovernmental phenomena have shifted over time, moving somewhat away from governments to the nongovernmental sector on a shared basis, where a host of public-private partnerships, shared administration, marketization, privatization, and decentralization is the norm (Fredrickson 1999; Loughlin 2000).

RESEARCHING PUBLIC MANAGEMENT NETWORKS

A research tradition is building in the intersecting arenas of governance and intergovernmental management networks. The earlier IGM works include studies of local networks in workforce training by Hanf et al. (1978) and Chisholm's (1989) study on managing across governmental boundaries in transportation systems. The more recent work of Radin and associates (1996) on federal–state rural development councils is highly related. Wright and Cho's (2000) panel surveys of state administrators examine policy changes as a result of their operation within intergovernmental networks. Meier and O'Toole (2001) model the impact of network management on the performance of Texas school districts. In an earlier work, O'Toole (1996) identified the different skills and competencies that managers need as they deal with the changing intergovernmental context. Finally, Agranoff and McGuire's (2003a) research on intergovernmental networks for economic development in cities also looks empirically at how public managers build and operate within governance structures.

A tradition of managing within networks is also emerging. Provan and Milward's (1991, 1995) work on network governance structure and network outcomes is central because of its focus on effectiveness. As evidence of new managerial roles, Mandell (1999) identifies a set of management styles and instruments that differ from those employed in traditional bureaucratic settings. Bardach's (1998) multiple case studies of interagency collaboration attempt to build a theory of network management. An anthology edited by Kickert et al. (1997) examines different strategies for managing policy networks. Finally, Agranoff and McGuire (2001b) pull together extant concepts in network management in an attempt to capture a paradigm that goes beyond planning, organizing, staffing, directing, coordinating, reporting, and budgeting (POSDCORB): collective vs. hierarchical idea generation and problem resolution; collaborative "groupware" based on social capital, shared learning, and a culture of problem-solving among role-based actors; and power balances and disparities based on knowledge, technical skill, organizing skill, and leadership.

These basic studies indicate important directions for future management research. They help to focus on what may or may not be essential to research; what differences, if any, there are in managing networks and organizations; and how IGR and the existence of government have changed the roles of the manager within public administration. In regard to this study, the focus shifts to the eight research questions raised in the previous chapter. The question relating to the changing boundaries of the state has been raised earlier in this chapter, as government appears to be sharing its domain with other entities. Here we need to focus on the problems involved in the loss of government jurisdiction, and in just what ways the boundaries of the state have shifted.

IS NETWORK MANAGEMENT DIFFERENT?

Our knowledge regarding how managers convene and operate in networks is based on quite limited evidence. We must begin by restating that networks, like other forms of interorganizational management, are considered nonhierarchical and are therefore highly based on exchange relations. The problem we immediately face is that, to date, no readily agreed-upon set of functional activities exists that is the hierarchical equivalent of POSDCORB. Bardach (1998) suggests that collaboratives are built on two platforms: one of trust, leadership, and an interactive communication network; the other of creative opportunity, intellectual capital, existence of implementation programs and agencies, and advocacy groups. These two platforms mutually build improved capacity to steer or guide the system toward objectives, which leads to a network that operates subsystems, and to continuous learning.

Kickert and Koppenjan (1997) identify network management as the steering of interaction processes, comprising three elements: intervention in an existing pattern of relations, consensus building, and problem solving. The major processes include: (1) activation—initiating interaction or games to solve particular problems or achieve goals; (2) arranging interaction—getting actors to participate; (3) structuring—building rules, norms, and a culture; (4) brokering—guarded mediation, and tapping and utilizing diverse ideas, insights, and solutions; (5) facilitating interaction—building in processes that are conducive to the development of strategic consensus building. Agranoff and McGuire (2001b) bring the network literature into similar stages: activation of players, framing tasks and issues, mobilizing to reach agreement and take action, and synthesizing the network by creating a favorable environment and enhancing conditions. Thus our search for a managerial process will fall somewhere between two poles. The first searches for the possibility of a new set of managerial tasks along the lines of the Kickert and Koppenjan framework, possibly a distinctive set of nonhierarchical management activities. The second pole takes the opposite tack, asking if the different POSDCORB tasks actually exist in networks but unfold differently in the absence of hierarchy and its attendant forces.

THE PROCESSES OF DECISION MAKING

The literature on networks addresses the particular processes through which decisions are made. Although the process is normally described as consensus oriented, it is more involved as it is heavily engaged in the mutual learning process. The most important elements of network decision on the surface appear quite similar to those in hierarchical organizations, such as shared learning processes. Innes and Booher (1999) suggest, however, that a new mind-set is needed in networks to overcome long-standing habits of producing specific agreements or actions. The interactive learning process is similar to Senge's characterization as "people . . . continually learning how to learn together" (1990, 3). He suggests that learning organizations require five core disciplines: personal mastery, mental models, shared vision, team learning, and systems thinking. Like learning organizations, networks require similar collective cognitive capabilities, since "the intelligence of a network lies in the patterns of relationships among its members" (Lipnack and Stamps 1994, 210).

Negotiation is a parallel process that supports decision. Bardach refers to a "culture of joint problem solving" that includes an "ethos that values equality, adaptability, discretion and results" (1998, 232). Part of this ethos is overcoming bureaucratic tendencies (hierarchy, stability, obedience, procedures) through a lively sense of possibility. Bardach also suggests that "collaboration is a matter of exhortation, explication, persuasion, give and take. To collaborate is to negotiate" (1998, 232). Negotiations have to take into account all interests—personal, organizational, partner organizations, and the collective (Galaskiewicz and Zaheer 1999). Negotiations within networks seek consensus only after members have fully explored issues and interests, and only after significant efforts have been made to respond to differences creatively (Innes and Booher 1999). Such processes are supported by accommodation and by the dualism manifested in the fact that the agency delegate to the network and the network delegate to the agency can be the same person. Weiner (1990) concludes that when negotiating, such dual loyalty necessitates a totally new mind-set and value stance for managers who work within transorganizational systems.

These processes appear to be held together by behavioral science techniques as similar to those employed in single organizations. Weiner (1990) suggests that in transorganizational (network) management, techniques similar to organization management are normally employed, including group problem solving, force-field analysis, action planning, team building, process consultation. But Weiner asserts that more is required in networks. First, in network management empowerment is based on information rather than on authority. Second, in network management existing organizational structures are dependent variables for network systems. Several organizations working together can be fashioned into new systems, using the flow of information to link transorganizational systems.

HOLDING THE NETWORK TOGETHER

If the public manager cannot depend on a legally based hierarchy, what tools are available to engage in the public's business and what network dynamics substitute for the traditional role of the manager in enforcing legal authority? One widely held belief is that trust is the network's substitute for mandated authority. Trust in collective behavior is linked to fiduciary obligation. Such responsibilities are essential in holding networks together because they impose the obligation to broadly attend to the concerns of others beyond the boundaries of specific, measurable transactions (Barber 1983). Trust does not require common belief, but obligation and expectation. Ferguson and Stoutland (1999) break down such expectations into four trust dimensions: participant motives, not exploiting or betraying others; competency, possessing the knowledge and skills to do what is expected; dependability, holding the necessary resources; and collegiality, showing respect and fairness.

Trust is required as organizations in networks attempt to redefine their legal-based (hierarchical, contractual) relationships (Nohria 1992). Sabel suggests that mutual obligation and expectation is key: "Trust-based governance structures have rich, consultative institutional structures whose very existence belies the assumption that the agents expect their actions automatically to be harmonized by the confluence of belief" (1992, 67). Indeed, Fountain (1994) suggests that trust as a social relation may be on par with exchange as a lubricant in network behavior.

Others maintain that the public or collective good, as manifested in a shared belief or common purpose, contributes to the network's cohesiveness (Alter and Hage 1993). Mandell (1999) refers to the sum of these qualities as a program rationale, the mind-set or commitment to the whole that holds a network together when hierarchical methods of coordination and control are not operative. From this perspective, program structures are not merely aggregates of individual organizations; analytically and practically the network itself is more critical than the component organizations and, at a certain point, focus on the individual organization is relevant only to understand how and why each organization contributes to the overall effort (Provan and Milward 1991).

Mutual dependency, particularly that oriented to the availability of resources, provides another explanation of cohesion. The interorganizational literature from the past few decades suggests that actors in a network are in some form of interactive dependency, usually based on resource exchange (Pennings 1981). Most organizations in a network are thus strategically interdependent, but some are more resource dependent than others (Rhodes 1981; Yuchtman and Seashore 1967). All interorganizational interactions—communication as well as joint activity—are ultimately and fully dependent and are seeking an adequate supply of resources. This orientation is the defining activity and is equated with forces of control within networks. The extent of commitment and resources shared may vary greatly, as parties possess different measures of resources (funding, expertise, support, human resources) to move networks forward.

Leadership and guidance ability in networks as self-managing systems is another contributor to network cohesion. It is commonly understood that network leadership and management require the "principles of 'soft' guidance" as replacements for command and control (Windhoff-Héntier 1992, 3). The principles of steering ability are critical in holding the network together (Kickert and Koppenjan 1997), although institutional rules that guide the behavior of actors within networks are also necessary to support such steering (Klijn and Koppenjan 2006). Network managerial tasks take advantage of network self-management propensities, using minimal coercion and resources, "balancing social forces and interests and enabling social actors and systems to organize themselves" (Kooiman 1993, 256). It is clear that in all of these nonhierarchical processes, the manager becomes a partner rather than an administrator.

KNOWLEDGE MANAGEMENT IN NETWORKS

In an information era the acquisition, adaptation, and application of knowledge becomes a central function of networks. Indeed, most networks are largely in the knowledge management (KM) business. KM attempts to organize, codify, and structure what is known by those involved in the work of organized entities (Davenport and Prusak 2000). In the public sector networks are important brokers of knowledge; single organizations collaborate in order to find solutions unavailable to them as individual entities. The networks are potential human capital and data entities waiting to attack society's difficult problems. Their knowledge not only includes data and information, but also insights from problem solving that come from experience, judgment, skills, and hands-on application. As such, the knowledge that public managers need includes explicit and tacit knowledge. The former is that which can be written, codified, and transmitted within and across organizations; tacit knowledge is less formally transmitted in that it is embedded in senses, perceptions, intuition, and experiences that are hard to express and less frequently codified (Weick 1995).

Networks appear to engage in several commonly accepted KM techniques. For example, explicit KM includes web-based geographic information systems (GIS), technology studies, market studies, environmental impact studies, engineering reports, and information portals. Tacit knowledge involves such approaches as conferences, institutes, workshops, informal mentoring, formal mentoring systems, and apprenticeships. These appear to facilitate the work of networks and agencies that collaborate. They are also laboratories for analyzing KM in the public sector at the ground level.

NETWORK PERFORMANCE

The conclusion of this work will address the issue of whether networks make a difference. Performance has become an important public management issue, and it appears equally applicable to interorganizational entities. The degree to which the fourteen PMNs attain results that would not have been achieved by working in single organizations is an important productivity issue. There are also notable downsides or costs of networking, yet public managers devote their time to these endeavors. What is it that they are seeking?

In hierarchical organizations, performance or value can be attributed to effectiveness by analyzing success in achieving goals. Tests of success may have to be modified with regard to networks. Provan and Milward (2001) put forward four potential outcome benchmarks: the ebb and flow of agencies in and out of the network, the range of services provided, the strength of relationships between and among partners, and the evaluation of network administrative structure. Klijn and Koppenjan (2000) suggest that the goal achievement method has less credence because objectives are more autonomous with no central coordinating actor, and each of several actors may have differing objectives. They further argue that the use of *ex ante* formulated objectives is usually untenable because actors adapt their perceptions and objectives interactively, responding to other parties and to the environment. Also, if certain parties do not participate in the interaction process the chances are high that their interests and preferences will not be represented in the derived solution. As a result, network results need to be measured by the "*ex post* satisfying" criterion (Teisman 1992, 1995, quoted in Klijn and Koppenjan 2000), based on the subjective judgment of network actors. In the final analysis, the actors themselves have to determine the benefits derived along with considering the costs. This means that both substantive and process elements need to be weighed.

In previous work the primary concern in network performance appears to center on questions of whether collaboration adds value to the public undertaking. As Moore suggests, public managers seek to "discover, define and produce public value," extending discovery of means to focus on ends, and becoming "important innovators in changing what public organizations do and how they do it" (1995, 20). In a similar vein, managers in networks must "look *out* to the value of what they are producing," to paraphrase Moore. In Bardach's study of interagency action, he defines collaboration "as any joint activity by two or more agencies that is intended to increase public value by their working together rather than separately" (1998, 8). From an administrative standpoint, he asserts that collaboration can create social value in the same way as its hierarchical counterparts, differentiation and specialization. Collaboration results need to be assessed because any loss in efficiency due to political, institutional, and technical pressures diminishes public value. As such, we should not be impressed by the idea of collaboration per se, but only if it produces better organizational performance or lower costs than its alternatives.

PUBLIC MANAGEMENT NETWORK FEATURES

Who are these PMNs that are expected to add public value to policy and program concerns in the real world? What are they attempting to accomplish? What kinds of issues do they work on? Before this work digs into methodology and typology, the terrain of these networks requires explanation. While real, they are not the kind of entities that one normally finds listed in a telephone directory.

As table 1.2 and table 1.3 in the previous chapter indicate, virtually all of these networks cross governmental and nongovernmental sectors. Most operate with representatives of federal officials based at the field or state level, state government officials in the capitols or state regions, nonprofit executive directors or elected officers, representatives of trade organizations, and university-applied research or outreach institute officials. A few PMNs are organized at the state level only, with a mixture of state program heads and NGOs. Their federal connections are more indirect. The private sector tends to be more prominent in these PMNs, although in each case their focus remains on public programs and public policies. Most of the private organizations focus on public matters. Indeed, in every case it is really the "public's business" that these bodies are working on. As such, they are working with government on matters of governing. In a sense, all of the component organizations are public (Bozeman 1987).

These public organizations work in policy contexts where boundary spanning, linking, or partnering is central to their mission. Each PMN's participating organizations have as part of their core mission a heavy emphasis on working across agencies; thus they would be coordinating or linking regardless of the existence of a PMN. Their work is dependent on the work of other individuals in other agencies. They naturally reach outside their organizations' borders. In fact, in many other public arenas similar activities occur without benefit of a PMN. The PMN provides a regularized, broader-based, and focused vehicle for bringing potentially collaborative parties to the table.

ROUTINE WORK

The PMNs under study do the routine work of interagency policy and programs. Unlike high-level federal government–private partnerships, blue ribbon task forces of federal agency heads and NGO executives in Washington, or

National Academy of Sciences policy panels, these managers represent the foot soldiers of public management. Working at the so-called field level, they are trying to effect environmental or transportation or rural or Medicaid policy made in Washington and state capitols. They help give these programs a state government/ politics flavor, and try to adapt it to local, real-world circumstances.

Whether it is information, money, expertise, or access to services, the networks pool resources so problems are identified and explored. The mix of available resources is different for each partner, but all have some interest in the issue or problem at hand. The participating PMN partners have common interests and often have common objectives. Concerns for developing rural communities, helping small communities deal with water problems, achieving a metropolitan approach to transportation, explaining and fostering the use of e-government, and moving disabled people from institution to community bring partners to their networks. The extent to which similar goals keep agencies together and help forge solutions is a matter of investigation throughout this book. Each of the PMNs is attempting to face the kinds of problems that have contributed to the prominence of networks (O'Toole 1997). They address the more nettlesome policy problems, and they work in arenas where there are limitations on direct government intervention, thus requiring the involvement of NGOs. The subject areas of PMNs, such as metro transportation, become further intermeshed with political demands whose influence must be blended with technical needs. Second-order program effects also give rise to PMNs, as highways affect green space, development threatens watersheds, or rural out-migration leaves smaller water customer bases. Finally, the extensive overlays of federal mandates, state regulations, and local ordinances create a need to deal with problems related to transportation for the disabled, balanced land use, or wastewater treatment that meets local construction, state health, and federal environmental standards. This means that within a policy, "achieving something meaningful in any one program must mean adapting to several" (O'Toole 1997, 47).

CONCLUSIONS

Because this field of study is new, the PMNs' internal management processes may still be something of a mystery. All of the PMNs come together for the reasons stated, and they possess some level of commitment to making their programs work by working with other programs. They all share ideas and information, examine new technologies, and explore problems and identify possible solutions. Some go further in regard to the latter issue, indicating strategic options to solving problems and often actually enacting solutions. How these sequences develop into a management process is a primary focus of this study.

Also of great importance is that, in a way similar to most networks, the PMNs proved not to be the primary entities that implement any course of action agreed on. It is important to remember that action appears to remain in the realm of the agencies. When a network makes a decision on action, it is normally the person-power of the partner representatives or their staff that are involved in the execution. Some PMNs do have small, core staffs, transportation networks do have relatively larger staffs, but these people are normally dedicated to support services, information gathering and research, and follow-up of tasks. The actual actions are virtually always the responsibility of the organizations that are linking. In this implementation sense, networks' actions appear very different from the programming activities of the organizations that comprise them.

Our analysis now turns to the discovery of differences between organizations and networks, and the impact of PMNs on the public management process. In the next chapter we focus on the discovery process itself. How was the PMN study conducted so that the participating public managers could speak for themselves? What led to the typology based on activities/decisions that frames this book?

CHAPTER THREE

. . . .

TOWARD A NETWORK TYPOLOGY: METHODOLOGY OF THE STUDY

Darby does not make decisions, we share research and project information on the watershed.

The Indiana Rural Development Council is not a policymaking body, nor do we normally sponsor programs. Our role is to increase the ability of the many rural interests to deal with intergovernmental problems facing rural areas.

We don't directly make policy or program decisions, we steer small communities to those agencies that can make the decisions to help (them) solve their water problems. The Small Communities Environmental Infrastructure Group organizes the technological, educational, and financial strategies that Ohio small towns adapt in the water area.

KIPDA is the Louisville-Southern Indiana area body that establishes metro transportation needs and plans, and has a substantial role in allocating and dedicating federal and federal-state highway funds.

THESE OBSERVATIONS FROM PMN discussants demonstrate that the real world does not always work in the ways that academic or armchair observers claim. Fixed rules about the role of networks in policy and program adjustment did not prove to be the universal case, as the above quotes indicate. The PMNs take on many and varied collaborative tasks, and for some their role is more restricted than is often suggested. Using the observations of the practitioners involved in the PMNs, the fourfold classification scheme will be justified.

The study methodology is identified as the research typology is demonstrated. The case will be made for utilizing grounded theory as a means of discovering network management as practiced by its practitioners. The grounded theory approach used in this book lays out how cutting edge practice can be conceptualized in a way that is useful to academic and practitioner alike. Indeed, grounded theory can be an important method for public administration scholars interested in going beyond the trendy assertions in any number of subfields, inasmuch as it is a systematic way to probe structure and process at a real world level. Moreover, it is a first-line approach used by many scholars

(Frederickson and Frederickson 2006; Radin 2000; McGuire 2000; Yildiz 2004; Imperial 2004; Wondolleck and Jaffee 2000; Church and Nakamura 1993) in fields like performance management, environmental policy, economic development, and policy implementation.

The utility of looking at PMNs from the grounded theory perspective will be illustrated by focusing on an issue central to this study, that of their ascribed role in policy adjustment and/or service processing. Among the various roles ascribed to PMNs are those related to making policy accommodations among participating agencies (Kickert and Koppenjan 1997; Klijn and Koppenjan 2000; Kooiman 2003), including the adjustment of programs to fit specific localized applications (Hanf, Hjern, and Porter 1978). Also related are the so-called joint production activities (Alter and Hage 1993) that help public service clients, such as in human services, flow through systems rooted in divided policies (Jennings and Ewalt 1998; O'Toole 1997). These roles, if universal to networks, would mean that some form of interactive or collaborative network decision making that leads to policy adaptation among agency and/or between agency service sequencing would be present in all networks. In regard to interactive decisions, the previous literature on how networks make decisions based on soft leadership principles (Windhoff-Héntier 1992; Gray 1989) then led to the development of one research question for this study (chapter 1) and a bank of discussion questions on the collective processes involved in network decision making.

Discussions in the field, however, almost immediately suggested that some networks do not actually make decisions, at least on making policy adjustments or program sequencing decisions. Their roles were completely outside of this domain. As the previous quotations suggest, the discussants often answered, "We don't decide," or "In terms of agencies' programs, we do not decide anything," or "We may request that another agency do something that will help us meet our aims, but we never decide that anyone take action." Others said, "We inform and report. We do not decide in the way you asked." Still other managers said that their role was not to decide but to "learn about new GIS uses and to help others use them." What began to emerge was that for a number of the PMNs under study, their "big" decisions related to internal matters such as agendas, work plans, task force structures, annual conferences, meeting locations, and potential presenters.

This "on the ground" information meant that not only did our initial notions of PMN decision making have to be revised, but that the networks themselves had to be reconsidered. Their public roles and organized missions possibly lay entirely outside of the realm of policy and program. We had to dig deeper into the data, looking for a form of meaning that might lie outside of the previous literature. As a result of this deeper focus, grounded theory made it possible to explain how the fourfold typology of network types introduced in chapter 1 emerged from the data.

The methodology employed in this work along with identification of the four types of PMNs is the primary focus of this chapter. The PMN typology thus becomes the prime example of how grounded theory in the study is developed. First, the chapter introduces the concept of grounded theory and its derivative application, systematic case analysis. Then the process and sequence of data gathering is analyzed. Next, the all-important process of building theory from case data, using the context of this study, is discussed. This is followed by the sequence of moving from coding to deeper meaning by demonstrating how the typology was derived. The chapter concludes with a discussion of the utility of grounded theory for network analysis.

FROM GROUNDED THEORY TO SYSTEMATIC CASE STUDIES

It is obvious that there are different ways of "knowing" in basic and applied social sciences. Inquiry systems include many models, including those based on agreement (such as Delphi), deductive and inductive measurement, multiple realities, unbounded systems theory, and complexity theory (Mitroff and Linstone 1993). All of these modes of analysis may be called on to answer public management questions. In order to answer some of the more important questions in public network theory, the field must look to one particular form of inquiry, inductive analysis through grounded theory. Indeed, grounded theory methodology can help answer some big questions in the management of networks (Agranoff and McGuire 2001b). Basically, it is a way to look at networks empirically from the perspectives of those immersed in these arenas.

Few core social science grounded theory studies use a pure form of this methodology in framing research issues from the literature (Miles and Huberman 1994). The particular empirical approach applied to this study is a form of grounded theory that follows a qualitative but positivist systematic case data analysis mode. It is an approach adapted to public administration by this author along with Radin (Agranoff and Radin 1991) and has been used in a number of studies (Agranoff 1986; Radin et al. 1996; Radin and Hawley 1988, among others). Its extensive reliance on multistage coding in order to look for deep meaning distinguishes it from many other qualitative methods used in policy implementation, for example (Williams et al. 1981).

As is the case with other qualitative methods, grounded theory does depend on in-depth analysis. In other words, the researcher places great reliance on detailed knowledge derived from cases. One type of deep analysis is what Geertz (1973) calls "thick" description, that is, interpretive work that focuses on the meaning of human behavior to the actors involved (Feldman 1995; Pattakos 2004). For example, in the field of international studies and in public policy, constructivist methods for learning about the constitution of meaning and concepts has become commonplace in interpretive research (Wendt 1999;

Finnemore and Sikkink 2001; Feldman 1989, 1995). Dexter concludes, for example, that "interviews sometimes acquired meaning from the observations
which I made" (1970, 15). Another related approach is intuitional analysis,
which recognizes that every person has an inner source of knowing that can
be brought to bear on organized entities through participation (Franz and
Pattakos 1996). Many additional forms of detailed knowledge—insights,
apprehensions, hunches, feelings, and "vibrations"—are derived from such interpretive research that provides explanation, causation, and theory building
(Guba and Lincoln 1981).

The other grounded theory stream is the positivist approach, a methodology first developed within clinical settings by Glaser and Strauss (1967). They
define qualitative research as any type of research that produces findings not
achieved by statistical procedures or other means of quantification. Although
they recognize that survey data are quantified, they are often qualitative in
nature and then converted into numerical form. Other qualitative data, such
as research that tries to understand people's nature or that looks at thought
processes or emotions, lend to getting into the field and finding out what
people are doing and thinking. As Strauss and Corbin (1998) indicate, there
are actually three major components of qualitative research: the data, which
can come from various sources (interviews, focused discussions, observations,
documents); the procedures used to interpret and analyze the data (coding,
categorization, sampling); and written and verbal reports at conferences, in
journals, and in books.

Grounded theory then means "theory that was derived from the data, systematically gathered and analyzed through the research process" (Strauss and
Corbin 1998, 12). This puts data collection, analysis, and the theory that
emerges in a very close relationship:

> A researcher does not begin a project with a preconceived theory in mind
> (unless his or her purpose is to elaborate and extend existing theory).
> Rather, the researcher begins with an area of study and allows the theory
> to emerge from the data. Theory derived from data is more likely to re-
> semble the "reality" than is theory derived by putting together a series
> of concepts based on experience or solely through speculation (how one
> thinks things ought to work). Grounded theories, because they are drawn
> from data, are likely to offer insight, enhance understanding, and pro-
> vide a meaningful guide to action. (ibid., 12)

This puts the researcher at the nexus of both critical and creative thinking,
where the researcher is the instrument. "The credibility of qualitative methods, therefore, hinges to a great extent on the skill, competence and rigor of
the person doing the fieldwork" (Patton 2002, 14).

Grounded theory in practice has been adapted to the realities of doing research outside of the clinical and anthropological settings from which it emerged. This approach conventionally kept prestructured designs to a minimum. Clinical psychologists, social anthropologists, and social phenomenologists consider the processes they are studying to be too complex, relative, and elusive to be analyzed with tight research designs involving standardized instruments. They allow the conceptual framework as well as the theory to emerge from the field, and gradually bring out the important questions. However, Miles and Huberman (1994) recommend designs that pay prior attention to a conceptual framework, as well as research questions, sampling, and instrumentation that have a "focusing and bounding" role within a study (34) (see also Marshall and Rossman 1995; Maxwell 1996). This adapted grounded theory approach puts the qualitative researcher somewhere between designs based on deductive quantitative (ordinal, interval, and ratio data) testing of explicit theoretical propositions and descriptive and causal inference, and thick analysis of nominal data analyzed by inference (Collier, Seawright, and Brady 2003, 5). That is the approach taken in this study.

This focused and bounded inductive approach proves to be well suited to application in public administration and policy, as suggested earlier. It has been adapted particularly to case studies and comparative case studies. The public network research focused on here follows a sequence close to the field-study based approach developed by Agranoff and Radin (1991). It is identified as follows: (1) design by major concept and research question development; (2) sampling by case site selection; (3) formatting and outlining of the cases; (4) preparation of the guide for focused discussions in the field; (5) preliminary site orientation, particularly to gather documentation and pretest the guide; (6) final discussion guide; (7) site visits, including discussions, observations, and additional document gathering; (8) recording of postsite impressions; (9) development of cases by organizing information into categories of data; and, (10) cross-case analysis, development of conceptual findings, and theory construction.

DATA GATHERING INSIDE THE BOX

The scenario for data gathering in this study focuses on operational and structural issues that may reveal possible managerial differences between networks and organizations. The concept formation phase, which set the stage for questions regarding decision making and later the discovery of managerial differences, was based primarily on previous literature reviews conducted by Agranoff and McGuire (2001b, 2003b) and those discussed in chapter 2. The study began with the time-consuming task of searching for cases, that is, the sampling problem (Patton 2002).

Finding networks appropriate for the study was not simply a matter of looking in a government organization directory and choosing agencies whose missions fit the study's scope. Locating these networks involved following leads from federal, state, and local government managers; listening carefully when networks are mentioned in the course of other research; or remembering those that surfaced during the hunt for real-life teaching examples. The initial search for this project led to about three dozen possibilities. We visited their website home pages to see if they really qualified as networks. That reduced the number to around twenty. E-mail contacts that included an abstract of the study were made with a potential principal contact, followed by phone calls to answer questions, request permission to enter the space of the network, and acquire names of potential informants. If the answer was in the affirmative and if the body was a true network, documentation from the network's website and through mailings was gathered. After the initial document examination, the networks to be studied were selected.

The field study includes observation and limited participation, guided discussions with principal network actors, and document analysis. The latter included extensive review of each network's annual reports, strategic plans, action plans, major studies, legislation and executive orders, meeting minutes, conference programs, and other published sources. For each network two waves of discussions were conducted on-site in Ohio, Indiana, Kentucky, Iowa, and Nebraska. In several cases site visits were scheduled to coincide with observation at regular network meetings and, in four cases, attendance at an annual conference. Rather than interviews, guided discussions were employed where discussants were asked to respond to a standardized set of questions, but in a conversational form. All discussants received an e-mail copy of the study abstract in advance of each wave of discussion.

Discussions were held with more than 150 network staff coordinators and/or chairpersons/presidents, along with federal and state agency managers and program heads. In most cases network activists from substate and local governments and nongovernmental organizations were also included, as well as university researchers and program specialists. Because the study focuses on management issues, priority was placed on public managers, particularly those who work both in large bureaucratic organizations and in networks. A mixture of agency heads or state directors, program managers, program specialists, and agency liaison persons or "boundary spanners" was included. This inevitably led to a weighted or purposive sample that included larger numbers of federal and state officials who were managers, along with network chairs and coordinators. The topic under study seemed to justify this approach because the focus is not on building individual case studies that depict the structure and operations of the networks themselves, but on how managers from agencies might manage differently in networks. As a result, some very important network contributors were undoubtedly missed, although they were counted in the core total in table 1.3. Their absence was totally a function of the topic.

The use of mixed methods allowed for a richer and deeper understanding of a murky arena, the approximately 20 percent of public managers' time spent crossing organizational lines to do their jobs, in this situation working in networks. Discussants had a chance to reflect on the presubmitted study abstract and to answer in their own words. Face-to-face contact allowed the researcher to read more stimuli, such as nonverbal expressions, and to get instant clarification of any point made. Also, additional but valuable information not on the discussion guide was usually added, including political and administrative tactics that would not be offered in a closed-ended questionnaire response. No tape recorder was used, because the information was often sensitive. The discussions also provided the opportunity to find out who really carried the network through their knowledge and efforts. If unequal power or resources proved to be a relevant factor within the network, it was likely to come out in the course of discussions in ways that quantitative methods could never tap.

Meanwhile, the scientific documentation and information produced by the networks and gathered during phase one afforded a clearer understanding of parts of the subsequent phase two emphasis on knowledge management, network performance, and questions on the boundaries of government. Discussions from the first phase provided information on the interlinking of research and technology with interagency possibilities and, ultimately, action. Indeed, it increased our understanding of how information/knowledge is as essential to networks as is collaborative interaction. Finally, the observation opportunities, while uneven, helped not only in understanding relationships between the formal and informal but also to see how networkers both give and receive valuable information and knowledge. They also provided a level of personal contact with many actors beyond the scheduled discussion in a considerably more informal and personal way. Together, the triangulated document-discussions-observation data-gathering mode allowed an inside view without becoming a participant observer. Clearly this approach leads to a more holistic picture of these semiamorphous organized entities.

BUILDING THEORY FROM CASE DATA

In grounded theory, analysis of data depends on conceptualizing and classifying events, acts, and outcomes. "The categories that emerge, along with their relationships, are the foundations for our developing theory" (Strauss and

Corbin 1998, 66). The act of abstracting, reducing, and relating is what makes the difference between theoretical and descriptive coding, putting the analyst into a conceptual mode of analysis. This falls into the proverbial "easier said than done" situation. How does one move from one to five thousand pages of notes (filled-in discussion guides) and/or tapes to theoretical conclusions that have a ring of reliability and validity? As other analysts of grounded theory have suggested, constant comparison is the key. Data are subjected to continuous, cyclical, evolving interpretation and reinterpretation that allows patterns to emerge (Mohrman, Tenkasi, and Mohrman Jr. 2003).

In a classic paper on building management theory from cases, Eisenhardt (1989) suggests that theory building begins with careful sampling and crafting of instruments, followed by beginning the analysis while still in the field. Field notes and immediate observations in the field can be analyzed and tested later. Also, early field observations can allow for adjustment of the instrument, which is an allowable approach in qualitative analysis. This is followed by case study write-ups for each case, allowing "the unique patterns of each case to emerge before investigators push to generalize patterns across cases" (540). She suggests that cross-case patterns can be built by: (1) selecting categories or dimensions, then looking for within-group similarities coupled with intergroup differences; (2) selecting pairs of cases, then listing the similarities and differences between each pair; and (3) dividing the data by source, then triangulating among discussions, observations, and documents. This iterative-patterned analysis allows for the emergence of frameworks that can be supported by coded data through constructs sharpening, and by building evidence that measures the construct in each case. Next, hypotheses/theoretical statements emerge that fit with the evidence, a sort of replication logic, for example, treating the cases/constructs as a series of experiments. In effect they are analogous to multiple experiments, as opposed to the sampling logic of traditional, within-experiment hypothesis-testing research in which aggregate relationships across data points are tested using summary statistics. "In replication logic, cases which confirm emergent relationships enhance confidence in the validity of the relationships" (Eisenhardt 1989, 542).

The operational sequence of analytical development follows a natural progression from notes/transcripts to conceptual analysis. In this regard, Carney (1990) suggests that this can be accomplished by following a five-step data display sequence: (1) creating a text to work on (synopses and reconstruction); (2) trying out coding categories to find a set that fits (coding and analytical notes); (3) identifying themes and trends in the data overall (searching for relationships); (4) testing hypotheses and reducing the bulk of the data for analysis of trends; and (5) delineating the deep structure (explanatory framework). Fortunately several useful data transformation guides exist that cover the details of coding, data displays (such as Kelle 1995; Miles and Huberman 1994), and data interpretation (such as Patton 2002; Wolcott 1994). The data themes and extended explanations that climb Carney's (1990) ladder help organize the study. Appendix B begins with a more detailed analysis of the research sequence. For those interested in the more advanced grounded theory analytical techniques such as time-ordered matrices, sequences of activities, explanatory effects matrices, causal networks, and clusters of cross-case displays, one must consult detailed manuals, such as Miles and Hubermann's (1994) *Qualitative Data Analysis*. All of these data handling/data display approaches are possible when grounded theory is employed.

DEMONSTRATING FINDINGS: NETWORK TYPOLOGY AND DECISION MAKING

The portion of the research results related to the network typology is presented here in order to illustrate how this type of qualitative data gathering can be used in working form to build theory. It is derived from a portion of the network decision-making findings. The process began with one question from the discussion guide: "What processes does your network engage in order to reach agreement and ultimately decisions?" Some responses to this question appear earlier in this chapter. Related findings are systematically reported through three vehicles: First, a series of coded and matrixed categories and a repackaged data presentation are illustrated, both in this chapter and in appendix B. Second, parallel summary text on the question follows. Third, a supporting vignette, demonstrating one network's protracted decision process, illustrates the richness that narrative analysis alongside data presentation can bring to grounded theory.

The detailed process of how the decision question was applied is contained in appendix B. It illustrates, table by table, how the analysis proceeded from a raw or unordered list of codes to an ordered list. This was followed by an all-important but unordered matrix of nine levels of decisions, produced here as table 3.1. An examination of this table reveals that among the nine different coded categories of decisions, some networks engage in only a few of the lower-numbered activities, whereas others do more; one—Iowa Communications—engages in all nine activities. More information on how this table was integrated to the development of the typology is in the textual explanation in appendix B. This multisequenced coding process (appendix B) allows the analyst to see many characteristics, including some that fly in the face of essayists' analyses of networks. For example, the tables in appendix B and table 3.1 conclude that the premise that public networks make policy adjustments and decisions does not hold true for all networks. The supporting text indicates that only four of the fourteen actually do, and three others come close. What do networks do?

The other networks do other things, such as information exchange, capacity enhancement, and strategic guidance, which led to the typology.

To illustrate, the summary text for table 3.1 and appended material is presented. The fourteen PMNs were ultimately arrayed numerically from low to high, which led to the informational, developmental, outreach, and action categories that emerged as explained in appendix B. Their formal definition has been presented previously in table 1.1. Basically, informational networks partner to exchange policy and program information, which may or may not lead to subsequent agency action. Developmental networks also engage in these activities, but also build member capabilities. Outreach networks come closer to taking policy/program action, because they blueprint interagency strategies while also engaging in capacity and informational activities. Finally, action networks make the types of interagency policy/program adjustments ascribed to networks in the literature and engage in most of the other activities listed in table 3.1. As a result, based on this decision-making framework it is clear that not all networks are alike, and these differences are potentially significant in a substantive way in understanding networks.

In this way second- and third-order data matrices are possible, using the typology based on the types of decisions or nondecisional agreements or understandings. They too are built after preliminary codes are established and recoded, and subsequently compared with the types of decision- or non-decision-based agreements made by each of the networks. It makes possible two-by-two tables, in effect, comparing type with other operational characteristics such as the establishment of decision-support databases. This decision/nondecision matrix, also featured in table 3.1, informed the research that networks have very important roles in technology and scientific exchange, and that for most networks their web-based links go far beyond their home pages. This opened up an extended avenue of inquiry in phase two of the study, that of networks' roles in knowledge management. Thus, the back and forth of data display and seeking of meaning within the data yields core findings that link raw qualitative data to theoretical conclusions.

The sample offered in the following vignette illustrates the potential richness that can come from grounded theory and parallels prior substantive text. In this case it is a decision-making account or reconstructed narrative from the field notes, based on several discussants' accounting of the Des Moines Metropolitan Planning Organization's (MPO) plan and project-funding decision processes. With a core city and many suburbs of variable growth, there are numerous potential conflicts if acrimonious decisions and long-standing feuds are allowed to jeopardize the MPO's role in developing a metropolitan perspective. The network's stability could be threatened. As a result, they have adopted elaborate decision rules for project funding that all network partners have

(text continues on page 48)

TABLE 3.1 Types of Actions/Decisions Made

Network	[a](1) Network Information Exchange	(2) Agendas/Network Work Plans	(3) Scientific Reports/Studies	(4) Forums/Enhancement and Assistance	(5) Web Link Info. Systems Development	(6) Strategic Blueprint/Fund Leveraging	(7) Plan Review	(8) Mutual Policy/Program Adjustment	(9) Network Policy-making
Darby	Quarterly meetings	Meeting locations	Only by the partners						
Des Moines Metro	Quarterly meetings		Special reports		Basic info. only		Transportation improvement plan; if requested for community	Continually, for metro orientation	Transportation plan fund awards
Enhanced Data	Monthly meetings	User-driven	Staff-prepared market plans		Manages state web portal		On use of state website	Negotiations w/agencies	Web-portal use policy and fee structure
Iowa Communications	Only one-to-one among users	Annual strategic plan	Technology reports	Technical assistance to users	Major point of public contact	Special: telemedicine, emergency management, public health, telejustice	By publicly appointed board	With state, fed., and local govt. users	Network operations by a public board

continued

TABLE 3.1 (continued)

Network	[a](1) Network Information Exchange	(2) Agendas/Network Work Plans	(3) Scientific Reports/Studies	(4) Forums/Enhancement and Assistance	(5) Web Link Info. Systems Development	(6) Strategic Blueprint/Fund Leveraging	(7) Plan Review	(8) Mutual Policy/Program Adjustment	(9) Network Policy-making
Indiana Economic Development	Economic conditions	Scope of research	Project reports				Occasionally on request of Dept. of Commerce		
Iowa Enterprise	Annual workshop	Assistance work plan		Special topic forums	How to get access to assistance	Some one-to-one coaching			
Iowa Geographic	Biannual conference	Work plan	New GIS applications	Quarterly report at meetings	Over 30 applications				
Indiana Rural Council	Meeting briefings	For work groups		Annual meeting; Water and Community Visitation Taskforces		2002 Rural Strategy (advisory only)			
Kentuckiana Agency	Monthly meetings		Special Project Reports	To local governments	Extensive support databases		Transportation improvement plan; special project plans	Continually for area focus	Transportation plan fund awards, large fed. projects

Lower Platte	State of the river; district reports	Annual work plan	Only at the district level		Web-based GIS		Informal
Partnership for Rural Nebraska	Annual Institute	Education/ training agenda	Nebraska rural poll	Joint training events	Site for rural reports/news		
Small Communities	Committee meetings	Plan of research	Technology transfer committee		Training committee maintains assess info.	Finance committee meets quarterly to set community strategies	
USDA/ Nebraska	Informal only	Annual coord. plan			USDA links	Formally in water and wastewater, informally in other areas	Constantly, on multiple funding projects
317 Group	Intermittent meetings and special sessions	Only if legislative amendments needed	Impact studies, waiting list studies	Future sessions at IU decision laboratory	Through ARC and INARF policy group	Through DDARS of FSSA-state agency and contact case managers	2003 Legislative Audit/Report

[a]Numerically ordered from least to most involved

bought into by prior agreement. On the other hand, plan voting is weighted, particularly by population, but nevertheless predetermined. While a protracted process, it helps keep the parties working together as a network. The Des Moines Metro vignette demonstrates how text prepared from the discussions can provide interesting reading to supplement the coded data. In this case, it illustrates a special mode of protracted decision making that some networks engage in to reduce potential conflict and maintain themselves as a collaborative.

Des Moines Metro's Decision-making Process

The Des Moines Metro's process combines information, politics, and fixed decision rules to maintain itself as a network and to take a metropolitan perspective. First, the long-range planning process relies heavily on the consensus-oriented work of its Technical Committee, which includes some members that overlap with its Policy Committee. When the Technical Committee reports on a draft of the plan, only minor adjustments are made before the Policy Committee takes an actual vote. Second, individual community funding projects are voted on only after the Technical Committee has examined their feasibility and suggested consensus-based adjustments. The staff then assigns a priority number based on a predetermined rotating principle. These rotation principles are based on population impact and time span since the last project was funded for a community. Third, an informal process of persuading community representatives to go along with metropolitan priorities in the plan is engaged by the Policy Committee chair (a western suburban city council member) and vice-chair (a state representative from an eastern town-suburb), and the secretary treasurer (a city manager from a town that is becoming a northern suburb). In particular, there is the issue of moving the city of Des Moines's nine (of thirty-one) representatives to act on anything that may benefit the suburbs. Fourth, voting is through a predetermined weighted process, a formula that includes feasibility, rotation, and population, that gives the core city the most votes but a minority in the overall process. This formula virtually predetermines the vote, and while it has not satisfied everyone, it has reduced a great deal of political friction. Overall, the sequence of long-range priorities, technical screening, informal persuasion, and the voting formula help keep the MPO together as a collaborative. Indeed, the highest degree of acrimony reported was related to an operations issue, when the Policy Committee approved a move of the MPO offices from the City of Des Moines Planning Department to a west suburban office complex.

The next steps also involve further reducing the bulk of the data to provide an analysis that leads to categories, and ultimately generation of theoretical conclusions and additional hypotheses. For example, one clear theoretical direction is that because all networks do not make the type of policy adjustments that observers claim they do, the framework of the four different types of networks can be cross-analyzed against a value-adding outcomes scheme presented in the final chapter. This provides a more accurate accounting of why networks exist and what public functions they perform. In other words, this examination into deep structure allows the research to move into an explanatory framework of network performance.

CONCLUSION: INSIDE THE LINES AND CIRCLES

If public administration is to treat networks seriously (O'Toole 1997), then more attention needs to be paid to what managers do and why they do it. As McGuire suggests, "A research agenda in network management must include three components: (1) a description of the behaviors chosen by the network manager; (2) an explanation of why managers make such choices; and, (3) an evaluation of these choices" (2002, 599).

One can now add to this mix the idea that networks must also be differentiated by the kind of work they do. The study of networks in public management cannot be studied without some internal grounding. We must listen to those who till the fields as well as to the academic community. If working collaboratively through entities like networks is an increasingly important aspect of the managerial task, greater attention must be paid to the operations of organization boundary spanning. The study of networks as applied to governance and public administration appears to have gone beyond the initial stage where consciousness of boundary spanning, collaboration, mutual adjustment, and new roles for government are recognized. It is time to move into the next phase, where these assumptions are tested.

While there is no one best way to study networks scientifically, they must be studied. In Western cultures, we too often adhere to deductive scientific methods, anecdotal and descriptive examples, or essays of observation as the major means of learning about phenomena. Deductive models tend to be narrower in scope, but provide useful information on how certain inputs are associated with selected outputs. They can be rigorous and explanatory, but tend to be devoid of context. Descriptive analyses provide valuable context but often miss important links among variables. Finally, essays cannot directly link inputs to outputs. They raise important questions but offer no substantiation beyond isolated examples.

The focused or conceptual framework form of grounded theory can add to the mix. Although grounded theory network studies normally consider smaller numbers of cases than large-scale deductive studies (but larger than essays), they can examine a reasonable number of variables (Goggin 1986), account for what goes on within, and associate and causally relate inputs to outputs (Miles and Huberman 1994). As managers in the public sector spend increasing amounts of transactional time in networks, thus transforming knowledge and resource inputs into outputs that are designed to add value, more must be learned about these emergent processes. One means is through embedding grounded theory qualitative methodology.

CHAPTER FOUR

. . . .

INFORMATIONAL AND DEVELOPMENTAL NETWORKS

Partnership for Rural Nebraska does not make . . . decisions on program questions, nor have we ever engaged in the part of our founding mission statement that involves public policy analysis.

NOW THAT THE grounded theory typology of networks has been developed, it is time to describe the four types. The nature of networks—what they are, who they are, what they do—can best be understood by focusing on each one. This will allow for a first sorting of the rhetoric and realities of the basic nature of PMNs. For the reader unfamiliar with their operational features, this also provides a basic introduction; for the experienced networker, the approach provides a reality check. This chapter and the next then present the key features of networks, and explain why each PMN falls in one of the four categories. Eight of the fourteen PMNs are highlighted in these chapters; all fourteen form the analytical core of the remainder of the study. Chapters 4 and 5 introduce the PMNs but additionally make the case for why the study networks are of a particular type.

The informational and developmental networks covered in this chapter are grouped together because neither type approaches policy issues or makes the program adjustments for which networks are commonly known. Neither type deals with public policy or public service delivery in a direct way. Although they may engage heavily in exchange or in enhancing partner strengths, they do not become involved in direct collaborative or strategic actions. As PMNs, information networks come together to collaboratively exchange information, learn the depth of problems, and hear how individual agencies are solving problems. Developmental networks are prone to extensively exchanging information, but they also mutually develop management/policy/program capabilities and engage heavily in capacity building. These skills can be brought back to home agencies so they can individually or dyadically solve problems that have cross-organization implications.

The Darby Partnership in Ohio (Darby) and the Indiana Economic Development Council (Indiana Economic Development) are highlighted as informational networks. The featured developmental networks are the Partnership for Rural Nebraska and the Iowa Geographic Information Council (Iowa Geographic).

THE DARBY PARTNERSHIP

Darby grew out of efforts to protect the Big and Little Darby Creek watershed, located in a six-county area of central Ohio. The eighty-eight-mile stream, with 245 miles of tributaries, flows into the Columbus-Franklin County area, one of the fastest growing metropolitan areas in the Midwest. The Darby Partnership meets quarterly, "shares information and resources to address stresses to the streams, and serves as a think tank for conservation efforts in the watershed" (bigdarby.org). Darby Creek is one of the top ten endangered rivers in the United States, and has been designated as a U.S. and Ohio Scenic River under federal and state acts. In 1991 the Nature Conservancy declared the Darby watershed "A Last Great Place" in the western hemisphere. The Darby Partnership includes federal, state, and local agencies; nongovernmental organizations; and private citizens. Although Darby's mailing list includes over 100 organizations, a core of about thirty agencies, jurisdictions, and allied organizations regularly participate in Darby's activities.

The evolution of Darby, from its inception as "Darby Partners" in 1991 to its current form as the "Darby Partnership," underscores much of its work as well as that of its core agencies. Since 1943 Ohio counties have had local Soil and Water Conservation Districts (SWCDs), which are charged with developing comprehensive plans for conservation of natural resources. They are technically assisted by the U.S. Department of Agriculture/Natural Resource Conservation Services (NRCS), which shares the same offices. In 1995 the six county SWCDs of the Darby Watershed (Logan, Union, Champaign, Madison, Pickaway, and Franklin) began to turn their attention to special conservation efforts, particularly for farmers. This led to partnering with the Ohio EPA and the Ohio Department of Natural Resources to develop a plan for the Darby Creek watershed, which made the cooperating agencies eligible for watershed improvements funding.

An important result was the inclusion of the Darby Creek Watershed as one of seventy Hydrologic Unit Areas in the United States. A host of new agencies were subsequently brought in as a result of implementing the hydrologic plan: U.S. Department of Agriculture, NRCS, and the Farm Services Agency [now USDA/RD], the Ohio State University Extension; Ohio Department of Natural Resources (Scenic Rivers and Forestry Divisions); SWCDs; Ohio Environmental Protection Agency; Ohio State University College of Landscape Architecture; The Nature Conservancy (TNC) of Ohio: U.S. EPA, Region 5; U.S. Forest Service; and U.S. Fish and Wildlife Service. In 1991 the TNC agreed to provide facilitation and administrative support for Darby, thus launching this PMN (The Darby Book, undated).

Darby has a limited agenda of actions, all primarily geared to listening to partner reports at quarterly meetings. A typical meeting involves updates on key research projects, reports from subareas and affiliated groups, proposed remediation plan reports, and technical support (such as stream bank preservation) demonstrations. As one state official related, the structure is "a close-knit collaborative effort of a lot of agencies, private entities, and citizens. Basically everyone has their say in the partnership, but it is not like we are voting members or anything. It is primarily an information dissemination organization" (Manskopf 2000). When the initial contacts were made with TNC about entering into Darby's space for this research project, some doubt was expressed that it qualified as a network, given their lack of direct impact on policy or programs. During the initial site visit, several discussants expressed uncertainty as to what role it did play beyond information exchange. "While a number of our partners like the SWCDs, Ohio EPA, and USDA have a great deal of influence over policy, the Partnership does not. We inform one another about what we are doing." Another described Darby as "an umbrella that touches the work of many related groups in the watershed, in the sense that it provides a place for the exchange of projects." Another told project evaluator Dick Manskopf, "The Darby Partnership is a place where information can be exchanged without the need for judgment and so people can come to their own conclusions about what the information means to them" (2000).

Darby clearly serves as the clearinghouse for the many projects and watershed organizations that are part of the USDA Hydrologic Unit Area project. For example, the author's first knowledge of Darby's existence came as a result of an introduction to an allied group, the Operation Future Association (OFA). This project organized, developed, and encouraged environmentally sensitive farming practices. Housed at TNC, it was a spin-off of Darby's efforts to bring landowners and agencies together. A current allied effort is the Darby Environmentally Sensitive Development Area External Advisory Group, which is studying ways to avert negative growth impacts from rapid growth in western Franklin County. This spin-off subgroup is focusing on riparian buffer restrictions, storm water management planning, conservation development regulations, and adequate public facilities, such as roadways. It provides a prime example of the type of groups that participate in and report within Darby.

Another particularly important partner is the Hellbranch Watershed Forum Cooperative Agreement, signed in May 2002. This is an interjurisdictional agreement in the eastern part of the Darby watershed, the most urbanized area.

This agreement grew out of an informal group, the Hellbranch Forum. The Hellbranch Agreement will engage in research and planning, and make policy and regulatory recommendations to the affected local government jurisdictions. At the western end of the Darby Watershed is Darby Creek Watershed Taskforce, formed in spring 2002. This organization focuses on nonpoint source pollutants . . . It employs a full-time coordinator, who holds awareness workshops and has developed a template for a comprehensive plan based on SWCD plans. A Darby-related voluntary group formed in 1972 is the Darby Creek Association, a nonagency, citizen-based group. It serves as an advocate for watershed-related issues, including conservation practices, multijurisdictional planning, and reducing the negative aspects of development. Numerous additional efforts, such as the land-acquisition efforts of TNC and Columbus/Franklin County Parks and Recreation, transportation planning by the MPO, Metropolitan Organization for Regional Planning Consortium (MOPRC), and efforts of federal, state, and local governments including the SWCDS also make up the scope of work activities at Darby.

Darby has gone through a series of progressive transformations. According to Korfmacher (2000), who has studied Darby extensively, it has moved from a primary focus on agricultural practices to much broader concerns. These include industrial expansion impacts, highway construction impacts, and rapid residential development. This focus is evidenced by the current discussions of flood plain regulations, regional planning, storm water controls, and even a 1999 proposal by the U.S. Fish and Wildlife Service to establish a wildlife refuge within the watershed.

While relatively limited in scope compared to a number of the other PMNs under study, Darby undoubtedly represents many voluntarily derived networks that primarily exchange information. As such, collaboratives like Darby cannot be written off because they do not make policy or service adjustments. Participants related the importance of putting a range of watershed issues in broader perspective through the informative meetings. This has proved to be an important educational tool. Darby is also considered responsible for launching a great deal of informal networking between meetings. Its website is noted as an important source to consult, as all of the allied partners post information there. Environmental forums as well as association and project meetings that cannot be attended by all participants are summarized through these sources. It has become a comprehensive first point of contact (see also Korfmacher 2000). Darby's effects are more indirect, in the sense of influencing partner decisions by expanding the pool of information as well as by raising awareness of who is doing what. Korfmacher has captured the essence of Darby as an informational network: "The partnership played an important role in sparking and supporting diverse efforts to preserve the Darby despite having no strong central source of funding for projects, no authority to implement or create standards, and no concrete goals. Simply by providing a neutral forum for discussion, the partnership exposed members to ideas, information, and potential collaborators they otherwise would not have encountered. This in turn influenced the actions of member agencies and their organizations in the Darby watershed and beyond" (2000, 60). Clearly Darby follows the type of nondecision/action-related tenets identified with regard to informational networks. It informs but does not decide.

THE INDIANA ECONOMIC DEVELOPMENT COUNCIL

The Indiana Economic Development Council (Indiana Economic Development; www.http//iedc.org) is a public-private partnership composed of business, labor, education, and government leaders that work together to reach consensus on key economic issues, and develop long-term strategic advantages for the state. Indiana Economic Development's most visible activity is the creation and updating of Indiana's strategic economic development plan, now revised approximately every four years. The Council is a 501c(3) not-for-profit corporation created by the Indiana General Assembly in 1985. Under its 2004 corporate charter changes, Indiana Economic Development is governed by a twenty-one-person board of directors, which includes the governor, lieutenant governor (who in Indiana directs the Departments of Commerce and Agriculture), and the chief operating officer, with the remainder composed of gubernatorial appointees. The governor serves as the chairperson of the board; the vice chair is a person engaged in private enterprise (Articles of Incorporation 2004).

The council began in 1985 with a sixty-four-person board, a sort of Who's Who in state education, labor, business, and government. In 2004 the board was reduced in size because of difficulties in assembling quorums of the state economy's leading notables. Its first two presidents (CEOs), who served during 1985–1989 and 1989–2001, were well-known figures in academia and in state economic development. From 2001 to 2003 there was no president. In mid-2003 a new president, with a professional background in information systems and finance and who holds local elected office, was appointed. In 1986 the Council became the host agency for Indiana's Small Business Development Centers (SBDC) program, which it continues to sponsor. In the same year it published its first economic development strategy, "Looking Forward." This strategic plan was followed by "Hoosier Horizons" in 1990, "INvesting IN Indiana" in 1993, "Break-Away Growth" in 1999, and "A New Path to Progress" in 2005.

Indiana Economic Development operates beyond its strategic plan by partnering with many organizations and agencies and with numerous projects. In addition to sponsoring the SBDCs, it has been heavily involved in *Ladders for Success,* a coalition that studies the impact of state and local welfare reforms. Another coalition, *Future Skills Now,* was designed to work with industry through local employer skills alliances to identify jobs with higher skill levels and higher pay that need to be filled, and to identify the skills needed to fill them. In partnership with Purdue University and the Indiana Manufacturers Association, the Council recently conducted a study of Indiana manufacturing to obtain baseline information about the state's manufacturers, evaluate how firms are impacted by labor market conditions, and assess the strategies firms are using to maintain and enhance their competitiveness. The Council regularly helps substate regions engage in their planning processes, normally with the financial help of Indiana Department of Commerce (DOC) and sometimes the U.S. Economic Development Administration (USEDA).

Most recently, Indiana Economic Development began to look into high-speed communication access in partnership with DOC and the Central Indiana Corporate Partnership. This "broadband project," as they refer to it, included mapping existing service access and networks across the state; testing the performance of dial-up connections to the Internet; and surveying homes and businesses on Internet usage, technology choices, and predictions about future demand for advanced telecommunication tools. Indiana Economic Development does a great deal of work in partnership with DOC, such as research on process improvements in advanced manufacturing and the characteristics and needs of high-growth companies; compiling state rankings in indexes that measure economic performance; and producing an online listing of the economic development programs in the state.

Underlying the ebb and flow that drives Indiana Economic Development are gubernatorial or state agency requests, as well as shifts in emphasis over time. Initially the Council put a great deal of effort into building basic databases. By the turn of the century it became clear that these efforts duplicated those of others. As a result, it now uses its website to provide links to new and popular projects and national business journals. A second website has been created, dedicated to the communications infrastructure project INdiana INterconnect (www.indianainter=connect.org) (2003 Annual Report). Its initial focus was on larger picture economic trends such as international trade, high technology, basic industries, and employment of hard-to-employ individuals.

Over the past few years a shift has occurred toward issues that will enhance Indiana's foundations for twenty-first-century economic development. The broadband or telecommunications competitiveness effort is a prime example. After the showcase conference in July 2003, the study and issues became a DOC priority. Related concerns include a project to introduce GIS tools and benefits to Indiana communities, an evaluation of local government tax abatement and tax increment financing for the state legislature, and studies of the potential of biotechnology in agricultural processing.

As a research arm, the work of Indiana Economic Development is thus to inform the economic development decision-making processes in both the private and public sectors. Indiana Economic Development speaks to hundreds of stakeholders, at least indirectly. Its strategic plan is to put information on the table that other key actors do or do not incorporate into their own decision strategies. The Council itself makes no direct policy or strategic recommendations and does not propose legislative changes, steering clear of its government and private-organization sponsors' turf. Its low profile was underscored by an involved respondent, who concluded, "We are most useful when no one is scared of us." Whether dealing with the larger economic trends and strategies or more recent economic infrastructure rapid responses, Indiana Economic Development is unlikely to be anything more than a core information arm for the state of Indiana.

The third informational network, the Lower Platte River Corridor Alliance (Lower Platte), is also a watershed conservation network. Like Darby, Lower Platte (www.lowerplatte.org) is a network of three conservation districts and seven state agencies created to promote research, exchange information, and raise the consciousness of stakeholders along the Lower Platte in Nebraska. It also engages the work of federal agencies, such as the U.S. Army Corps of Engineers, the U.S. Geological Survey (USGS), and EPA. Quarterly Alliance meetings are convened to share the partners' progress reports on programs and projects. The partners assist counties and communities along a hundred-mile stretch of the river (roughly from above Lincoln to Omaha) regarding the natural resource impacts of their decisions. Any actions taken as a result of Lower Platte exchanges or research are by the state agencies, conservation districts, or other local governments.

THE PARTNERSHIP FOR RURAL NEBRASKA

The Partnership for Rural Nebraska (Partnership for Rural Nebraska; www.cari.unl.edu/prn1) is a cooperative agreement involving state-based rural development entities to address rural opportunities and challenges, provide the resources and expertise to enhance development opportunities, and work together to meet those challenges. Partnership for Rural Nebraska's mission statement underscores its character as a developmental network: "The Partnership for Rural Nebraska was created to improve the effectiveness of resource utilization statewide. The core partners are committed to integrating efforts and coordinating resources to enhance rural research, policy analysis, program delivery, education, and professional development" (www.cariunl.edu/prn1/aboutus.htm). Its core partners include the University of Nebraska, Center for Applied Rural Innovation (CARI), the State of Nebraska, Department of

Economic Development (DED) and Rural Development Commission (RDC), USDA/RD in Nebraska, and the Nebraska Development Network (NDN), an association of regional planning organizations. Other agency members who have been involved with Partnership for Rural Nebraska over time are the USDA Natural Resources Conservation Service, Nebraska Departments of Environmental Quality and Health and Human Services, and the University of Nebraska Center for Rural Research and Development.

The Partnership for Rural Nebraska was created in 1995 by an executive order of the governor of Nebraska for the state agencies, and a memorandum of understanding among the federal government and other parties. Rural development is obviously a key issue in Nebraska, and involves many players. Partnership for Rural Nebraska came together when the major players found that while they had similar foci, they had somewhat different but overlapping goals. USDA/Nebraska, for example, has a number of lending and grant programs in infrastructure and business, as discussed further in chapter 5, but in the 1990s also began supporting community development programs. The RDC emphasized five areas: small business development, value-added agriculture, information technology, youth development, and community building. This agenda overlapped with DED, USDA/Nebraska, NDN, and, to some extent, CARI. In 1995 a new governor's staff called in the top DED staff, RDC, and NDN to brainstorm about sharing funds and people. The University and USDA were then brought to the table. Initial leadership was placed in a governance board of appointed members from USDA, State of Nebraska, and the University. Its operations were guided by a coordinating team, consisting of two representatives from each core partner.

The Partnership's ongoing activities include an annual meeting; the Rural Institute; workshops and seminars sponsored by the Education Committee; *Rural News Bits*, an electronic newsletter that lists partner programs and funding opportunities; an annual poll conducted by CARI for Partnership for Rural Nebraska; a shared-staff program that promotes cooperatives; some sharing of partner staff; and numerous opportunities to bolster communication among the various entities. These activities are designed to implement Partnership for Rural Nebraska's ten founding goals: ensure long-term partnering and community-based capacity-building; develop a common rural research agenda; conduct common needs assessments; enhance rural policy analysis and improve understanding of federal, state, and local policy issues; create an integrated and ongoing strategic planning process; move Nebraska to a customer-driven rural development program delivery system; engage in shared education and professional development; create a system for shared resource acquisition and management; establish a unified targeting process for rural development resources; and establish and implement an integrated program and performance evaluation system (Partnership for Rural Nebraska Charter).

The flagship activity of Partnership for Rural Nebraska is clearly the annual Nebraska Rural Institute. This three-day meeting is, in effect, a state con-
vention of rural development professionals and volunteers. The Institute
brings together practitioners, community leaders, and academics. The program content and delivery is a blend of academic, practical, and community-
based experiences that include onsite sessions and mobile workshops. The
Institute rotates to a different part of the state each year, and is cosponsored
by regional organizations. One regular cosponsor is the area development
group affiliated with NDN; in 2004 this was the Southwest Regional Group.
Around 1,000 people have attended these meetings, including a number of
foreign participants.

Partnership for Rural Nebraska leaders point out that the primary barriers
to success involve "changes in administration at [the] federal, state, and university, and shifting budgetary situations among the partners [that] have
brought changing political agendas, new priorities, and threatened funding.
These changes have required adjustments in the project" (Cooperative Extension Examples of Engagement 2003). One discussant related that Partnership
for Rural Nebraska has consistently been impacted by various core actors re-
assessing their roles, and trying to become larger players in rural development.
"Our governor wanted to put his personal stamp on rural development, the
Rural Development Commission was the lightning rod, and he tried to
'rebrand' that group. He generated a competing policy action and put it on hold
with regard to Partnership for Rural Nebraska." The Rural Development Commission exists on a limited budget but has been merged into DED; it is no
longer listed as a core partner. The evolving trend of Partnership for Rural
Nebraska has been dictated by politics. Throughout 2003 the State of Nebraska
was facing budget cutbacks and withdrew some of its support, particularly for
the regional groups of NDN. On the other hand, partners like the University
and USDA/Nebraska have been steadfast in their support and in maintaining
the Partnership's original mission. Partnership agency staff have thus served
over the years as lobbyists for continuation of the project.

One of the most dramatic changes in Partnership for Rural Nebraska came
in May 2004, when NDN and Partnership for Rural Nebraska formally merged
into Partnership for Rural Nebraska. As discussed in chapter 6, the governing
board of Partnership for Rural Nebraska was expanded to include a representative from each of seven NDN regional groups. This merger came in part because of complimentary missions and overlapping memberships. The other
main reason was that DED terminated its seed grant funding for the regional
groups. The NDN regional groups are largely composed of planners, community development specialists, and other local officials. They meet regularly to
share resources, upcoming conferences, and trainings; provide community and
organizational updates; and discuss future issues. A Partnership for Rural

Nebraska Regional Group Subcommittee was developed to provide liaison and integration between the two groups.

Partnership for Rural Nebraska's ten original goals have been achieved with regard to its developmental roles. It engages an exchange of ideas and development of partner skills and abilities more than policy issues or a common research agenda. The Rural Poll and CARI work on needs assessments are original, but their reports do not make policy recommendations. They merely represent information that others can act upon. Partnership for Rural Nebraska thus does not engage in policy analysis on a systematic basis (although CARI does to some extent), no integrated strategic planning process exists, nor has unified resource targeting or integrated program and performance evaluation been undertaken. The Partnership's strengths come in other areas. It has met its goals related to partnering, sharing, coordinating movement to customer-driven delivery, and shared resources/management. Most of all, it has met the goal of developing a shared education and professional development program.

In operation if not in design, the Partnership for Rural Nebraska is a prime example of a developmental network. It goes beyond the sharing of information to enhance the operating capacities of its partners and the rural community of Nebraska. It is designed to "improve the effectiveness of resources that support local-based rural development efforts statewide" (CARI Programs 2002). In addition to the highly successful Rural Institute and annual Rural Poll, the *Rural News Bits* newsletter is received by over 6,000 people working in Nebraska Rural Development. A 2002 reader survey indicated that 76 percent of respondents indicated they use its information and only 15 percent indicated that they received the same type of information from other sources (CARI Programs 2002). From 2001 to 2003 the Partnership for Rural Nebraska focused on value-added agriculture. It proved to be a hot topic; the result of the enhanced communication was the improvement of the overall pool of technical research and information approaches, and the enrichment of practices among the federal, state, local, and university partners. These efforts enhanced the capabilities of the broader set of rural development organizations. In the words of one longtime Partnership for Rural Nebraska leader, "Without a virtual structure that provides for the connections Nebraska would have suffered more. We are more dynamic and overlapping rather than competing. [The Partnership] is consistent with our populist culture and settlement patterns. Culturally, we look to self-help and people working together."

THE IOWA GEOGRAPHIC INFORMATION COUNCIL

The Iowa Geographic Information Council (Iowa Geographic) (www.iowagic.org) was established by former-governor Terry Branstad's Executive Order Number 65 in July 1998. The order is designed to "coordinate the various activities in geographic information systems (GIS) and related technologies in order to better exchange and share information and to enhance the stewardship of geographic information in the management of public resources" (Iowa Geographic Information Council 1998). The Council consists of representatives from federal, state, county, regional, and local governments, colleges and universities, and the private sector. "The breadth of the Iowa GIS council model is unique, with its local government, university, regional organizations, and metropolitan planning organizations" (ibid.). Iowa Geographic has a twenty-five-member board that represents each of these functional sectors, along with general membership available to all Iowa citizens. In 2003 the Council was transformed from a state-chartered entity to a 501c(3) nonprofit organization to better reflect its evolution into public-private partner status.

The Council meets quarterly, normally over the Iowa Communications Network [(Iowa Communications), see chapter 5], to discuss state-based GIS issues. Meetings combine Council business with educational presentations on available data sets, project updates, and other GIS issues. Iowa Geographic's mission includes: (1) acting as a clearinghouse for GIS information and expertise in Iowa; (2) encouraging the development of open GIS standards; (3) facilitating the voluntary exchange of data among Iowa GIS users; (4) encouraging the use of telecommunications networks like Iowa Communications for exchange of ideas; (5) improving policymakers' knowledge of GIS and related technologies; and (6) serving as a focal point for intergovernmental efforts to receive additional funds, especially federal funds, for GIS development in Iowa.

Iowa Geographic's history is one of gradual movement away from state government. The idea for coordinating GIS began as far back as 1994, when its first president was a doctoral student in planning, and the executive director of the Iowa Rural Development Council, which is housed in Iowa's DED. He joined with a group of Department of Natural Resources technical staff and a county engineer and began to meet to discuss the Internet and GIS use. The group developed a list of people who used GIS, and held an initial meeting to see if there was interest in creating a council similar to those of other states. At the time GIS was just starting to use PCs, but the cost of software presented an obstacle. There was a need to pool or share costs, and to have a vehicle to coordinate efforts. An initial meeting was held at the State Department of Transportation in Ames; attendance was standing room only. This enthusiasm led to the start of an informal users group for exchange of information, which led to the creation of a website and a conference. In 1998 the State of Iowa was approached for support, as was Iowa State University (ISU) Extension. Initially reluctant, the State agreed to help after some lobbying, and put the Council's work within their IT plan. ISU Extension proved to be supportive from the start.

The original executive order called for "administrative staff support from the Office of Information Technology Services." A GIS coordinator was hired out of that office to work with government agencies at all levels. In 1999 a new Iowa chief information officer was appointed, but he reportedly distanced himself from the Council and all of its activities, including funding of the state GIS coordinator. After several frustrating months discussions were held with ISU Extension, resulting in the formation of a 2001 intergovernmental agreement between the university and Iowa Geographic. The Council moved from the state government to ISU. The agreement included Extension's support of a half-time GIS coordinator. The website/clearinghouse was maintained by the ISU GIS facility. Notwithstanding project support, formal relationships with state government information agencies declined further. Iowa Geographic's experiences in pursuing grant funds for its Ortho Infra-red project and other co-ordinated purchases of aerial photography convinced the Council that it should become a nonprofit organization while continuing its relationship with ISU.

Iowa Geographic's activities demonstrate its capacity-building or developmental classification. First, in addition to Iowa Geographic information, the Iowa Geographic web-based GIS clearinghouse provides links to other key GIS sites in the state, a GIS Resource Guide to help identify GIS contacts and educate users about GIS, and an Image Map Server with aerial photos and other digital imaging. Second, Iowa Geographic publishes an online quarterly newsletter that transmits information on Council business, upcoming training events and seminars, and short news items on GIS applications. Third, the Council sponsors a biannual GIS conference on a university campus. The 2003 conference involved a total of fifty-eight different sessions. According to the coordinator for that conference, all of the sectors involved in Iowa Geographic interests are represented on the program, and programs are geared to different levels: those who have almost no knowledge about GIS and its uses, those currently setting up GIS programs, and those who are regular users. Conference papers and/or presentation abstracts are available online through the Clearinghouse. Fourth, the Council arranges specialized courses on GIS uses and software, particularly for city and county officials and planners. It also works with state agencies, such as with DOT to incorporate GIS into long-range transportation planning processes.

Two activities represent the hallmarks of Iowa Geographic. The half-time state GIS coordinator works directly with local governments to introduce GIS to their systems and provide geospatial and mapping services, along with long-term system maintenance. This author was able to observe an interaction in a small city facing rapid urbanization and growth management. The program involved extending existing map limits to include new annexations/water lines, and producing an environmentally sensitive topographical map of these areas. The long-term GIS application will include delineation of property lines, identification of the number of acres in each area designed for future annexation, identification of parcel owners, and a complete mapping of property use. The GIS coordinator is constantly on the road, helping communities build strategic geospatial data, along with hardware and software plans for the local government.

The other project is the Ortho Infra-red and Digital Ortho Quarter-Quadrant photos of the entire state. The primary work of Iowa Geographic's Remote Sensing Committee, which gathered extensive input on potential use, was proposed in 2000 to the Iowa Geographic Board. A vendor was recommended to produce color infrared aerial mapping for the entire state to the one-meter square. Triatholon, a Vancouver, Canada, subsidiary of an American company, was selected to do the work. This $1.4 million project was delivered on time and is now available to a variety of users, including the Iowa Geographic Image Map Server. The project was funded by over fifty-four partners: one-third state government (DOT, DNR, university), one-third federal (U.S. EPA; U.S. Fish and Wildlife Service), and one-third private sources in local government.

The Council has been able to overcome a number of financial and political obstacles to build capabilities within the GIS community. As the foremost successes, leaders point to the coordinated purchases of aerial photography. Instead of a series of individual purchases, a statewide program meets many needs and avoids duplication. It performs educational functions in seminars and conferences through the Clearinghouse, and most importantly its partnership with ISU Extension that provides a "Johnny Appleseed" start-up program for local governments. It has also been active on the national and regional scene with similar GIS statewide networks. Iowa Geographic leaders also recognize its many challenges. "We need better liaison with state government. It has not been good since our state GIS Coordinator moved out of the State Department of Administration." Another said, "A relationship needs to be established with the CIO of the state. John Gillispie, head of Iowa Communications, has just been given that additional role. That link needs to be redeveloped." Iowa Geographic is reestablishing its strategic plan and trying to regularize its newsletter, which had faded from existence. Some committees have also been inactive, such as those on weather and climate, and emergency 911. "We need people who want to take charge," claimed one activist. As each piece is put into place, it furthers Iowa Geographic's role in building GIS capacity in Iowa.

Two additional developmental networks should be introduced here. First is the Indiana Rural Developmental Council (Indiana Rural Council), one of over thirty such federal-state-local-NGO state-based bodies that address rural concerns, build rural organization capabilities, and identify intergovernmental solutions in the social and economic arena that its component partners can pursue. Its work in rural leadership development, infrastructure and housing resource identification, and enhancing community development capacity makes it another developmental network.

Also in this category is the Iowa Enterprise Network (Iowa Enterprise), a group of federal, state, and university representatives as well as small business owners, who have attempted to provide consultations and build the skills of people who work in home-based businesses. Its primary work has been in holding conferences and skill-sharing sessions; more recently it has begun to study microbusiness problems, such as business succession in small towns. Iowa Enterprise found it difficult to involve home-based business people over the long run. During the study period the network's capacity-building actions were brought under the auspices of the Small Business Committee of the Iowa Rural Development Council.

CONCLUSION

The PMNs described in this chapter demonstrate the major activities or operations of informational and developmental networks. Both types are primarily engaged in information exchanges. The developmental networks go one step further by actively engaging in programs that expand knowledge pools and create enhanced potential for component agencies to solve difficult problems. However, as PMNs they do not engage in either joint strategy or policy/ program making, or interactive program adjustment. In an information society where considerable disconnects exist among information holders, and between those responsible for solving public problems and those that acquire disparate technical information, information sharing and capacity building are hardly unimportant.

Bridging the gaps of agency and organization knowledge and capabilities is hardly an insignificant undertaking in the network era. These two types of networks formalize the myriad of lateral exchanges that occur—dyadic, triadic, and so on—into formal bodies that bring in many more potential actors. Moreover, they are ongoing entities that allow for the focus and continuity that dyadic and other ad hoc relationships do not. Issues like rural development, community development, watershed protection, and economic strategymaking reach far beyond a few core organizations. During the 1990s recognition of these forces triggered the move to convene the various actors in more regular forums that involve government and NGOs.

Despite falling short of concrete decisions and policy adjustments or even in developing strategies, the potential for action on the part of one or more partners in each of these types of networks is possible and often likely. The Darby Partnership has many spin-offs. The Hellbranch project, for example, grew from a spin-off forum to an action plan and intergovernmental agreement to control growth and preservation of the western part of Franklin County. Indiana Economic Development's broadband strategy study has become a major priority for the Indiana DOC and many other organizations within the development community. Partnership for Rural Nebraska and CARI's survey work on rural water problems has led to major programs in the Departments of Environmental Quality, DED, and the USDA/Nebraska. Developmental networks do more than exchange information and knowledge, they create knowledge bases for further use. Like many of the other networks discussed in the next chapter, they build capacity by organizing and developing useful information/knowledge for agencies, NGOs, and policymakers.

The question of why these networks avoid policy/program or action-related strategic blueprinting can be raised. Why do they identify and share information on problems, and why do some enhance problem-solving capacity but stop short of the actual solving of the problem? The answers go somewhat beyond the scope and methodology of this grounded theory study. One can speculate, however, that the disparate stakeholders in watershed networks and in economic development may preclude anything that approaches real action. For example, landowners and environmentalists thrown together with federal land state agencies can result in a daunting combination. Another reason may be turf. The Partnership for Rural Nebraska partners, for example, have legally charged mandates and entrenched programs. Operating in this way, they can look at the bigger picture and disseminate valuable knowledge through their networks, but may not be poised to make formal decisions. In the same fashion, with the exception of state information policy, Iowa Geographic sees itself as promoting and developing, not addressing individual agency problems or specific recommendations. Even with regard to Iowa's state GIS information policy, the Council only wants to reinstate it as a priority, it does not want to control policy directly. This is regarded as the province of the governor's office and the major agency users. These two types of networks and their disparate members have circumscribed missions, which lead them to avoid a larger policy/program role. These issues are revisited in the final chapter.

CHAPTER FIVE

. . . .

OUTREACH AND ACTION NETWORKS

The 317 Group has been in the business of developing public policy toward the disabled from the start. Only we don't make it directly. That is the job of the legislature. Three seventeen provides the tools and develops the frameworks of disabilities policy, that is, residential alternatives.

OUR STUDY OF PMNs moves to those that actually become directly involved in policy and programs, as we focus on outreach and action networks. As identified, outreach networks provide new and interactive programming opportunities for participating agencies and organizations as they strategically blueprint interactive activity that is implemented by the partners. This distinction involves informal reciprocal agreements, as these networks jointly decide on activity and their partners exchange information and technologies, propose sequences for programming, exchange resource access opportunities, pool client contacts, and enhance access opportunities that lead to new programming avenues. The fourth and final type of network, the action network, makes the kind of policy/program adjustments most common in the literature. Here the partners come together to make interagency adjustments, formally adopt collaborative courses of action, and/or deliver services, along with all of the other network activities such as exchanges of information and technologies. Three PMNs introduced in this chapter are outreach networks whereas the remaining four are action networks.

THE SMALL COMMUNITIES ENVIRONMENTAL INFRASTRUCTURE GROUP OF OHIO

Formed in 1990 by water program funders, the Small Communities Environmental Infrastructure Group (Small Communities; www.cpmra.muohio .edu.sceig.htm) represents one of the oldest of several state-based bodies devoted to helping small towns (www.scwie.org). The group brings together federal and state agencies, local governments and local government NGOs, service organizations, and educational institutions in order to help small communities meet their water and wastewater infrastructure needs. Small Communities' organizations provide regulatory, technical, financial, and educational assistance for projects, working toward coordination of efforts to assist small governments with developing, improving, and maintaining their water systems. This group of Ohio-based experts holds quarterly meetings to discuss the needs of small communities, and identify appropriate and feasible responses or remedies. Additionally, Small Communities has published documents and compiled a list of Internet resources related to the installation, repair, or expansion of environmental infrastructure (Small Communities 2002). Small Communities is a nonchartered, informal PMN.

The impetus for the founding of Small Communities came from the executive director of the Ohio Water Development Authority (OWDA), a state organization that funds around 60 percent of all water and wastewater projects in the state. The director had previously served as deputy director of Ohio EPA, and was in contact with many federal and state government funders who were aware that in small towns the demand for resources exceeded supply. There were many funding sources available to communities in the 1980s, such as a revolving state fund for water infrastructure and a public works discretionary program with funds of around $10 million per year, but there was no easy way for a small town to access these and federal funds. "If a small town had a problem it was a seven year process of coming together and finding a solution. It was a total 'bottom-up' process of learning what the problem was, possible solutions, costs, and so on. There was no direction from the state." After two of the funders looked at state-level interagency groups in Arkansas and West Virginia, it was simply a matter of lining up the players.

It was clear that OWDA and EPA had a number of potential interactions with many other organizations such as USDA/RD in Ohio, USEDA, Ohio Department of Development (Small Cities Block Grant-CDBG), and with private sector lenders. "No one had a vested interest in small town water problems. . . . A problem comes to one is a problem to all . . . we thought there was a lot to learn if a whole series of people work[ed] on it." Another founder said, "Small towns have few staff and they were forced to contact each funder. They often had to knock on ten to fifteen doors. They have limited resources and they have engineering consultants to touch all the bases (on construction and compliance), so they know those ropes. But that leaves the 'how to finance,' and that's where our group of funders came together." Another founder went beyond the finance issue. "I want to find out what others in my capacity are doing . . . water and sewer in Ohio is complex. It involves engineering and technology, rules and regulations, grants, loans, the works! I did not want to miss anything." As a result, the group began with both financing and education efforts. The OWDA model of creating financing and technical partnerships to solve problems was adapted to Small Communities. Over the years OWDA had engaged in partnerships in the area of brownfield remediation, industry attraction, municipal water and wastewater, coastal erosion (Lake Erie), and others (OWDA 2002, 14). The group followed this pattern to develop Small Communities, as OWDA convened and hosted the initial meetings.

Small Communities is held together by a myriad of partners. At the core are the funders: OWDA, Ohio EPA, Ohio Department of Development (Small Cities CDBG), Ohio Public Works Commission, USEDA, USDA/RD, Ohio Governor's Office of Appalachia, and a private sector banker representative. At the table as nonfunders are various representatives of Ohio's regional planning commissions and local development districts. Ohio higher education is also involved. Three rural centers—Bowling Green University, Ohio University, and Miami University—are involved in the training of elected officials. Miami University's rural center also maintains Small Communities' website and electronic bulletin board. Ohio State University's College of Agriculture (Natural Resources and Extension Departments) plays a major role in curriculum development, particularly in the areas of community development, grantsmanship, water plant manager training (finance, operation, maintenance, wastewater testing), and piloting training. The Ohio Rural Water Association offers USDA-funded circuit riders for small towns, and the Ohio Rural Community Action Program (RCAP) offers USDA-funded technical community development staff and maintains a compendium of all water project funding sources in the state. A number of other water infrastructure interests are also at the table from time to time: engineering consultants, state associations, agricultural extension agents, and the Ohio Departments of Health and Natural Resources.

This network's goals and objectives reflect its nature as an outreach network. Its three stated goals are to: "provide useful information for small community leadership," "assist small communities in identifying the most appropriate resources to help them resolve problems associated with environmental infrastructure," and "developing additional technical and financial resources" (Small Communities Goals and Objectives 2002). Its supporting objectives include: producing new or revised curriculum materials for "Water Systems for Small Communities"; developing drinking water and technology transfer curricula; providing funding guidance for up to thirty small communities annually; conducting a follow-up survey for communities that received financing strategies in 1997–2000; implementing a new Appalachia Environmental Infrastructure Strategy, discussed below; exploring streamlining interagency application procedures; identifying one new technology; providing information about new and underutilized technologies; identifying the data requirements for a system of cost summary of wastewater re-use; reviewing and recommending improvements to Ohio EPA rules and policies and offering guidance on technical matters, including environmental and engineering considerations; developing a decision tree or checklist to determine if an onsite system is more practical than a central sewer system; searching for a community that would pilot an onsite system; organizing a small communities self-help manual; and engaging in liaison with the Ohio Rural Development Partnership (Ohio's Rural Development Council) (Small Communities Goals and Objectives 2002). These actions clearly demonstrate that Small Communities is not only involved in exchanging and developing information and in building capacities, but takes a further step by orchestrating strategies as it works with small communities.

The core of Small Communities and its character as an outreach network lies in the work of its Finance Committee. It meets every other month, taking up the cases of each community one-by-one, with two to four communities presenting at each meeting. Normally the community will bring its water plant manager, mayor or other elected official, and its engineering consultant. At the table are the major funders, particularly OWDA, Ohio EPA, CDBG in DOD, USDA/RD in Nebraska, USEDA, Ohio Public Works Commission, and the Governor's Office of Appalachia. A typical project profile submitted in advance to the committee contains a project description, projected costs and user rates, current funding commitments, current user rates and connections, and current project status including engineer's report.

One regular attendee describes a typical session:

> It is very much case-by-case. Each town has a different problem. We try to help with knowledge, particularly for underserved . . . who are years and millions from a solution. We try to explain to them how to go through the process, what order . . . these part-time mayors are unaware of the different criteria, for example CDBG's low-moderate income, and so on. For some it's first steps, and we tell them to start with a planning grant. We tell them loans secured by long-term financing are the normal course of action. If they don't have an engineer, we suggest that and provide a list of cost-effective consultants. For communities that are farther along we suggest a path of funding, usually by those at the table, including requirements, timelines and deadlines, and more. After we meet with them, it is up to the community and their consultant to make the necessary applications.

At the meeting that I attended, one applicant (Burr Oak) asked questions concerning feasible water rates to retire projected debt, compliance with regulations, and projected end costs. Questions were also raised concerning mergers with adjacent water systems. In one case a proposed package was formulated with USDA/RD in Ohio as the lead funder, to be supplemented by EPA and CDBG funds. USDA then said it could not act until previously requested costs per end user—operation and maintenance costs, sales to other water systems, and rates data—were supplied. EDA reminded the community that it does not fund residential areas unless a significant jobs retention and extension impact could be demonstrated, and without projected investment the probability of EDA funding was not encouraging. CDBG then responded that without documentation of low-moderate income (prov. 5310) and an eligible county government as a legal applicant they would not participate. Burr Oak was asked to return with the requested data, but they were also encouraged to explore financing with Ohio EPA and OWDA.

At the same meeting a simple strategy was quickly forged for a tiny community whose water plant had flooded. Only $125,000 was requested. Because it was not in a flood plain it had no insurance. The request was to build on the $13,000 already received from FEMA. The Public Works Commission offered a grant from emergency funds, with a one-to-two-day turnaround in application processing. The other 10 percent would be available in the form of a 2-percent-interest loan from Ohio EPA, and a small grant offered by the Governor's Office of Appalachia. These examples demonstrate both a simple and complex example of Small Communities' strategic blueprinting.

Small Communities faces a number of challenges and opportunities. First, its efforts to deal in the area of technology have lagged behind those in education and financing. Its technology transfer effort has been sporadic. The group had planned to post a series of technology transfer fact sheets on its website, but it has not materialized. The Technology Transfer Committee has been inactive. On the other hand, a number of technology work groups have demonstrated success. One highlight is Shenandoah's peat bio filter cluster drainage system, which demonstrates Small Communities' work in strategically adapting technology along technical, legal, and financial fronts. Through the interactive work of an engineering, financial, and legal interdisciplinary work group, a feasible, cost-effective, and environmental permit-ready system was piloted. This strategic blueprint is now ready for transfer to other communities.

Second, the financial strategy effort has reached over two hundred communities, normally around twenty-four per year. Follow-up surveys and the small number of repeat communities indicate very high rates of success. On the other hand, in recent years a notable number of Finance Committee meetings have been cancelled because too few communities have come forward. It is not clear whether this is due to some level of saturation of small towns, more accessible information on the Internet, better use of consultants, or some other reason.

Third, the training curriculum has advanced to a level of multiple modules, seven one-day sessions over seven weeks. Materials now include highly usable workbooks. The training program for water plant operators is outstanding, and emphasizes both conservation and efficiency. It is operated by a division of the Ohio State University School of Agriculture.

Fourth, as is the case with other states, Ohio is struggling to find ways to deal with onsite management of wastewater in rural clusters of thirty to forty houses. Now that the Shenandoah experiment is near completion, Small Communities will take the lead in developing a model funding package for other communities.

Fifth and finally, Small Communities leaders feel they have to do more to identify and develop expert reviewed practices in all of its areas of education, technology, and finance and post them on their website, making them available to local officials, consultants, and development specialists. These activities would extend the strategic development activities of Small Communities to a larger number of communities.

INDIANA 317 TASK FORCE/GROUP

This nonchartered PMN is composed of public officials, NGO executives and staff, and a university institute director who developed and maintained Indiana's attempt to transition institutionalized developmentally disabled persons to the community. Later self-identified as the 317 Group, the key actors of the Indiana 317 Task Force originally formulated what became Indiana Senate Bill 317 of 1997, which shifted money from state institutions to follow residents into the community. Medicaid moneys subsequently bolstered this effort, as programming to assist in transition/community services expanded rapidly. In 1999, the U.S. Supreme Court in *L.C. and E.W. v Olmstead* in effect required that states make serious efforts to eliminate unnecessary institutionalization and to begin to reduce the numbers of people waiting for services. Olmstead plans are now in place in all but fifteen states. Indiana 317 has become this state's operational response to this decision (INARF 2005).

The original 317 committee was a Governor's Task Force that met in 1997–98 to develop a comprehensive plan for community-based services. Chaired by the Secretary of the Department of the Family and Social Services Administration (FSSA), it was composed of state government officials, NGO trade or advocacy associations, nonprofit and for profit providers, citizen members, and university representatives. Meetings were well attended and very open, as each member was able to express his or her views. A series of five regional meetings were held to explain the basic community approach and to hear local views from consumers and their families, potential consumers, and providers. The process was very data-driven, with reports on financing mechanisms, trends, community service waiting lists, and comparisons with other states. The trade associations supplied flyers and other materials on deinstitutionalization. A proposal was submitted to the governor and to both legislative houses (FSSA 1998). The essence of the final proposal as submitted included person-centered planning and funding, redirection of funding from larger settings, quality assurance, building community capacity, and securing the necessary financing to meet demand. The lobbying phase was carried out by the CEOs of two major trade associations, Arc of Indiana (formerly Association for Retarded Citizens) and the Indiana Association of Rehabilitation Facilities (INARF). Also involved were key handicapped-citizen leaders and others from the disability community.

After enactment funding for the 317 Plan provided $39.2 million in new state funding, implementation was then assigned to FSSA. Medicaid officials initially resisted funding this program, first claiming that person-centered services were not reimbursable. The FSSA secretary ultimately persuaded them. She also formed an informal systems change group that met monthly to go over the numbers, categories, and spending patterns, and to make contact assignments. The 317 Group emerged from the original task force and the systems change group, a work group to maintain the sustainable elements of 317 both inside and outside of government.

This succeeding 317 Group is composed of those who have an ongoing stake in program continuation. First are the key trade associations, INARF and Arc, plus other groups like the Council of Voluntary Organizations for the Handicapped, Indiana Case Management, and the Indiana Parent Information Network. Second are state officials including the FSSA: the director of the Division of Disability, Aging, and Rehabilitative Services (DDARS); director of Bureau of Developmental Disabilities; director of Bureau of Quality Improvement Services; director of Medicaid; Director, Office of Medicaid Policy and Planning; and director of Level of Care, Office of Medicaid Policy and Planning. Third is the director of the Governor's Planning Council for Developmental Disabilities, a federally funded state agency that is independent of FSSA. Fourth are private and for-profit provider representatives. Fifth are citizen/consumer representatives. Sixth is the director of Indiana University's Indiana Institute on Disability and Community (IIDC), a research and service unit that is unattached to any university academic department or school. It is one of two federally funded University Centers for Excellence in Developmental Disabilities in Indiana.

The 317 Group is sustained outside of government by the efforts of Arc and INARF, with support from IIDC and the Governor's Planning Council. While this PMN has no formal budget, these four entities jointly funded a 2004 external study that analyzes financing trends in Indiana since 317 (Braddock and Hemp 2004). Arc has staff people dedicated to publicizing 317, and one person who works with families in institutions to explain community options. These activities are funded by the Governor's Planning Council. INARF has a policy research task force composed of 317 Group members and nonmembers, which is investigating such related issues as case management, institutional budgets, best practices in community-based services, and the impact of state budget reductions on 317/Olmstead compliance. Finally, IIDC has sponsored a series of 317 focus groups for both consumers and advocates at its electronic Collaborative Work Lab.

The 317 Group has been able to ride the wave of widespread support for its concept and program. A four-year report to the state legislatures MR/DD Commission indicates that most of the original 317 targets for shifting funding and community living have been met. It has bipartisan legislative support. Senator Marvin Reigsecker, who chairs the MR/DD Commission, cited the 317 program as "a great example of what can happen when you lay aside politics and work together" (INARF 2003, 2). Its biggest problem has been shortfalls in funding and a related inability to make a dent in Indiana's long waiting list for services, which currently numbers around 10,000 people.

The 317 Group continues to extend the program's momentum. In late 2004–early 2005, its lobbyists were faced with the task of explaining the program and its impact to a new gubernatorial administration and to thirteen new legislators. A series of fact sheets were prepared. All legislators were invited to eleven 317 forums around the state, held by Arc/INARF. Arc/INARF sponsored a freshman legislator breakfast in which each legislator was seated with a constituent family and a provider CEO. In addition to the level-of-care improvements already introduced into 317, the Group wants to add two additional components: emergency services for those on waiting lists, and wage parity for provider staff as a boost to the infrastructure of services. The aim is to raise the state matching funds to at least $118 million, maintaining Medicaid, so that money can follow a person out of the state institution and the waiting list can be reduced. In fact, the Legislature did appropriate $31 million in new funds for emergency services, and added almost $23 million for day services and $3 million for supported employment. This increase of $57 million for the developmentally disabled came with a projected minimal 5.2 percent increase in Medicaid spending. The 317 Group has thus successfully returned to a legislative advocacy phase.

The remaining outreach network is the USDA/RD in Nebraska (USDA/Nebraska). As in other states, USDA/Nebraska is the primary financing arm of the U.S. Department of Agriculture in rural (nonfarm) America, through the provision of guaranteed loans, direct loans, and grants in utilities services, business and cooperative services, and housing, community development, and infrastructure. Nonnationally competitive funds for Nebraska approached $85 million for fiscal year 2004. The Nebraska program devotes one full-time person to coordinating its staff outreach effort, is involved in a joint water and wastewater funding consortium, and is among the most active players in Partnership for Rural Nebraska (now merged with the Nebraska Development Network). Most importantly, USDA/Nebraska is among the most active state programs in partnering and establishing virtual organizations like the Nebraska

Value Added Agriculture Partnership, and the Readiness, Education, Awareness Collaboration for Homeowners. It normally engages with other entities in virtually every grant and loan program transaction, along with program-to-program collaboration.

THE KENTUCKIANA PLANNING AND DEVELOPMENT AGENCY

The transportation arm of the Kentuckiana Regional Planning and Development Agency (Kentuckiana Agency) serves as the Metropolitan Planning Organization (MPO) for the Louisville area, three counties in Kentucky, and two in Indiana. Kentuckiana Agency not only houses the MPO, but serves as the area development district and the area agency on aging. Kentuckiana Agency Transportation Division staff serves the MPO, the PMN studied here. As will be demonstrated, Kentuckiana Agency is composed of federal, state, and regional transportation officials; local government elected officials; and local government professional staff. The MPO is responsible for implementing the U.S. Transportation Equity Act for the 21st Century (TEA-21) for the metropolitan area. Spread over two states, the five-county area corresponds to the EPA nonattainment area or air pollutant zone, the area projected to be urbanized by the year 2020, and the transportation management area by the Federal Highway Administration (FHWA). Supported by Kentuckiana Agency staff that provides planning and technical assistance, the MPO looks at all transportation needs, placing emphasis on bicycle, highway, paratransit, pedestrian, and public modes of transportation. The multijurisdictional body of officials is responsible under TEA-21 for the MPO Transportation Improvement Program (TIP), which involves short-term allocation of federal funds (almost $34 million in fiscal year 2003) for local projects, as well as the long-range plan for the area, which must incorporate all externally funded projects.

Kentuckiana Agency represents the amalgamation of three prior area based planning cooperative arrangements, a council of governments, a comprehensive metro transportation planning organization, and an area development district (housing and aging, and transportation) of the State of Kentucky (Vogel and Nezelkewicz 2002). It merged in the early 1970s when the Kentucky Department of Transportation threatened to withdraw funding and a consolidation was negotiated. It corresponds to the broader parameters of the three agencies: Jefferson, Oldham, Bullit, Spencer, Shelby, Henry and Trimble Counties in Kentucky, and Clark and Floyd Counties in Indiana. Five of these counties—Jefferson, Oldham, Bullit, Clark and Floyd—remain as the Kentuckiana Agency jurisdiction area. When the Intermodal Surface Transportation Efficiency Act (ISTEA) of 1991 was passed and the power of MPOs was enhanced, the five-county MPO network was created. Legally, the Transportation Policy Committee, composed of federal, state, and local officials, is the MPO, a "relatively autono-mous body within Kentuckiana Agency" (ibid., 114).

The structure of Kentuckiana Agency is made up of several layers that pre-pare, deliberate, and approve the TIP and Long Range Plan. First is the Kentuckiana Agency Transportation staff, approximately ten full-time and five part-time employees. They are responsible for all of the data analysis, traffic and other counts, and amalgamation of plans from the various jurisdictions.

The second layer is composed of the federal, regional, and state officials who serve technical, consultation, and advisory roles throughout the TEA-21 pro-cess. The Planning Process Memorandum of Understanding (1999) identifies the Transit Authority of River City (TARC), the Kentucky Transportation Cabinet (KYTC), the Indiana Department of Transportation (INDOT), the Air Pollution Control District of Jefferson County (APCD), the Kentucky National Resources and Environmental Protection Cabinet (KNREPC), and the Indiana Department of Environmental Management (IDEM). In addition, several fed-eral officials from the U.S. DOT Federal Highway Administration based in each state and, to a less-involved extent, mass transit and air quality officials from UMTA/DOT and EPA are also involved in various aspects of the process.

The third layer is the technical planning, engineering, and research staff from each of the MPO jurisdictions, along with other technical experts who work with Kentuckiana Agency staff to exchange data and provide technical review, coordination, and assistance, particularly through the MPO Transportation Technical Coordinating Committee (TTCC). This is a very influential pre-decision body in the case of Kentuckiana Agency. Federal, state, and regional officials also work closely with the TTCC.

Fourth is Kentuckiana Agency's Community Transportation Advisory Com-mittee, consisting of representatives of area interest groups. They provide ad-vice on community concerns impacted by transportation planning. The MPO also has special advisory committees, such as the Bicycle and Pedestrian Advi-sory Committee.

The fifth layer is composed of the chief elected officials (or their designees) of each unit of local government (cities and counties), who along with a few other designated officials make up the bulk of the Policy Committee and have voting power on the Transportation Improvement Program (TIP) and Long Range Plan. This includes about a dozen officials, Louisville and most of Jefferson County having merged in 2003, plus other designated officials (INDOT, KYTC, and the Regional Airport Authority) (KIPDA 2004). As a re-sult of these multiple players and actors, the MPO involves a broad network of officials and public employees working on TEA-21 processes.

The MPO becomes highly involved in a number of activities that culminate in the TIP and Long Range Plan. Along with this, TEA-21 reserves a substan-tial portion of surface transportation block grants to MPOs in those urban areas with populations over 200,000. In integrating these transportation needs, the staff and officials become heavily engaged in decision-based research tools such as travel model development; air quality analysis/consultation; the congestion management system; long- and short-range transportation studies for particular jurisdictions; and collection of data and database maintenance on traffic counts, socioeconomic data, bicycle and pedestrian facilities, geographic data, travel model data, and a project management information database. Kentuckiana Agency staff also oversees a ride-share agency responsible for administering a regional carpool, vanpool, and transit promotion and services program. At typical Policy Committee meetings, presentations on special studies and workshops are followed by both TIP and Long Range Plan action. Meetings are organized by Kentuckiana Agency staff in consultation with officers, and are carefully orchestrated with supporting documentation. "We take care of the administrative details for the meetings as completely as possible, so the technical experts and elected officials can decide with ease and rapidly," reflected a staff member.

Kentuckiana Agency elected officials and professional staff from state and local governments are generally positive regarding the MPO's role in forging a metropolitan perspective. Long-term involvement of technical staff has added continuity and has allowed for the emergence of a consensus group that has fostered a metro perspective. One longtime county planning director stated that the technical group looks "to the staff to see what is important. We don't manage them, we manage together." The technical group is important for educating "all of the engineers and planners. I am an engineer. Transportation is not my thing. It helps me to understand issues like pedestrian concerns that I otherwise would not think about. Besides, a lot of good planning tools are bounced around when we meet." Several studies and programs, data collection projects, planning tools, and knowledge-based models support Kentuckiana Agency's work on the TIP and Long Range Plan. Elected officials bring together cities, small towns, and county governments into a body where "each can speak their mind but look to the two-state area." Another city council member said, "I feel comfortable pushing our projects and looking at the bigger picture. I need to be there so our small town is not left behind, but while I am there I also try to do what is best for the Louisville area." As a two-state MPO, Kentuckiana Agency has the more-involved step of dealing with two sets of state agencies and federal offices located in the states. According to MPO officers and staff, this has not proved to be a formidable task. "We have two sets of consultations and processes and we have to be concerned with what people from two states want. It takes more time. Sometimes we let Indiana go its own way. Sometimes they are not concerned with Kentucky issues. But we need to be together for the larger perspective. That is the way it is." Kentuckiana Agency combines the various jurisdictions and agencies into a quasi-government body, in this case

an action network that allocates key federal resources in its area (Vogel and
Nezelkewicz 2002, 123–27).

IOWA COMMUNICATIONS NETWORK

The Iowa Communications Network (Iowa Communications) is a statewide
fiber optic network connecting all ninety-nine counties in Iowa. Iowa Communications links schools, hospitals, state and federal government agencies,
public defense armories, libraries, and higher-education institutions, using full-
motion video, high-speed Internet connections, and data and voice services.
It is primarily used as a tool for distance learning, telejustice, telemedicine, and
state and federal agency service needs. Each Iowa Communications classroom
contains the equipment to convert incoming light waves into video programs,
and outgoing (originating) programs into light so that the signals can be transmitted over the network.

The central hub of Iowa Communications is located at the Joint Forces
Headquarters Armory (Iowa National Guard) northwest of Des Moines, where
technical staff monitor the system that activates the sites connecting program
senders and receivers. The full-motion video aspect of the network connects
770 classrooms throughout the state, including almost 400 K–12 schools, more
than 30 postsecondary institutions, and around 50 libraries. According to Iowa
Communications, training programs offered by universities, colleges, and community colleges have helped over 9,000 teachers, medical professionals, librar-
ians, state employees, and other Iowans. The voice, data, and Internet system
operated by Iowa Communications serves 12,000 public sector users (telephone, fax, station or modem numbers) in the Des Moines metropolitan area
(Iowa Communications FAQ 2004, 4).

Although this entity can be labeled a network, it is different from the other
PMNs in that it is a state code agency that interacts with the other elements
of the public sector. "We are a resource that started with schools, libraries, and
medicine. Now we are reaching out to other areas of government, most recently
homeland security. Iowa Communications is a 'test bed' for the National Guard,
and for public health and other security programs." As will be demonstrated,
Iowa Communications interacts in an interorganizational/interagency fashion
along a number of lines, making it both a transmission network and a PMN.
Iowa Communications is the only fully state-operated telecommunications
network in the United States.

Iowa Communications' mission is "to provide authorized users the highest
quality and technically advanced educational, medical, judicial, and government telecommunications services" (Iowa Communications 2003 Annual Report, 1). Iowa Communications services include full-motion video, which

allows participants at sites hundreds of miles apart to interact dynamically as if in the same room; Internet access at affordable rates and with reliable customer service information; and low-cost voice and data service for state and federal government and educational users. One Iowa Communications executive reported that Iowa Communications is a public utility, a state agency, and an enterprise of government. "We get only $1 million out of a $23 million operating enterprise. The rest comes from the sale of services. We are a solution to their [agency telecommunications/data needs] applications . . . and problems. . . . They are not mandated to use Iowa Communications . . . I have to compete pricewise to get their 'voluntary' patronage."

It is Iowa Communications' operations with agency users that demonstrate its operation as a PMN. As an action network, it makes the final policy decisions and adjustments through ITTC and its executives but it does so by interactively working with its agency/educational clients. This occurs at three levels. First, at the executive level concerns regarding policy as well as basic concerns are worked out between Iowa Communications executives and agency heads. "A lot of my day is with department heads over policy level issues. We serve the legislature, judiciary, federal authorized users, National Guard, Postal Service, Federal Reserve Bank, libraries, hospitals, clinics. Although we are approved by FCC as a common carrier and therefore eligible for a universal service discount for our users, we have to meet their needs. We are both a vendor and a partner in state government."

The second level is the interaction between agency managers responsible for information services and Iowa Communications executive staff, particularly the two deputy directors. The Department of Human Services (DHS), for example, needs data transmission services over an areawide network that involves over 150 locations (field offices, state institutions, and so on). The DHS capitol complex uses Iowa Communications as their telephone carrier, and it also uses Iowa Communications television transmission for training and meetings in all ninety-nine county offices. Iowa Communications' next step is the development of wireless capacity to increase the mobility of DHS staff. The Department of Emergency Management uses a host of Iowa Communications services: operation of 911 service, nuclear power plant protection, data networks in Iowa's frequent floods, and numerous disaster briefings since September 11, 2001. The Iowa Department of Education, along with IPTV programming managers, work with Iowa Communications staff regarding broadcast issues.

The third level is at the technical or operational level. Here operating staff at the user agencies and schools interact with Iowa Communications staff. Another technical component, part of the network since 2003, are the private telecommunications providers who carry Iowa Communications beyond the fiber optic cable sites to classrooms and libraries in more remote locations. In Iowa a total of 156 private telecom providers existed in 2004, virtually all of them with a tiny customer base and reach. Technical operating problems are ordinarily solved at the Iowa Communications' help desk. The most important concerns at this level involve scheduling, such as classroom use, arranging for video refinancing, e-mail connections among agency staff, posting notices, and accessing reports. Much of this technical-person-to-technical-person connection is routine as the switching and connecting is performed, but often when a problem occurs there is a great deal of one-to-one contact between Iowa Communications people and the public user. "Over the years we have built up important 'trust' relationships with our customers. We try not to hide behind the technology and say that 'no one can do that' and try to convey the notion that we can make the switches to link their requests into the network," one technical Iowa Communications staff person stated.

Iowa Communications is not universally loved by its key political, agency, and industry publics. It has been audited and studied by the legislature and state auditor several times. The private telecoms characterized it as an unfair competitor, and have successfully lobbied to limit its use to existing schools, libraries, and agencies. Local governments, for example, are precluded from linking with Iowa Communications although use rates would be considerably lower than on the private market. Iowa Communications has brought in a new executive director from the private telecommunication sector. He has tried to refocus the debate by presenting Iowa Communications as a financing structure, a capital asset that would allow the state to retain its telecom capacity while letting a nongovernment entity hold the physical asset and invest in the physical aspects. This is necessary because Iowa Communications' low rates make it impossible to raise sufficient capital improvement/upgrade money, and it is unlikely there will be more legislative backed bonding authority. As a result, a concept was presented in late 2004 to "sell Iowa Communications assets," which would allow fiber cable located outside the Des Moines area and certain backbone equipment to be sold to the private sector (Iowa Communications, Sale of the Assets 2004). While the future ownership of Iowa Communications is uncertain, its continuing operation as a network among public sector users appears assured in the near term.

Two additional action networks are part of this study. First is another MPO, the Des Moines Area Metropolitan Planning Organization (Des Moines Metro). Des Moines Metro is quite similar to Kentuckiana Agency in that it involves the same type of federal, state, and local government officials in Iowa's largest metropolitan area. It is composed of officials from thirteen cities and four counties in the metro area, along with relevant federal, state, and regional transport and transit officials. It is also responsible for implementing the Long-Range Transportation Plan and approving TIP funding.

The final action network studied here is the Enhanced Data Access Review Committee (Enhanced Data) of the Indiana Intelnet Commission, which operates the integrated telecommunication network of the state and accessIndiana (www.IN.gov), the statewide digital telecommunication system. Enhanced Data governs use of the accessIndiana web portal, reviews agency agreements, establishes agency and other fees for its use, and promotes the use of the state's computer gateway. Composed of state officials and public members, Enhanced Data has been the facilitation point for automating such state functions as state park reservations, tax payments, drivers' licenses, and vehicle renewal. In regard to web portal use, it is the major point of contact with state legislators and state agencies.

CONCLUSIONS

Unlike the informational and developmental networks, the PMNs discussed in this chapter are involved in forms of interagency strategy and policymaking. Outreach networks like Small Communities, USDA/Nebraska, and the 317 Group stop just short of formal policy and program decisions. They work across agency and organization lines to formulate, propose, and, to some degree, simulate strategies. The actual policy/program decisions are made by the agencies that network within these PMNs. They do not make collective decisions, but collectively they point to potential courses of action. It is decision or direct action that distinguishes the four action networks. They formulate and propose strategies but also take action on them. The two MPOs make important decisions regarding what is and what is not in their long-range plans, and thus what is to be federally funded over a period of time. They allocate millions for improvement projects. Iowa Communications officials network with their agency users, who together decide on the operation of the system. Enhanced Data works interactively with state agencies to make their use and rate decisions. Each of these networks brings together officials from several agencies and levels of jurisdiction; each has an agenda that includes their participants and interests, and a public agenda that transcends their interest. Thus, either in a formal or indirect way, these PMNs demonstrate the characteristics attributed to networks in the literature.

What makes outreach networks stop short of making the official action related decisions, thus limiting them to blueprinting strategies? Researching this issue directly is again beyond the grounded theory methodology that allowed the typology to emerge. The participants' words suggest that in large part it is due to barriers embedded in law and presented by legal mandates, funding rules, eligibility criteria, and eligible grantees/recipients. Moreover, some of the federal and state officials involved in these PMNs are legally precluded from being involved in interorganizational bodies that make program decisions. As a result, the local governments that come before Small Communities must work with them to find a path, but the governments themselves must pursue the suggested course of action. In this respect, Small Communities and its counterparts in other states have even struggled with common application forms. By the same logic, USDA/Nebraska can devote considerable effort to outreach and coordination with their grant and loan clients and with other organizations, but their rules preclude that next step. The reality for the 317 Group is that the real policy is made by the Indiana legislature, the governor's office, and the Indiana State Budget Committee. They are able only to outline and propose the appropriate steps that the developmental disabilities community has agreed upon.

Statutory support seems to be the underlying difference for the four action networks. Each has a legal mandate to incorporate projects in a plan or to allocate federal funds, to regulate web portal use and set rates, and to operate a public telecommunications enterprise. Each involves multiple agency and jurisdiction representatives who network to make the policy and program adjustments needed to accomplish their mission. Indeed, these PMNs are mandated to make the kind of policy/program decisions normally ascribed to networks. Does this mean that all action networks have a statutory base? That assumption needs to be investigated further, particularly in light of the fact that other PMNs were originally enabled in a statutory fashion: Indiana Economic Development, Iowa Geographic, and the 317 Group. These PMNs do not have such legal mandates or formal decision power.

Now that the fourteen PMNs have been introduced and the typology that emerged has been empirically outlined, questions about the operation and impact of these bodies remain. The analysis turns to how PMNs are managed and whether the typology demonstrates any differences. Key questions related to differences between hierarchical organization management and network management will also be explored.

CHAPTER SIX

. . . .

COLLABORARCHY: A DIFFERENT KIND OF MANAGEMENT?

The Rural Development Council has a board, bylaws, strategic plan and all of the other things but we really operate like a rural town meeting . . . normally consensus is allowed to rise to the top. After all, we are made up of the top-level rural administrators in government and private-sector leadership.

IN THIS CHAPTER we take a close look at how PMNs are managed, a subject about which little is known (Kickert and Koppenjan 1997; Koppenjan and Klijn 2004; Agranoff and McGuire 2001b, 2003a). Indeed, this is an area where there is considerably more speculation than empirical research. The grounded theory research approach allows for a look inside the PMNs to see how they are managed, and to explore the degree to which these managerial approaches differ from those of hierarchical organizations.

These networks are not randomly organized or ad hoc bodies but are self-organizing entities that are normally enabled or chartered, have distinct nonhierarchical authority structures, employ regularized cross-agency communications systems, and have distinct internal power structures along with a set of internal arrangements. In some ways the organization of these PMNs resembles those of nonprofit organization structures with boards and committees, but in other ways the PMNs resemble the more open hierarchies of today's bureaucratic organizations with their teams, task forces, and work groups. In general, the PMNs are organized to facilitate the kind of collaborative decisions needed from knowledge-era workers. I term these structures "collaborarchies." Indeed, in many ways their structures resemble those of the more-open hierarchies that equally depend on collaboration.

The first of the key questions raised in this chapter deals with how network management differs from the management of emerging organizations, particularly the differences between network actors' home organizations and that of networks. It then moves to the bases of authority or their equivalent in networks. This section also discusses staffing patterns. The subsequent section looks at modes of communication, both within the PMNs and externally. Network strategic direction and planning, along with program implementation, is taken up. Then the basis of work ordering and grouping is examined, an activity known as organizing in hierarchical organizations. Finally, questions of trust are focused on, an important operating premise for cohesion in collaborative undertakings.

Where relevant, the different types of networks will be compared. The different types of PMN decision making were already analyzed in chapter 3, as the typology was developed. Since the fourfold explanation of decision making is the most sensitive to the typology, its findings in regard to operations can be added to this chapter. Some other decision-related management differences will also be noted here. The chapter conclusion contains an explanation of how network structures are collaborarchies; that is, hybrids between voluntary organizations with boards and officials, and collaborative structures like work groups and committees within contemporary bureaucratic organizations.

COLLABORATIVE ORGANIZATIONS

However tempting it may be to compare and contrast network management with a classical paradigm like Weber's (1947) legal-authority-based hierarchical organization, or Gulick and Urwick's (1937) POSDCORB, the fact is that in the information/human capital era organizations themselves resemble those ideals less and less. Even for heuristic purposes it would appear less useful in the twenty-first century to compare hierarchy with network (Powell 1990), when a hierarchy probably looks less like an organization in this time of the emerging bureaucratic organization. Organizational structures themselves have become more flexible and permeable over the twentieth century (Clegg 1990). This has two important implications for understanding PMN management. First is that the public administrators and program specialists who work in bureaucracies are now more attuned to internal organizational experiences that are less rigid, cross the divisional boundaries of their own structures, reach out to other agencies of their government, and involve an increasing number of intergovernmental experiences. Second, this experience with a changing bureaucratic paradigm has brought on a host of cross-boundary transactions, including network experiences. Boundary-spanning approaches—grants, contracts, regulatory interaction, cooperative agreements, joint ventures, and the like—are now regular bureaucratic transactions.

A fair comparison would thus be between network and the emergent organization that faces the challenge of knowledge and resource management within, and also externally collaborates on a regular basis. Any number of the newer management books in the past decade stress these themes, particularly how collaboration is changing the operation of the traditional organization (for example, Drucker 1995; Campbell and Gould 1999; Pasternack and Viscio 1998; Davenport and Prusak 2000). Among the most thorough and thoughtful of this genre is *The Conductive Organization* by Saint-Onge and Armstrong (2004). They define the conductive organization as "an organization that continuously generates and renews the capabilities to achieve breakthrough performance by enhancing the quality and flow of knowledge and by calibrating its strategy, culture, structure, and systems to the needs of its customers and the marketplace" (213). Obviously addressing primarily business organizations, Saint-Onge and Armstrong discuss numerous organizational processes, including the importance of creating partnerships through internal-external interaction, building alliances and coalitions, forming and reforming teams across function and organization boundaries, and collaborating to actively manage interdependencies: "The capability to effectively manage complex partnerships is growing in importance as organizations are reconfigured. Organizations are becoming more and more involved in complex value-creation networks, where the boundaries between one organization and another become blurred and functions become integrated. It's becoming a critical organizational and leadership capability to be able to create and leverage participation in network-designed and delivered solutions" (191). In such organizations, it is usual for the professional and managerial staff to collaborate, learn, share, and execute their responsibilities.

Groff and Jones maintain that today's organizations contain more and more people who share knowledge. "Collaboration groups consist of formal and informal, often self-organized, groups of employees who possess complimentary knowledge and share interest in particular problems, processes, or projects in their organization"(2003, 20). Moreover, they suggest that sharing knowledge is not a zero-sum game. "Unlike conventional assets, knowledge grows when it is shared. The main limitation to infinite knowledge growth is the currency of the information economy—attention" (ibid.). They also underscore the importance of Metcalf's Law (utility = $[nodes]^2$); that is, the usefulness of a network equals the square of the number of users (Metcalfe 1996).

Today's public administrators in particular experience connectivity in dealing with the operations and practices of nonprofit organizations. The past half century has seen an expanding network of alliances between the national government and a host of public and private bodies—other levels of government, private business, banks, insurance companies, and, increasingly, nonprofit agencies (Salamon 1995). These nonprofit organizations are part of the core of the third sector in government and business. They are characterized as structured organizations that are located outside of government, are not designed to distribute profits to owners/investors, are self-governing, and involve substantial voluntary effort (Salamon 1995). Nonprofit organization personnel and processes—boards, planning and technical staff, community-based task forces, strategic planning—are exposed to government officials through interaction with those officials that administer grants or contracts with government. In turn, government interaction has affected nonprofit organizations; they have "become more broadly representative of community interests, as the organizations they serve have to deal more actively with their environments" (Smith and Lipsky 1993, 41). In general, nonprofit organizations are known for their flexibility in operation and the application of traditional managerial techniques such as budgeting, governance, information management, and human resources to widely varying situations (Wolf 1999, 20). The growth of government nonprofit interaction brings another important set of organizational experiences to the network experience.

It is within these contexts that public administrators, association executives, and program managers/specialists work today. Within agencies and organizations, conventional processes such as legal powers and duties, rules and procedures, and hierarchical authority remain and form a continuing overlay of organizational concerns. These continuing procedures put important boundaries on what can be done, particularly for public agencies. But the overlays of cross-boundary collaboration and interorganizational contact are also very real. Knowledge-era public sector managers operate in both contexts, with legal hierarchical authority that increasingly has more connectivity than earlier in the twentieth century. Thus it is in this era of the changing conductive organization that most participants bring management experience to PMNs; these are the organizations to which network management should be compared.

MANAGEMENT DIFFERENCES IN NETWORKS

"It is different. At (the MPO) I am like a board member or part of a committee. Here (at the county) I'm the executive. We have an organization to run, from policies to personnel hearings." A county department head in the same MPO put it this way: "This department has a system of roads, 5,000 or so of rolling stock, traffic operations, permitting, capital improvement projects, mapping, all of which support mission-related services. We have a hierarchy, politicians to deal with, and lots of procedures. The (name of MPO) is completely different. It is regional, not local, and operates by consensus, based on detailed technical analysis." A federal official stated, "In my program we have sign-offs, grant reports, funding, and so on based on section 5303. At the MPOs we are at the table, more as a member of a technical team." In one outreach network a community agency head said that "inside there is a different context, players, different processes. We have staff, internal mechanisms, structures . . . at the (names PMN) it is the newer staff that are out of college and out on the edge of things . . . we became new partners to make change in new ways."

When administrators from different agencies come together to solve problems or share information with one another, most operate differently than in their home agencies. One informational network leader said, "Inside, I manage a program, and I have a line role. When in a partnership I dispense and exchange information." Another stated, "I am a typical 'fed,' with administrative structure, rules, programs . . . whereas in this [network] group, the activity is exchange, equal input." Another state official stated, "At the network there are no bosses, many players." A federal official stated, "We do loans, fund and operate programs within the agency. At the network we build capacity." Another state official said, "We do programs and contracts here. In the network I am not the answer." All of these responses suggest that another kind of management is going on in these networks.

To many respondents, however, this management is an extension of the work they do within their organizations. "It's hard to separate (agency and network)! We are brought here (action network) to see the big picture. We need to be concerned about other jurisdictions' roads, at home our roads." An outreach network participant put it this way: "In the human services field we need to collaborate and network. As executive of this organization, I spend a lot of my time in meetings and networking . . . with many different groups . . . we may use different strategies in our organizations and need to spend a lot of time talking and working things out between our interests." Another executive in the same network said, "Here I run a nonprofit organization, and we have had a lot of success, but 'big things' rarely get done by one. They transcend one organization's interest. The informal group settled on some basic premises; these guiding principles pointed to continuing collaboration. That's the way it usually works, through networking from the inside-out." Another state agency official, a liaison with allied agencies and organizations, said, "In the conservation/environmental field there is no one engineering or policy solution. There are many. I am the agency's 'rep' to the (informational network) because we all have a stake in the watershed and can all contribute. Many of us have done this cross-program work for years. This body just formalizes what we have come together to do since 'conservation became environment.'" Finally, another professional staff member of an outreach network said that involvement "legitimizes what I do as I explain and work from program to program."

Nevertheless, this kind of management is somewhat different. First and foremost, agency representatives come to the table as delegates from their agency and form a pooled authority system that is based more on expertise than on position. Despite differential informal authority, in most of the networks studied official authority is more or less one delegate, one opportunity to influence the recommended agreed course of action. One federal official said, "I am the orchestra leader in [agency], in the Council I am a partner." Authority generally flows in the following manner: Designation as an agent to the network usually brings a measure of delegated authority, the ability to speak on behalf of the agency and to commit agency resources. That seat at the table provides the venue to offer home-agency information and technical expertise to the joint experience. Potential resources—funding opportunities, access to programs, new technologies, and educational opportunities—are entered into the transactional mix. These inputs are added to the discussions, which are joint learning experiences based on exchange. If the network then takes a form of action— as, for example, outreach and decision networks do—accommodations are made. In this sense, authority is based on expertise and the ability to reach agreement as a collective. These agreements carry more moral weight, as opposed to legal authority, because they have the backing of many experts and managers even though traditional program authority normally remains in the participating organizations. One state official concluded that "while [the network] provides the input, and we work as a team, and try to reach agreement, . . . this agency is the final decision maker."

NETWORK AUTHORITY AND POWER

If the agency retains the ultimate decision, what gives the network the sustainability to go beyond delegated authority and potential power to develop its own sense of legitimacy and hold some degree of operating power? In a basic sense, most networks, even those that are chartered, appear to be voluntary in that they represent the coming together of organizations, and their representatives work on issues of mutual concern. Does something else hold them together? Whether chartered or not, a set of power bases proves to be a very important cohesive device.

Authority

Is there a formalized equivalent to legal-based legitimacy and hierarchical authority in PMNs? For all but the three nonchartered PMNs the answer is yes, and in most cases the major mechanisms are borrowed not from bureaucracy or hierarchy, but from associational life or intergovernmental relations. Table 6.1 displays the authority pattern for each; that is, the equivalent mechanisms for each PMN. In the first two columns, their enabling authority and their stated rules and procedures, if any, are displayed. Except for the three nonchartered PMNs, most networks have some sort of legally based operating authority in the same way as a government agency or nonprofit agency is enabled. For the eleven chartered PMNs, the most common enabling vehicle (third column) is either intergovernmental agreement under state statutory guidance, or as a nonprofit 501c(3) organization under federal and state regulation. Six were formed by intergovernmental agreement, and three either as a 501c(3) exclusively or, in the case of Indiana Rural Council, as both an intergovernmental and a 501c(3) organization. Although they are networks, three others—USDA/Nebraska, Iowa Communications, and Enhanced Data (for USDA only its outreach program)—are rooted in state or federal code. That leaves Darby, Small Communities, and the 317 Group as nonchartered organizations.

Because the very nature of networking involves organizations coming and working together, it is perhaps no surprise that the intergovernmental agreement is a preferred vehicle of enablement. On the other hand, the typical agreement is interlocal. It is quite unusual for an agreement in the United States to involve a combination of federal, state, and local government officials, along with the nongovernment sector. The 501c(3) allows the PMN to be formally recognized as an organization and become a potential conduit for funding. Because they both deal with the bringing together of disparate entities, these two mechanisms provide a form of status before the law that is important in an organizational society.

What takes these networks beyond their charter status as collective bodies? The fourth column in table 6.1 identifies the formalized rules and procedures of the fourteen PMNs. The three nonchartered networks plus Lower Platte and Enhanced Data have no formal rules or documented procedures. This does not mean that these six do not have regularized procedures. Small Communities, for example, has established formal but unwritten procedures for presentation at its Finance Committee meetings. As pointed out in chapter 5, towns must present a one-page summary with criteria, followed by a presentation by the water plant operator and/or an engineering consultant. Its Steering Committee follows an established sequence of committee reports, special projects, agency reports, and a review of the work plan. There are no written procedures for the other networks. Only three—Iowa Communications, Des Moines Metro, and Indiana Economic Development—have rules or bylaws for operation. One PMN, USDA/RD, uses its annual work plan as a way of establishing its outreach procedures of operation.

What does all this suggest? When it comes to formal authority, most PMNs do not extend themselves much beyond chartering or enabling. These entities need the pooled resources and expertise emanating from many organizations. They do not want to become bogged down in parliamentary procedures that impede exploration, discovery, and potential solutions. They try to avoid entrapment in their own procedures in order to maximize the flexibility that networks promise (Alter and Hage 1993).

TABLE 6.1 Bases of Nonhierarchical Authority

PMN	Type	Enabling Authority	Stated Rules and Procedures
Darby	I	None	None
Indiana Economic Development	I	501c(3) not-for-profit	Purposes, members, and board in Articles of Incorporation
Lower Platte	I	Interlocal agreement—Nebraska State 13-801-827	None
Iowa Enterprise	D	501c(3) not-for-profit (2004—Business Committee of Iowa RDC)	Board and Council membership until 2004
Indiana Rural Council	D	Intergovernmental Agreement/ 501c(3) not-for-profit	Council membership established
Partnership for Rural Nebraska	D	Intergovernmental Agreement	Charter sets board and teams
Iowa Geographic	D	Executive Order/501c(3) not-for-profit as of 2003	Board membership from various GIS sectors stated

Small Communities	O		None
USDA/Nebraska	O	State program of federal agency	Based in Annual Program Plan
317 Group	O	None (originally governor's task force)	None
Iowa Communications	A	Iowa Statutes and Administrative Code	Rules and procedures of operation in Administrative Code Sec. 8D.11
Enhanced Data	A	Indiana Code 5-21-6 ch. 6	None stated; quorum stated in law
Kentuckiana Agency	A	Intergovernmental agreement; TEA-21 statute	Planning process memorandum of understanding; delegates authority from Kentuckiana Agency board to MPO
Des Moines Metro	A	Intergovernmental agreement (Iowa 28E); TEA-21 statute	States' voting and nonvoting membership criteria and ratios (by jurisdiction); defines planning area; bylaws

The issue of differences among the four types remains. Clearly, noncharter status falls into the informational, developmental, and outreach category. Two of the four nonchartered networks are of the outreach type. One would have expected more to belong to the informational category, but that is not the case. The presence or absence of rules and procedures is also dispersed among the categories. One distinction does hold, however, if one returns to the third column of table 6.1. All four action networks are based in law: Iowa Communications and Enhanced Data in state law; the two MPOs in U.S. law, TEA-21. Their action potential has the legitimacy of law, similar to that of a bureaucratic organization. Although they are networks of federal, state, and local officials, the MPOs' authority to allocate federal TIP funds and to incorporate local projects in their long-range plan is rooted in federal law. Iowa Communications sets rates and interacts with its public sector partners based on its enabling statute and administrative code. As illustrated in the previous chapter, Enhanced Data's powers with regard to other agencies are clearly stated in Indiana Code 5-21-6, ch. 6. This is an important distinction that, at least among the fourteen PMNs, sets them apart as networks that can directly make policy and program adjustments. The other ten networks do not possess that authority.

Power

To look for power within the network, one must look beyond authority and procedures. This issue is somewhat clouded by the rhetoric and literature on networking, where the focus has been on equity in participation-based joint decisions. They are often characterized as "coequal, interdependent, patterned relationships" (Klijn 1996, 93). On the other hand, Burt finds that in networks some sit in positions of extensive opportunity contexts, filling "structural holes" and creating unequal opportunity, while others are less able or willing players (1992, 67). Organizational representatives also differ with regard to the resources they bring to the network; thus different resource dependencies and power differences exist (Rhodes 1997). Clegg and Hardy suggest that "[we] cannot ignore that power can be hidden behind the façade of 'trust' and the rhetoric of 'collaboration,' and used to promote vested interests through the manipulation and capitulation of weaker partners" (1996, 679). The analysis, therefore, turns to concerns of power in this exploration of network management.

Considerable light can be shed on this question by examining four operating phenomena revealed by detailed coding across the PMNs: network champions, staffing patterns, the bases of internal political influence, and the bases of internal technical influence. Table 6.2 displays pooled, within-case perceptions by discussants regarding their characterization of internal power and authority, in each of the PMNs. It suggests that networks do indeed possess discernible power structures, and that such structures are of a differentiated nature. The first column identifies the presence or absence of a network champion, a person or, in a few cases, two people most responsible for establishing, moving, and orchestrating the network. During the research period, all but two networks, Indiana Economic Development and Iowa Enterprise, had at least one such person, and four had experienced two champions. The two networks that struggled the most and were both reconstituted after periods of dormancy had no champion. This undoubtedly contributed to their struggles, a view their participants confirmed during discussions.

A state program head of a federal agency in one of the rural development networks stated that every network must "have a catalytic leader who has a passion for it." Another state official said, "We need an overall champion, and each subcommittee project needs a mini champion!" Even though authority is more equal in network members and is also based on expertise, someone still needs to come forward and help orchestrate a vision, follow through on the work plan, contact key partners, orchestrate meetings, and so on. Ordinarily this is someone who holds an administrative position in one key agency, can command needed but modest professional staff resources, has control over potential donated in-house clerical and communication resources, and has the technical or professional respect of the other members.

A network champion can be but is not always the convener or chairperson. Often it is the director of one of the participating agencies who, through staff time, holds the modest network records, operates the listserv, and maintains the website. In other cases it is a volunteer who has the capacity to do the work within the home organization; for example, a federal or state agency/program or unit of a college or university. In a few cases the role of champion has rotated with the chair, who is expected to be a temporary champion. The risk is that "with an inactive chair we go a year or so with very little activity." As in the case of many voluntary organizations, success depends on a visible and dedicated leader. Behind most long-term networks lies the energy and work of a network champion.

Networks also need persons with political influence within the body to help sustain them. Because these are not organizations but are composed of representatives of organizations, they depend on donated effort that can be transformed into political power. The second column of table 6.2 identifies the basics of the network's internal political influence, people that are identified by others as promoters, whose presence, participation, and resource commitment send a message that "this [network] is important and that is why I am here." While network influence is said to flow from role and expertise rather than position (Weiner 1990), our participants felt that assumption is not completely true, as some of the positions that sustaining participants hold put them in a more powerful and influential place than others.

The data in table 6.2 represent each PMN's pooled assessment of who has political influence. It is clear that every network depends on influential representatives. The watershed networks rely heavily on their conservation districts and state agencies. The rural development bodies rely heavily on USDA/RD in their respective states and their departments of economic development. Some, such as Iowa Communications and Indiana Economic Development, look to key gubernatorial staff. The 317 group depends on the head of the state agency DDARS, and two association CEOs of Arc and INARF. Finally, the MPOs both rely on their staff transportation managers, Policy Committee officers, and Technical Committee officers. The pattern is the same regardless of the type of PMN.

Networks appear to need these influential promoters around their champions. One network promoter referred to himself and others like him as "vision keepers. . . . These are the people at the middle or working level of federal and state agencies where the links up and down have to be made." As members who work with programs on a daily basis, they have the agency knowledge to share with others. They provide a program and the organizing energy that champions need to keep the process going. They become involved in developing joint information events and activities, and engage extensively in information sharing, attend meetings to access information and emerging technologies, and communicate the network's concerns to their home agencies. Each network needs three to six promoters representing a range of different agencies. Many who are involved in the PMNs related that it would be difficult to be a successful champion, or even think of a viable network, without the complementary and essential work of the promoters or vision keepers.

All of the PMNs are in the business of information exchange, and most are also in the business of discovering, adapting, and applying technology. Most come together to share information and to learn about technology. Many even pool and sometimes adapt technology. Iowa Geographic is a prime example, as it uncovers and adapts GIS technology from the very complex Ortho Infrared project to helping a local community map its growth corridor. This requires people with expertise in GIS who differentially lend their technical abilities to Iowa Geographic. That phenomenon is reflected in the third column of table 6.2, Bases of Technical Influence. Each PMN follows this pattern of a few people adding the most to the technical mix. One MPO discussant put it this way, "There is a core, key players, of engineers and planners and others from the Technical Committee that work closely with the staff. The core is where the foundation is laid and the real work is within that (core-member-led technical) subgroup." The MPOs then rely on Technical Committee activists, including state and federal officials and other transit/highways experts. In Small Communities the core players are the key funders and university-based researchers. Indiana Economic Development relies heavily on external consultants and university-based members. Iowa Geographic depends on the head of the Iowa State University GIS Facility, DNR and DOT GIS specialists, and one or two heavy GIS users from local governments. These professionals—program heads and specialists—weigh in on the work and form the core of technical power within the network.

In a network, power could not flow in any other way. The work of Small Communities is premised on finding adaptable solutions to intractable water problems, only some of which can be solved by financing packages. New water/wastewater technology brings university-based and agency-based engineers to look for scale-based solutions. If technically feasible, the legal-regulatory and financing people become involved. This brings technical people to the core of network influence. "We can only help a large number of small communities if the engineering and technology people step forward and find a way. Then the rest of you can work on the dollars and the permitting. Success depends a lot on what I would call 'technical activism.'" Although Iowa Enterprise has struggled to bring in home-based businesses to its fold, it is the core of small business consultants, SBDC specialists, USDA/Nebraska loan experts, and university-community development people that "provide the very expertise that those home-based business people do not have." Another discussant stated that without those people and their one web master contributing their efforts, "Iowa Enterprise would have fallen under the lack of inertia that busy home-business people brought to the group. It was not so much lack of enthusiasm, but the ability to know what to do was not there for our members. Some of us just had to use our expertise and experience to do it for them." It appears that every network involved in technical problems must be sustained by a technical core.

Some level of staffing also appears to be part of the equation. The fourth column of table 6.2 describes the varied staffing patterns among the PMNs. Darby, Partnership for Rural Nebraska, and Iowa Geographic have part-time staff assigned to other duties in one lead organization of the network. Iowa Enterprise, Small Communities, and the 317 Group have only pro bono staffing picked up by one organization. Lower Platte, Indiana Rural Council, and USDA/Nebraska have a full-time equivalent coordinator or executive director. That leaves five PMNs—Indiana Economic Development, Iowa Communications, Enhanced Data, Kentuckiana Agency, and Des Moines Metro—that have a full-time staff. With the exception of Indiana Economic Development, all are action networks; funding undoubtedly allows for the staff to carry out their mandated missions. More important than the number of staff is the role of staff. While it clearly varies between the networks, the staff can also be agents of network power. When there is a staff, more than the support system is

(text continues on page 100)

TABLE 6.2 Elements of Network Power and Operating Authority

PMN	Type	Champion	Basis of Political Influence	Basis of Technical Influence	Staff
Darby	I	√	TNC (The Nature Conservancy/ Ohio), state agency program heads, SCWD district managers	Ohio EPA and DNR program representatives, engineers, local planners, SCWD field staff, USDA/NCRS field staff	Part-time (TNC) Darby coordinator
Indiana Economic Development	I	—[a]	Governor's office, IN Dept. of Commerce executives, IN Dept. of Administration	Contract economic development researchers, contract planners, university-based economic development researchers, state agency statistics and data analysts	Nontechnical staff of five
Lower Platte	I	√	3 Natural Conservation Resource district managers	State agency program representatives (designated by their directors), engineering and scientific personnel from districts, federal specialists: NCRS, USFWS, USGS	One full-time watershed coordinator

Iowa Enterprise	D	—	Iowa SBA office director, Iowa Dev. Authority director (cooperatives), SBDC state program acting director, executive dir. Iowa RDC	Small business consultants, SBDC staff, web development consultant, USDA/Nebraska loan program heads, university-based development specialists	Pro bono staffing/SBA until 2002, Iowa RDC (2002–)
Indiana Rural Council	D	√√[b]	Indiana lt. governor, USDA/ Nebraska state director, Dept. of Commerce deputy director, deputy commissioner of agriculture	University-based community development experts, Indiana Agricultural Leadership Forum, Purdue Extension deputy director, federal and state program heads	Executive director (program manager added in 2004)
Iowa Communications	A	√	State legislators, governor's office, State CIO, Iowa Dept. of Public Education, IPTV (public television), university and colleges	State agency information officers, DEM, DAS, DOT, DPHO, Iowa National Guard, Univ. of Iowa Hospital deputy director, chief education officer, IPTV/ Department of Education	Administrative, sales, and technical
Enhanced Data	A	√	Indiana Dept. of Admin., State IO, governor's designee, Internet exec. dir., state librarian	accessIndiana technical staff; state department information specialists: DNR, Revenue, FSSA, Motor Vehicles	Uses accessIndiana staff

continued

TABLE 6.2 (continued)

PMN	Type	Champion	Basis of Political Influence	Basis of Technical Influence	Staff
Kentuckiana Agency	A	√	Kentuckiana Agency transportation manager, MPO officers, officers and activists on Technical Committee	State and federal transit and highway staff in two states, local government engineering and transportation planning experts, information specialists	Ten full-time and six part-time staff
Des Moines Metro	A	√	Des Moines Metro executive dir., MPO officers, Des Moines city council member, officers of Technical Committee, state legislator, city manager	State and federal transit and highway staff in Iowa, local government engineers and planners, local government executives, Des Moines Transit and Airport executives	Seven staff
Partnership for Rural Nebraska	D	√√[b]	USDA/Nebraska state director, DED deputy director, University of Nebraska–Lincoln rural research institute director, dir. of rural Development Commission (until 2003)	State agency (partner) program heads, Nebraska Development Network activists, USDA/Nebraska program heads, rural development researchers at universities	Part-time (UNL institute) coordinator

Iowa Geographic	D	√√[b]	State agency and university-based GIS/information systems directors: ISU, DOT, DNR; extension director	ISU GIS facility director, DOT GIS specialist, DNR GIS specialist, experienced city and county GIS users	Half-time State GIS coordinator
Small Communities	O	√	OWDA exec. dir., Ohio EDA, USDA/RD, Ohio DoD, Ohio Public Works finance program heads	State and federal agency program heads and engineers, university environmental researchers and training specialists, community development specialists	None, pro bono staffing
USDA/Nebraska	O	√	USDA/Nebraska state director, USDA/Nebraska deputy director, Partnership for Rural Nebraska/Nebraska Development Network officers	USDA grant and loan staff, state development association staff, state program heads, area and local development professionals, private lending	One program director devoted to outreach efforts
317 Group	O	√√[b]	Indiana DDARS (FSSA) head, INARF and Arc executive directors, university-based center head	DDARS staff, Medicaid staff, INARF and Arc professional staff, Governor's Planning Council and university staff	None, pro bono staffing

[a]Champion until 2000.
[b]More than one champion.

involved; the political and technical power bases are touched as work is orchestrated. In a nonhierarchical body where the activist core is working mainly in the home agency, the work of staff is as critical as it would be in a voluntary organization. "Without (name of staff director), despite his need to be in control, we would not move along the way we do, and no doubt there would be more nonproductive conflicts." Another said, "Our (staff person) does more than arrange everything, she sees to it that the right people are there for the right decisions and that they push the program in the right direction." A participant observed, "(name of former staff person) was so energetic and invested that the (PMN) appeared like it was 'her baby' instead of our (name of group). To get anything done you had to go through her." Staffing must clearly be put into the power equation.

With the exception of the work of Milward and Provan (1998), very little research has been done on power in public networks. Milward and Provan found that network effectiveness was linked to stakeholders' control of power among community mental health centers. Here we find power to be real within the network, but distributed among champions, promoters, technical influentials, and staff. Decisions are brokered, as the collaborative literature suggests, but within the context of this shared, nonhierarchical power. In effect, the important building blocks of collaborarchy involve at least four components of power—champions, promoters, experts, and staff.

It is important to note that we have only identified the sources of collaborarchy power, not the ratio or balance among each element. Here one can only speculate. As discussants relate, beyond the facade of consensus and collaborative management stronger partners do take advantage of weaker partners. Some organization representatives sit in positions where their knowledge, financial resources, organization position, or legal authority accrues power within the collective (Agranoff and McGuire 2001b). While such power can be used to impede consensus or dominate, in collaborarchy it is often used to forge general agreements, along the line of Clarence Stone's (1989) urban work on the power of possibility. Like modern organizations, today's networks rely on technical power. For example, in the rural development networks—Indiana Rural Council and Partnership for Rural Nebraska—the USDA/Nebraska, university extension, and state economic development departments tend to be powerful and committed actors where technical questions are treated as coequal with issues of program and policy. Their partner members do a great deal of the persuasion and ultimately the technical adjustment work required to foster the common mission by getting others to make the adjustments needed for essential consensus. On the other hand, the absence of the support of any of the "big three" can slow progress in these networks (see also Radin et al. 1996).

STRUCTURED COMMUNICATION AND PROMOTION

Unlike organizations that have built-in mechanisms of hierarchical communications based on face-to-face and distributed written communications, networks have the challenge of creating contacts outside of hierarchical structures. We now know that they have nonhierarchical structures including staff personnel, champions, promoters, and a technical corps through whom members can channel their contacts. Later in this chapter it will also become clear that they often have formalized corps of officers and work groups. In a sense, communication channels substitute for the hierarchical structure in participants' home organizations. It is through this array of actors that the patterns of communication flow. Networks can use the printed word as well for both internal and external communication. Like most contemporary hierarchical organizations they can access electronic contact, a tremendous advantage for entities that are not only located in multiple sites, but are not held together by any formal or informal organizational communication system.

The communication practices of the PMNs are identified in table 6.3, which provides an overview of their electronic and print approaches. It demonstrates the critical role of electronic connection for networks, whose partners/activists are at scattered and remote sites and meet face-to-face much less frequently than organization members. The table contains both internal and external modes. Clearly all PMNs have taken advantage of electronic communication; all use e-mail for internal communication among the members, and all but one—317 Group—have a website reporting the existence of the PMN. Indeed, it is perhaps no accident that the era of the network and the electronic connection era coincide.

With participants spread over so many organizational sites, e-mail allows for instant contact among partners. Moreover, e-mail reduces the one-to-one communication typical of phone calls. One network actor can communicate with many. Finally, the listserve capacities of each network maximize the contact potential, allowing for rapid network expansion along the communication dimension. Notices of meetings, announcements of relevant events and programs, and newly available technologies are all transmitted this way. "They save a lot of telephone tag, and contact with one can be contact with all."

The website allows the network a form of public identity. For nine of the PMNs, meeting announcements, meeting minutes, project reports, data, and key news related to the partners are web-posted, circulated, and made available for all involved in the network. The material is also publicly accessible. The last four columns of table 6.3 focus on various means of external communication in newsletters, publications, news releases, and project reports and studies. Here a varied pattern emerges. Seven PMNs employ a newsletter; most are

TABLE 6.3 PMN Communication

PMN	E-Mail	Internal and External Website	Internal Web Posting	External Newsletter	External Publications	News Releases	Project Reports/ Studies	Comments
Darby	√	√	√	—	√	—	—	Reports by partners; TNC does publicity
Indiana Economic Development	√	√	—	—	√	√	√	Contractor reports
Lower Platte	√	√	√	√	√	—	√	Web-based GIS
Iowa Enterprise	√	√	—	—	—	—	—	Business succession study in progress
Indiana Rural Council	√	√	√	√	√	—	√	Rural strategy
Partnership for Rural Nebraska	√	√	√	√	√	√	√	*Rural News Bits*; Rural Poll; CARI studies
Iowa Geographic	√	√	√	√	√	—	√	Newsletter dormant since 2002; color ortho-red posted on web; Iowa Communications for meetings

Small Communities	√	√	—	—	√	Learning materials; OWDA electronic bulletin board
USDA/Nebraska	√	√	—	√	—	Annual Report
317 Group	√	—	—	√	√	DDARS; Arc and INARF carry most communications
Iowa Communications	√	√	√	√	√	Legislators, CIO, agency briefings
Enhanced Data	√	√	√	—	√	Market reports and public contact prepared by accessIndiana staff or Internet Commission
Kentuckiana Agency	√	√	√	√	√	E-mail for data transmission; numerous project reports
Des Moines Metro	√	√	√	√	√	E-mail used for data transmission; numerous project reports

electronic at this time (one is dormant). All but three regularly issue publications of different kinds. For example, Darby circulates *Darby Book*, a manual on the history of and ecological threats to the watershed, as well as information on conservation and mediation practices. Iowa Communications has a number of publications including *FAQ/Iowa Communications*. Half of the PMNs regularly issue news releases, usually announcing their studies, programs, forums, and related newsworthy events. All but three PMNs regularly issue project reports or studies that emanate from their work groups to the public. For example, Indiana Rural Council circulated their 2002 *Rural Development Strategy* conducted for the state legislature. The MPOs regularly issue reports based on study group efforts on alternate modes of transportation: bicycle, pedestrian, trails, and light rail. There appears to be no pattern of differences in communication between the four types of PMNs. It does appear that, with the exception of Enhanced Data and Small Communities, there is a great deal of public contact among the outreach and action networks. This is also where the staffing component tends to be the highest, which may be a reason for more extensive external communication. Overall, most of the networks make substantial attempts at external contact.

Beyond a modest amount of publicity through electronic venues and an occasional brochure and newsletter, external network promotion constitutes the primary public relations activity for most PMNs. Acts of development and maintenance such as research reports and new technical tools are the major elements of public promotion. A natural contacting of nonnetwork, likeminded agency managers, specialists, and knowledge holders regarding commonly held aims or interests moves champions and vision keepers, along with the political and technical core, to engage in a defined involvement that brings in others. Those who benefit personally/professionally/organizationally will come forward and add their participation, and occasionally become vision keepers. Media advertisements, news releases, newspaper and magazine articles, and other aspects of mass publicity can create some visibility, but appear to be rare forms of public contact for network building.

Patterns of Interaction

The real interaction in networks comes through organizing and operating. First, electronic means are not substitutes for face-to-face communication, particularly at network meetings. Here the network business and transactions are approved and communications operations are regulated. The networks less commonly use the kind of formal work schedules or major project designs that single organizations are familiar with. As in the two watershed networks, studies are often conducted, after which the partners hear the results, ask questions, and are then free to bring the studies back to their agencies for implementation. With the exception of the transportation and watershed networks, little that comes to the table is really controversial. As chapter 3 clearly indicates, real decisions are not really core issues for many networks.

Another important dimension of contact is between the network participant and the home organization. In this case PMN discussants report that internal agency/organization contact is a combination of face-to-face interaction and e-mail messaging. This boundary-spanning aspect of communication is essential because one must regularly interact at home to be an effective bridge between home organization and the network. A PMN activist knows a great deal about the programs, regulations, technologies, funding rules, and other workings of the agency. "Others in the network will turn to you with questions and expect answers." This requires some involved level of interaction within the home agency that often goes beyond informing; it may involve adjusting and deciding. In this sense the boundary-spanning activity is intra-organizational as well as interorganizational in domain. "Do the lateral networking within your agency," said one state program director. "If expertise is called for that you cannot supply, bring the right person (from the home agency) to the meeting." This is particularly important as PMNs exchange, explore, and adapt technical knowledge. One state program director who is part of the technical core of his network said, "It is your responsibility (as agency representative) to see that the right need for technical information from your agency is satisfied."

Network communication is also considered necessary with organization executives/CEOs/program heads. Clearly partner involvement relies on the tacit support of most partners' agency heads. It proves hard for anyone in the hierarchy to devote scarce agency resources—time, personnel, information, expertise—if the person at the top has not bought into the idea of agency presence in a network. "Our (name of PMN) is struggling right now because it was the idea of a Republican governor two governors ago. The previous and current Democrats see less of a need for such a body." As a result, in this situation appointed department heads were reported as offering only token support. On the other hand, another network coordinator stated, "The only way we have survived political resistance from local people is that the state and [special] district chief executive officers are steadfast in their support of this joint undertaking." In this case the executives are not directly involved, but they have committed dollars to support a coordinator and have made their staff available for network activity. Top-level support is essential promotional activity. This requires the network representative to be in some regular contact with the agency head. "I make it a part of my regular briefings with the director to let him know what is going on in the Partnership." Another staff director said, "The governor's office and the director's office of (department) are part of our regular round of discussions. They give us direction and we give them feedback."

This portrayal of the major modes of communication suggests that networks have similar bridging needs to that of organizations. As collaborarchies, these bridges require somewhat more effort because the natural internal channels are not always there, but bridging is nevertheless equally essential across the boundaries of organization. Three conclusions therefore stand out with regard to PMN communications: First, like conductive organizations, networks as collaborarchies must constantly reach across to communicate with a number of external publics. This reach increasingly involves multiple channels. Second, unlike organizations, the internal channels must be self-created through the network's contacts with government agencies, NGOs, related networks, and the general public. Beyond the participants' organizations there are fewer built-in channels. In terms of the clientele of each partner organization, communication is normally shared with network partners, inasmuch as the partners implement agreements. Moreover, some are protective of contact with their clients. Third, while both organizations and networks can and do take advantage of electronic mail, web postings, electronic data transfer, and electronic reporting, but electronic modes appear indispensable to networks, facilitating those self-developed channels that come more naturally within organizations that have managers, divisions, bureaus, and programs. Collaborarchies depend on nonnatural or fabricated communication channels.

STRATEGY PLANNING AND IMPLEMENTATION

Do networks adapt similar strategic imperatives as that of hierarchical organizations, or do their self-managing programs lead them in another direction? Strategy refers to the broad goals and the actions required to accomplish such direction. For the emergent conductive organization, strategy can be broken into components: an outreaching strategic intent and imperatives that addresses core internal responsibilities; how public value will be created; and how knowledge access and exchange will be generated (Saint-Onge and Armstrong 2004). In this chapter the focus is on strategic intent and core capabilities, exploring how organizational representatives come together to self-guide their PMNs.

In practice a variety of approaches are taken into account. Table 6.4 examines and summarizes the more standard strategic and planning approaches taken by PMNs. It is easy to see that these closely resemble the practices undertaken by most contemporary public agencies and nonprofit organizations. Like most organizations, PMNs try to engage in the various aspects of strategic planning and goal setting, but much less frequently undertake programming internally and implementation is normally carried out by partner agencies. PMNs' vision, mission, and goals are analyzed in the table's second column. Most networks do come together and articulate a vision (column two); all but one have adopted a mission statement; and twelve regularly adopt goals. With the exception of Small Communities, all have at least two of these three strategic imperatives. In many ways, adoption of these tools signifies the broad purpose for which the group has become a collaborative and contributes to the cohesive forces needed in the absence of legal mandates and ascribed authority.

Strategic directions are examined in column three of table 6.4. As one moves from informational to the other types of networks, it is obvious that with the exceptions of Indiana Economic Development and Enhanced Data, the strategic directions become more long-term and are more likely to resemble organizational approaches. Whereas Small Communities plans only for specific projects and Enhanced Data has no strategic objectives, the other five outreach and action networks orient their plans over the long term, based on specific principles. By contrast, the informational and developmental networks plan less comprehensively and three do not engage in these activities at all.

With regard to more concrete work plans or project objectives identified in the fourth column of table 6.4, all but two engage in either work plans or set objectives, either on an annual planning basis or for specific projects. Again, if one looks at outreach and action networks, the work tends to be more comprehensive albeit short-term, as opposed to those based on ad hoc projects. Although one may not find the same kind of detailed regular strategic tools in every network as in most bureaucratic organizations, in many ways PMNs resemble the tools of voluntary organizations.

Planning in all of the different types of networks is typically vision and problem driven. "The work plan is a catalyst for what we do." The partners articulate what they want to work on and the collective body, by agreement on a token vote, adopts it. For example, the Partnership for Rural Nebraska has a Steering Committee composed of administrators and an Education Committee made up of program specialists. The former group agrees on the network's work program whereas the latter plans an annual Rural Institute. At one time an executive committee composed of the ratifiers on the overall agreement approved the programming decisions made by program and second-level staff, but this has been done away with. In each PMN process, it is a matter of finding and tapping available expertise and delegated authority. Planning then becomes more a case of organizing what the network has decided to do. One network coordinator related, "In my other work, in this (home) organization, we administrators lay out what we need to do to make programs work. In the [network] a committee plans everything."

Implementation or programming is primarily external to the core of the network. Returning to table 6.4, the two right-hand columns (5 and 6) focus on this issue. Nine of the fourteen networks do not conduct any of their own

TABLE 6.4 Strategic Tools/Programming

PMN	Vision/ Mission/Goals	Written Strategic Directions	Work Plan/ Objectives	Internal/ External Programming	Location of Programming
Darby (I)	M G	—	—	E	Strategies for parts of watershed by partner organizations
Indiana Economic Development (I)	V M G	Clusters within strategic plan	Three-year and project work plans	E	Implementation of three-year plan by state agencies and private sector
Lower Platte (I)	M G	—	Project	E	Lead role by three NRDs
Iowa Enterprise (D)	M G	—	—	E	By RDC committee
Indiana Rural Council (D)	V M G	For each of major activities	Annual work plans	I/E	Two small grant programs by separate, non-PMN committees; major program efforts met externally
Partnership for Rural Nebraska (D)	V M G	Developed and revised periodically	Individual projects, e.g., Institute, Rural Poll	I/E	Only Institute and Poll programmed internally
Iowa Geographic (D)	V M G	Periodically revised strategic plan	Project work plans	I/E	Some software development internal; remainder external

Small Communities (D)	G	For specific projects	Annual objectives	E	All strategic directions implemented by agencies
USDA/Nebraska (O)	M G	Five-year long-term plan	Annual work plan and action plan	I/E	Combination of own and external programming
317 Group (O)	V M G	Original task force principles plus new components	For each of seven individual strategic components	E	Programming by state agencies and NGOs
Iowa Communications (A)	V M G	On assets, usage, financing, regulatory review	Special initiatives, e.g., sale of assets	I/E	Transmission by Iowa Communications, programs by users, programming by agencies and organizations
Enhanced Data (A)	V M G	—	For access fees and surcharges	E	Most by accessIndiana and Intelnet Commission
Kentuckiana Agency (A)	V M G	TIP/long-range plan	Annual work program, project plans, plan objectives	E	By individual jurisdictions
Des Moines Metro (A)	V M G	TIP/long-range plan	Annual work program, project plans, plan objectives	E	By individual jurisdictions

programming; five experience limited internal operations. A look at the last column, which describes the location of programming, reveals that for those that do some implementation it tends to be rather minor. Indiana Rural Council, for example, operates two small rural community grant programs, authorized by the Indiana Legislature in 2003. They are staffed by Indiana Rural Council but run by separate committees, totally independent of the PMN. Indiana Rural Council has no role in these programs. All other programming is through their partner's organizations. Another example is that of Iowa Geographic, where some software development, such as the Ortho Infra-red project, is internal to a network committee. Other programs, such as the local government outreach effort, are operated through Iowa State University Extension and the (website) Resources Guide by the Iowa State University GIS Facility. Two examples where there is a more balanced mix are USDA/Nebraska and Iowa Communications, but even in those cases, operation of network programs relies as much on external entities as it does on internal groups. For the informational networks, programming relies entirely and exclusively on partner organizations and agencies. That, along with their nondecisional status identified in chapter 3, helps define this category.

Every one of the networks thus experiences primarily external implementation. The common core of internal programming is very small. Network implementation typically involves meeting arrangements, the listserv, and a website. Most of the networks studied either have a small staff presence— usually one coordinator— or receive program support from the home agency of the current chair or president. The real PMN programs that flow from the work plans of a network happen in the agencies themselves. For example, both the rural development and natural resource networks rely on substate, state, and federal agencies to do the actual remediation and development work needed to deal with their challenges and agreed courses of action. The 317 Group relies almost exclusively on the state agencies and nonprofit organizations to follow the strategies that they develop. The rather detailed plans of the MPOs that lead to approved programs and funds allocated are, in the end, carried out by local governments. In the same fashion the Iowa Communications Network, also an action network, is the data transmission and narrowcast agency for dozens of federal, state, and local government agencies that are responsible for their own programming. One state official reported, "I have less control over what is done by the members because they are agencies and I can't tell them what to do."

All of the strategic and implementation approaches depicted in table 6.4 are part of the leadership and guidance ability necessary in self-managing systems like networks. It is more or less understood that network leadership includes the "principle of 'soft' guidance" as a replacement for command and control (Windhoff-Héntier 1992, 3), a prime tenet of collaborarchy. This type of steering contributes to holding networks together, and provides important signals to participants that their involvement has meaning and direction. It is part of the network's propensity to engage in "balancing social forces and interests and enabling social actors and systems to organize themselves" (Kooiman 1993, 256).

NETWORK ORGANIZATION

At first glance, the structure of the PMN—boards and committees—makes them appear similar to voluntary organizations. These structures also look like the knowledge arrangements that are emerging within single organizations, that require more than the lines and boxes of bureaus, departments, and divisions. Like conductive organizations, network collaborarchies include arrangements or groupings of people and responsibilities into distinctive roles and relationships that are mainly geared to meet challenges by encouraging the flow of information and resources across organizations.

Beyond the power bases already covered earlier in table 6.2, PMNs are organized to perform the collaborative exchanges, engage in knowledge development, and take part in other joint efforts that engender their organization. Table 6.5 identifies how PMNs are organized, their internal arrangements and operational groupings. With their governing boards/executive committees, committees and subgroups, and contacts with other networks, they look very much like nonprofit organizations. As the second column indicates, ten of the fourteen have some form of a board, normally a governing board, or in the case of the MPOs their Policy Committee. The exceptions are the Darby Core Group of professionals (until the mid-1990s there was also a group of administrators); Small Communities' Steering Committee, which is not a governing board but a general oversight group; USDA/Nebraska's two administrator arrangement; and the 317 Group's informal steering group. The remaining PMNs follow the model of the voluntary association board of directors. Like an association board, PMN boards not only provide overall governance and direction, but symbolically represent the community of organizations that bring them together. Their officers and actions bear an aura of legitimacy similar to that of voluntary association boards.

Beyond the basic governing board or steering group, the PMNs are organized for their primary interorganization information/knowledge and problem solving. They are organizationally designed to support the strategic goals, objectives, and programs identified earlier. The third and fourth columns of table 6.5 identify the standing committees and work groups of the networks. With the exception of four, each has either a set of standing committees that

(text continues on page 117)

TABLE 6.5 PMN Internal Arrangement and Groupings

PMN	Governing Body	Standing Committees	Work Groups/ Task Forces	No. of Primary Interacting Networks, Contacts Associations	Comments
Darby	Core group of environ. specialists and planners	—	For particular efforts, e.g., stream bank erosion; farmer nutrient planning; tree planting	10	Until 1995, two core groups of administrators and specialists
Indiana Economic Development	Board of Directors/ Officers Executive Comm.	For three-year economic development strategic plan	Consultants; project advisory groups in many areas	6	Each project effort brings in multiple partners
Lower Platte	Board of 3 NRD execs and 7 staff agency	—	Special study groups; for GIS website	5	U.S. Army Corps of Engineers, USGS, EPA, Nat. Park Serv., area city and county govts., utilities boards

Iowa Enterprise	Board of Officers/Business Comm. of IA Rural Devel. Council[a]	Advisory Council of state and federal administrators	Web development; conference and program committees; study work groups	7	Until 2004 restructuring; after 2004 Board and Council merged
Indiana Rural Council	Governing Board from 5 sectors: federal, state, local govt., nonprofit, and for-profit	Executive Comm., five others for major program efforts	Task/work groups for several special efforts	14	Also separate membership award committees for two small grants administered by Indiana Rural Council
Partnership for Rural Nebraska	Governing Board (signatory executives) and Coord. Comm. (prog. admin.) merged in 2003	Coordinating Committee (until 2003), Education Committee	For Rural Institute and Nebraska Development Academy	10	Merger of Partnership for Rural Nebraska and its component, Nebraska Development Network in 2004
Iowa Geographic	Board representing six sectors: federal, state, and local govts., universities, nonprofit, for-profit	Newsletter, Remote Sensing, Strategic Planning, Conf., Climate and Environ., Cadastral and Education	Special workshop task forces	6	MPOs, Regional Planning Agencies, city and county govts., U.S. geological survey, national and regional GIS associations

continued

TABLE 6.5   (continued)

PMN	Governing Body	Standing Committees	Work Groups/ Task Forces	No. of Primary Interacting Networks, Contacts Associations	Comments
Small Communities	Coordinating Committee	Education, Finance, and Technology Transfer	Special work groups, Appalachia, on-site wastewater mgmt.	6	Local development districts, area planning agencies, rural associations, and U.S. Army Corp of Engineers
USDA/ Nebraska	State director and Community Capacity Building Program manager	Nebraska USDA/RD, State Field Advisory Council	Water and Wastewater Advisory Committee; Nebraska Cooperative Development Center; Affordable Housing Trust Fund; Technical Action Review; Readiness, Awareness; Collaborative for Homeowners	7	PRN, Nebraska Devel. Network, Nebraska DED, Nebraska Investment Finance Authority, Fannie Mae, USDA Rural Advancement Communities, Nebraska Value-Added Partnership

317 Group	Informal steering group of activists	None	Working groups on funding study; work lab focus groups; legislative program	5	DDARS also promotes special work groups that involve external 317 Group reps, e.g., matrix group (funding follows client task force)
Iowa Communications	Iowa Telecommunications and Technology Commission	Education (statutory), Telecommunications, Advisory, Tele-medicine (statutory)	Regional (statutory) Telecom Councils, Admin. Telecom Advisory Council (state and federal agencies), Telejustice Advisory Comm., Higher Education Advisory Comm., Library Network Advisory Comm.	9	Work groups non-statutory; all committees in various statuses of activity
Enhanced Data	Voting members of committee (9)	—	Work groups, INdebt (back taxes payment), License Watch (professional), Who's Your Legislator?, Bureau of Motor Vehicles license and registration	4	Regular contact with other states served by accessIndiana contractor

continued

TABLE 6.5 (continued)

PMN	Governing Body	Standing Committees	Work Groups/ Task Forces	No. of Primary Interacting Networks, Contacts Associations	Comments
Kentuckiana Agency	Transportation Policy Committee	Transportation Technical Committee, Coordinating Committee, Community Transportation Advisory Committee	Technical Comm. work groups: Bicycle/ Pedestrian, Project Special Funding, Transportation Enhancement Project, Pollution Attainment Projects, Walkability Projects	3	In constant interaction with area city and county governments and planning commissions
Des Moines Metro	Transportation Policy Committee, Executive Committee	Transportation Technical Committee	Roundtables: Transit, Bicycle and Pedestrian, Freight	6	In constant interaction with area city and county governments

[a]In 2004 Iowa Enterprise was folded into the Iowa Rural Development Council, retaining its activity as a member of the Indiana Rural Council Business Committee.

guides the day-to-day work of the group, an executive committee structure, and/or major groupings that focus on major network tasks. Indiana Rural Council, for example, not only has an Executive Committee of board officers, but has the following standing committees: Community Visitation, Housing, Infrastructure, Leadership Development, Agricultural Development, and Annual Conference. Similarly, Iowa Geographic has a series of committees that define their major areas of GIS development: Remote Sensing, Clearinghouse/ Resource Guide, Climate and Environment, Natural Resources, Cadastral, and Education. USDA/Nebraska utilizes a field advisory group. The MPOs both have technical committees; one also has a standing community advisory committee and the other has specialized roundtables. Some of these bodies are composed of board members only, but most bring in nonboard specialists and administrators, broadening the reach of the network beyond the core of officers and activists. For example, the Remote Sensing Committee of Iowa Geographic engaged dozens of agency representatives who use GIS to fund and develop the technical specifications for their Ortho Infra-red project. Similarly, the content of Partnership for Rural Nebraska's Rural Institute is planned and organized by its Education Committee, which expands to include regional-development and higher-education representatives from the area of the state that is hosting that particular conference. Similar to voluntary associations that have standing and ad hoc committees, PMN committees reach outside of their core participants and partners to include knowledge and resources whenever they may be found. It is in this sense that PMN committees are like knowledge-oriented organizations that organize to take advantage of cross-divisional, line staff, and consultant/clientele/customer expertise by bringing them into their working structures.

This similarity is even more evident in the numerous work groups and task forces that are internally organized by the PMNs, along with the primary contacts they have with related multiorganizational bodies. The work group/task force accounting is noted in the fourth column of table 6.5. All fourteen develop working groups that break down technical aspects or focus on specific resource or servicing problems. Some are designed to produce work efforts, such as Darby's conservation groups; others oversee or conduct research projects like Lower Platte's policy and degradation studies; some recommend aspects for smoother network operation such as Enhanced Data's work groups or Iowa Communications' advisory committees; and others, like those of Small Communities and the MPOs, look at the feasibility of technology or alternative approaches. Again, these groups involve many noncore network activists, and they carry a great deal of the detailed knowledge development work of the networks, as discussed in chapter 7.

These work groups also have a form equivalent to cross-departmental working groups, as the fifth column of table 6.5 suggests. It enumerates the number of interacting, multiorganizational bodies with which the PMNs are in regular working contact. These counts do not include the primary state and federal agencies or local government bodies that PMNs regularly interact with, but multiple organization associations of statewide significance, related networks, and consortia of associations. They range from three for Kentuckiana Agency, to fourteen for Indiana Rural Council. For example, among Small Communities' six overlapping groups are the national Small Communities Water Infrastructure Exchange, Ohio Rural Water Association, the Rural Community Assistance Program Network, and three private lending institutions. USDA/Nebraska's reach includes Partnership for Rural Nebraska/Nebraska Development Network, the Nebraska Value-Added Partnership, USDA Rural Advancement Communities, and the network of government-backed and private lending institutions. The networks under study are all involved in a series of related networks of allied interest in much the same way that today's knowledge-based organizations would partner with consortia or peak associations that possess the resources and information needed to achieve their strategic aims.

PMN organizing has been analyzed after studying the other management tasks because network structure appears to flow from all the other management activities. At the governance structure level the form of organization in a network more closely resembles a voluntary organization than a bureaucracy. Officers are selected on a rotating basis. That normally means tapping one who has been immediately active and has the technical and political respect of the other network activists. Often it is someone who can also command one's agency or university resources. Other officers may or may not be utilized, and their presence is more or less a formality beyond forming an executive committee.

At the working level, the PMNs more closely resemble today's knowledge organizations in structure. The real organization in most networks is within its standing committees and work groups where the basic work gets done. The particular structure for each network is the result of a self-organizing process where partners bring issues to the table and the group decides which specific issues it will focus on. Specialization and expertise are then pooled into task forums and working groups that involve network partners, activists, and many nonactivists.

Beyond their boards, network structures are rarely designed in the sense that they are laid out in advance. It is an incremental process. Discussants initially report that the process resembles herding cats. One state official asserted that eventually "our activities fall into categories, more or less, and we agree to a structure of some kind, at some time, about when we decide on our work plan." Working in a network structure is thus quite different for most managers, who are normally more heavily engaged in their own structures and operations. The only exception to this would be a notable number of agency boundary spanners, or staff who represent their department/agency nearly full time as a liaison person to other organizations and who are network participants. Only about 10 percent of the informants fell into this category. Even the boundary spanner who does different work is within a hierarchy with standard management processes as he or she communicates with the home organization. In the network, all managers face a nonhierarchical self-organizing situation where "jointly agreed focus and purpose prevails." As is the case with today's knowledge or conductive organizations, structure is not only less formal but is subject to rapid change with emergent challenges.

COHESION WITHIN THE NETWORK STRUCTURE: THE IMPORTANCE OF TRUST

More than structure holds networks together. If they are not legal hierarchically based, they are "structures of interdependence" (O'Toole 1997, 45) in which dependence manifests itself in ways that contribute to cohesion-based mutual action. A number of internal forces have been previously identified in this chapter, such as critical leadership factors contributed by champions, and the political and technical cores and staff. One can also point to the strategic contribution of interdependent actors working on common visions, missions, and goals, along with the strategic directions that PMNs take. To some, these collaborative adaptations are manifestations of a shared belief in a common purpose, or what Mandell (1999) identifies as a program rationale, the commitment to the whole that holds a network together when traditional methods of coordination and control are not operative. One MPO activist simply said, "We try to focus on the same purpose." Another stated, "People bond over transportation . . . all have their (project) needs . . . but all are also there for the common good." A state administrator in the 317 Group stated that "we all agree that the mission is important! There is not a lot of debate. There is agreement on direction." Another 317 Group member agreed, "We became educated to avoid our own history (of state institutions). In this fast-paced world we finish each other's sentences." From a program-rationale standpoint, this cohesive force is at a level beyond that of the individual organization; the focus on the individual organization is only relevant for understanding how and why each organization contributes to the overall effort (Provan and Milward 1991). The foundation of trust within the network is a central factor in establishing and maintaining network cohesion. As identified in chapter 2, trust in collective bodies like networks is linked to fiduciary obligations; they impose a commitment to attend broadly to the concerns of specific others.

Trust in the PMNs is developed in three major ways. First, most of the network's central players—political and technical core and staff—have known one another for a number of years. People working in developmental disabilities, environmental management, or transportation have much working experience in interagency or association-agency work. Some have moved from agency to agency, or organization to agency, or the reverse. One longtime state agency deputy director said, "In economic development we touch lots of bases, public and private sector. I have a project history with some of those people that spans lots of (gubernatorial) administrations."

Second, most PMN activists have numerous experiences with counterparts from other agencies and organizations in dyadic or triadic collaborative ventures outside of the network itself. "I don't always have to bring an issue before the Finance Committee (of Small Communities). Sometimes I just tell Rural Development (USDA) or (name) over in Community Development Block Grants to see what we can do together." Another related that "(a network champion) has been around for over thirty years, and he knows where the deals can be made, so he knocks on the state (agency) doors. He has not only built up a lot of familiarity, but respect and a belief that his part of the bargain is deliverable." Beyond these dyadic/triadic contacts are state and federal and association officials working with one another in other collaborative settings: interagency funding awards committees, task forces, councils and consortia, as well as the other bodies identified in table 6.5.

Third, both technical and program work within the PMN builds on the two previous forces, and reinforces the trust process. As each agency pursues its designated work and results are produced, people representing different organizations develop the respect needed to foster additional trust. "Even if we might disagree it is with respect for one another. We participate and address one another's concerns and projects because the rest of us respect those of us working closely together." "Some show up only when their projects are to be decided [on], but most of us are longtime members, there carrying the load and trying to help one another. There is a lot of trust." Another discussant said, "We hold together because we know that if we show concern for everybody's agendas and needs, we will be able to build up the kind of results that advance the overall good that we are really here for."

An additional observation from the data is that as one moves up the scale of network types, network trust is even more essential, particularly for those PMNs that blueprint strategies and make policy/program adjustments. The three informational networks involve broad sets of economic and environmental stakeholders, and because of real political and economic differences are less likely to engender high levels of trust among all involved parties. However, this would be less true for their political and technical core staffs, where working processes appear to lead to high levels of trust. Developmental networks are less likely to have conflicting stakeholders, but often have skeptics or less-committed participants on their boards. Here again the core groups are highly conducive to trust. As outreach networks blueprint strategies and thus establish numerous transactional relationships among agencies and organizations, and as action networks do their decisional work, trust would appear to be an imperative element.

Trust is not guaranteed by action. The Des Moines Metro has some difficulty getting representatives to think from a metropolitan perspective rather than from that of their own jurisdiction's interests. Their policy body, composed of elected officials and local managers, finds this particularly difficult. They also suffer from turnover of local elected official members. The organization's technical committee finds this to be less of a problem, as it is composed of appointed administrators who have worked together over time. The informational natural resource networks—Lower Platte and Darby—also find it difficult to promote mutual respect among conflicting interests. In these cases trust is harder to develop, though it appears to exist among the core of administrators; in the other cases a level of working familiarity if not trust is evident. The other networks, however, rely heavily on their interactive processes to orchestrate mutual obligation.

On the other hand, it is clear that for all the networks the process of mutual learning through exploration contributes to additional trust. "As we educate one another we take advantage of diverse backgrounds." When participants hear technical presentations by colleagues or learn about others' programs, they develop more than a passing level of understanding. They learn not only about the other agency and its programs, but are able to make deeper judgments regarding the competency of the agency, along with that agency's potential contribution to the network's mission. As participation in the network increases over time, individuals demonstrate an increase in key technical and managerial abilities, which in turn builds the collective confidence of the group. Indeed, the more knowledge that is extended, the greater the opportunity to increase trust in others' abilities.

Discussants in virtually all networks agreed that the consensus-building process builds trust: "We give up some autonomy for a new paradigm shift, collaboration. This leads to mutual understanding and a passion about partnering." As the details and positions are put on the table and adjustments are made, people feel more comfortable about one another. One federal official stated that a great group dynamic means "Don't let your power get in the way." Each instance of consensus cements this obligation-based trust.

Another operating rule in most networks is that trust is maintained by nonencroachment on any participating agency's domain. One state official put it bluntly: "Let each agency put their details and concerns on the table; respect each agency's needs and interests. They come first!" Most network actors state that it is better to keep agency agendas in the open, but when agendas do come forward it may be impossible to force an agency to change. Mild persuasion and minor adjustment may follow, but intransigence on the part of an agency, particularly a powerful one, usually means that a network must pull away from a controversial issue.

The individual information-sharing dimension of each network activity also cements relationships in a very subtle way. In Small Communities a key portion of every meeting is the time allotted for agencies to share their own experiences and agendas; this unfolds before they tackle joint outreach activities. Through this process, partners know what the others are undertaking; agendas are put on the table. In most of the networks meeting time usually includes an around-the-table report on those issues relevant to each agency or program. These exchange sessions allow all members to represent their organizations, whether they are official boundary spanners or not. The process of opening up one's agency to others advances trust.

As suggested earlier, trust can also be built through progressive results. "Start with something small and build from there" was a sentiment echoed by a number of discussants. Another suggested that it helps to start with low-risk efforts. As each network carves out the possible, results accrue that prove to the group that they can work together. Committee and work group efforts are critical here. When small groups work together on focused projects, it leads to a higher level of intimacy. If the work gets done, it breeds deeper understanding. Failure to do committee work, or failure to deliver a promised information component, a data set, or some other work necessary for network operation, contributes to loss of trust. Since networks rely primarily on the volunteer contribution of full-time administrators from organizations, each is expected to do his or her share and come through with any commitments made to the group.

Finally, extended time frame conferences or meetings are also important social platforms. Iowa Geographic has a biannual conference at a university where prepared papers and panel presentations are presented. Iowa Enterprise holds periodic conferences where self-help projects are demonstrated, along with useful presentations on maintaining small businesses. Partnership for Rural Nebraska's annual Rural Institute, planned by its component partners, is an established trust-builder. Indiana Rural Council holds a one-day annual conference, and in 2002 hosted the two-day National Rural Development Council Partnership workshop. These meetings bring the key actors together to plan the sessions; the sessions, formally and informally, provide the type of social and intellectual bonding that reinforces preexisting trust. These efforts build spirit, create visibility, and to many discussants add other trust-building activities to their PMNs.

CONCLUSIONS

The key to understanding management within networks lies within the occupational culture and norms of those who make up their structures. Each of the PMNs are composed of agency department heads, second-level administrators, program directors, program specialists, local elected officials, and NGO executives and technical staff. They bring into the network their experiences of working within large bureaucratic agencies and voluntary organizations. On the other hand, their formal organizations are themselves changing. As the information-based, knowledge-seeking demands of home organizations increase, bureaucracies and voluntary organizations are internally structuring themselves to facilitate collaboration. These internal forces in the home agency, along with experiences in nonformalized linkages and collaborative management across boundaries, are brought to the network experience. They shape the internal management structure of PMNs to a degree, resulting in boards, operating procedures, officers, staff, and so on.

It also appears that networks must go beyond the formalities of officers and rules in order to devolve a collaborarchy that holds the group together and provides means that support its actions. For developmental, outreach, and action networks in particular this includes its internal programming and external policy decisions and strategies. This is where staff, champions, a political core, and a technical core come in, giving the network the needed stability and order to command respect and allow knowledge work to proceed. Another plank in this platform is the network's strategic operations as they investigate and solve problems. This involves problem task forces and work groups or technical subcommittees. Only this organization, which comes as a result of work that is concrete and collectively agreed on, keeps people working with others outside of their own organizations. The network must encourage organizational representatives to be more than signatory participants; they must delve into the technical work of the PMN. Moreover, today's electronic contact through e-mail and web posting keeps contact among the physically distant participants more regularized, and involves more players, than before these electronic venues existed. Carrying out the various roles of networks depends on all of these strategic interactions. Together these social forces are important for the development of collaborative capacity, instigating exchanges, and engendering "cooperative dispositions and mutual understanding of the individuals who are trying to work together in a common task" (Bardach 1998, 307).

Networks are self-managed collaborarchies. They are clearly not randomly or haphazardly organized or structured, nor do they work without definable processes. The most active and productive of our fourteen networks are those that are able to reach beyond their good cause; they are able to convene multiple delegates to produce concrete action. As with organizations, this takes more than a good idea and the right people; it also takes more than strong leadership. Participation must be transformed into energy through network structures and process. Managers in networks do this by borrowing on their experiences in their increasingly open, knowledge-seeking bureaucratic and nonprofit organizations. Management in the collaborarchy is thus simultaneously similar to and different from management in hierarchical organizations.

CHAPTER SEVEN

. . . .

NETWORKS AS KNOWLEDGE MANAGERS

We have an Iowa GIS clearinghouse where anybody can share knowledge—maps, physical documents, hard data—in a PDS format. But it is underutilized. When I need to know how to do something I know whom to contact thanks to Iowa Geographic. Knowledge is transmitted through interpersonal contacts and lots of presentations at our meetings. We don't write it up . . . it's just there . . . it is more of a technical sharing at the point of use as a result of Iowa Geographic connections.

THIS IS NOT an atypical reaction to the way public managers in PMNs secure knowledge and information related to individual agency or network projects. Normally when one thinks of information and knowledge one thinks of data sources, the World Wide Web, intranets and portals, or the file cabinets and policy/procedure manuals of the past. But this is changing. A follow-up survey by the management consulting firm Bain and Company asked 960 company executives which management tools they used most. In the 1995–2005 decade the biggest changes occurred with those tools that rely most heavily on information technology: customer-relationship management, supply-chain management, and knowledge management. They are now used by more than half of all companies (*Economist* 4/9/05, 53).

As Cross et al. observe, "A significant component of a person's information environment consists of the relationships he or she can tap for various informational needs" (2003, 208). One engineering researcher, summarizing a decade worth of studies, found that engineers and scientists were roughly five times more likely to turn to a person for information than to an impersonal source such as a data base or file cabinet (Allen 1984, in ibid., 231). As cross-organization entities, networks become an important means of information and knowledge sharing, and of knowledge creation. Knowledge gaps and uncertainties regarding problems and programs remains one of the primary reasons why PMNs organize; how to manage these gaps between organizations is thus a critical function (Koppenjan and Klijn 2004). The knowledge-seeking activities of the PMNs rely heavily on the electronic and other information and communication supports identified in the previous chapter, as summarized in table 6.3.

This chapter explores knowledge management (KM) activities within the PMNs. The first section identifies the broad concept of KM and its criticality to network process and operation. The next section then introduces the KM techniques and activities employed by each PMN. It will become clear that virtually all rely on extensive external databases, create forms of own-source or network-created information/ knowledge bases, and that in a formal sense most KM efforts rely on fostering explicit knowledge. Tacit knowledge is recognized as important, but is bound up in their ongoing collaborative processes. Because of this tacit/explicit integration, knowledge is rarely documented nor are dedicated tacit KM venues often promoted. The last substantive section looks at how the PMNs combine explicit and tacit knowledge into a set of characteristic joint learning approaches that aid decision/action. Six different network learning modes are presented, from informal discussion to laboratory-like behavioral simulation approaches. The concluding section points to some aspects of KM that can be useful for public managers and NGO executives.

UNDERSTANDING KNOWLEDGE MANAGEMENT

In KM, the movement from data to information to knowledge is critical. According to Davenport and Prusak (2000), data refers to a set of discrete, objective facts about events, often in organized efforts like structured records of transactions. Information is characterized as a message in the form of a document or an audible or visible communication. Information moves around organized bodies through hard (wires, satellite dishes, electronic mail boxes) and soft (notes, article copy) networks. Knowledge is broader, deeper, and richer than data or information. It is highly mutable and highly contextual, but with greater utility. Davenport and Prusak define it in this way: "Knowledge is a fluid mix of framed experience, values, contextual information, and expert insight that provides a framework for evaluating and incorporating new experiences and information. It originates and is applied in the minds of knowers. In organizations, it often becomes embedded not only in documents or repositories but also in organizational routines, processes, practices, and norms" (2000, 5). Knowledge is within people, a part of the assets of the human capital that is so important in contemporary activities. Indeed, it is intrinsically human. "Knowledge derives from information as information derives from data. If information is to become knowledge, humans must do all the work" (ibid., 6). In effect, knowledge is both a process and an outcome.

It is also clear that knowledge blends that which can be documented or formulized with the intuitive sense of knowing how to complete a task, Polanyi concludes that knowledge is "formulae which have a bearing on experience" in the sense that knowledge is "personal knowing," ranging from map reading to piano playing to bicycle riding to scientific work, that requires "skillful action" (1962, 49). As a result, KM is considered to have two analytical components, explicit and tacit knowledge. Explicit knowledge is that which can be codified and communicated easily by documenting it in words or numbers, charts, or drawings. It is the more familiar form of knowledge. Tacit knowledge is embedded in the senses, individual perceptions, physical experiences, intuition, and rules of thumb. It is rarely documented, but "frequently communicated through conversations with the use of metaphors" (Saint-Onge and Armstrong 2004, 41). It includes know-how, understanding, mental models, insights, and principles inherent to a discipline.

Some believe that tacit and explicit knowledge stand in opposition to one another, but in fact they are two sides of the same coin. All knowing involves skillful action, and the knower "necessarily participates in all acts of understanding" (Polanyi and Prosch 1975, 44). To Tsoukas, explicit knowledge is always rendered uncertain without tacit knowledge. "It is vectoral: we know the particulars by relying on our awareness of them for attending to something else" (2005, 158). He continues:

> The ineffability of tacit knowledge does not mean that we cannot discuss the skilled performances in which we are involved. We can—indeed, should—discuss them, provided we stop insisting on "converting" tacit knowledge and, instead, start recursively drawing our attention to how we draw each other's attention to things. Instructive forms of talk help us reorientate ourselves to how we relate to others and the world around us, thus enabling us to talk and act differently. We can command a clearer view of our tasks at hand if we "remind" ourselves of how we do things, so that distinctions which we had previously not noticed, and features which had previously escaped our attention, may be brought forward. (ibid., 159)

Rather than focusing on operationalizing tacit knowledge, greater emphasis needs to be placed on new ways of talking, fresh forms of interacting, and novel ways of distinguishing and connecting. To Tsoukas, tacit knowledge cannot be "captured," "translated," or "converted," but only displayed and manifested, as it involves skilled performance; that is, KM praxis is "punctuated through social interaction" (ibid., 158–59). The quote at the beginning of this chapter clearly demonstrates that Iowa Geographic traffics heavily in the process of tacit-explicit knowledge conversion through operation, not codification.

The interaction between the two types of knowledge means that its potential for action is essential. Davenport and Prusak (2000) suggest that one of the reasons we find knowledge valuable is its proximity to action in a much more real-world sense than data or information. Knowledge should be evaluated by the decisions or actions to which it leads. Better knowledge can lead to wiser decisions/actions, efficiencies, and results. Moreover, knowledge can move down the value chain, informing information and data. Davenport and Prusak (2000) conclude that this action potential is based on the blending of experience, truth, judgment, and rules of thumb. A prime example of this essential mixture using a small-town cluster engineering system was presented in chapter 5.

What are the tools of KM? Stewart (2001) indicates that KM activities cover a host of organizational activities: building data bases, measuring intellectual capital, establishing corporate libraries, building intranets, sharing best practices, installing groupware, leading training programs, leading cultural change, fostering collaboration, and creating virtual organizations. Olshfski and Hu (2004) identify several additional practices: information portals, informal mentoring, electronic archiving, listserves of discussion groups, knowledge portals, regularly scheduled problem-solving sessions, knowledge maps or yellow pages, expert interviews, formal mentoring systems, apprenticeships, and decision support systems. Some organizations, public and private, now appoint a chief knowledge officer (CKO), who often incorporates the work of the previous chief information officer.

Stewart maintains that the essentials of managing explicit knowledge are easy and familiar: assemble, validate, standardize/simplify, update, leverage, ensure that users know about it and how to use it, automate and accelerate retrieval and application, and add to the base. Since tacit knowledge constitutes the "stock of intellectual capital" (2001, 124) it is harder to elicit such rules of thumb, but he suggests that it clearly involves processes of internalization, combined with other knowledge, sharing, and externalization. Techniques such as sharing best practices, fostering collaboration, mentoring, groupware, and problem-solving sessions clearly facilitate tacit knowledge acquisition. They are the instruments of handling the essential explicit/tacit knowledge interface.

The nature and process of KM is a subject that has only recently been raised in the field of public management. Most of the books on KM deal with business practices. Olshfski and Hu (2004) point out that of the 511 articles published since 1996 with KM as a key topic, only one appeared in a public administration journal; 276 were published in business literature and 196 in information technology journals, with the remaining 38 in other journals. It is not an unknown subject, however. Olshfski and Hu (2004) cite a 2002 Organization for Economic Cooperation and Development (OECD) study that shows many Canadian and European governments demonstrating interest and issuing reports. They also report that KM is attracting growing interest in U.S. public sector practice. They point to thirteen agencies of the federal government that have recently created a form of chief knowledge officer to serve as a catalyst for such activities, including the Department of the Army's knowledge portals and its virtual knowledge centers. These practices, along with their own public sector research among public officials in New Jersey, indicate that "the public sector is joining a conversation that the private sector has been engaged in for more than fifteen years" (ibid., 3).

What makes KM so central to the functioning networks? As maintained earlier, knowledge-intensive work requires the interaction of human capital. An informational/knowledge-based environment helps organizational members and network participants solve increasingly vexing and ambiguous problems (O'Toole 1997). We have also argued that collaboration across agencies and organizations is essential to solving an increasingly important problem-related requirement in both conductive organizations and in networks. Knowledge management architectures need to go beyond codification of information to foster learning through knowledge exchange or opportunities to share by connecting people, communities, and expertise connections (Saint-Onge and Armstrong 2004). This means interorganizational collaborative activity where shared interests broker complimentary knowledge that is otherwise difficult, costly, time-consuming, and perishable. "Sharing your knowledge . . . is not a zero-sum game. Unlike conventional assets, knowledge grows when it is shared. The main limitation to infinite knowledge growth is the currency of the information economy-attention" (Groff and Jones 2003, 20).

KM has become a core function of PMNs. Koppenjan and Klijn suggest that a normal first response to policy uncertainty in public networks is information collection, but research is limited because difficult problems normally carry different opinions with them and strong opinions can challenge the validity of the research. Moreover, scientific research has its limitations, and often raises greater complexities. Problems are often solved by cooperation and learning behavior that can be supported by KM. "Interaction processes are considered to be searches wherein public and private parties from different organizations, (levels of) government and networks jointly learn about the nature of a problem, look at the possibility of doing something about it, and identify the characteristics of the strategic and institutional context within which problem-solving develops" (Koppenjan and Klijn 2004, 10). As Agranoff and McGuire (2003b) conclude, the challenge of KM within networks is compounded by the constant intergovernmental changes of the past half-century, shifting policies and actions of state governments, and changes in such policy areas as economic development, environmental protection, and developmental disabilities. As policies, programs, and venues shift, so do the KM demands of governments and collaborative bodies like the PMNs.

KNOWLEDGE MANAGEMENT IN PMNs

The knowledge management role of networks is essential, as they broker and produce information that can be converted to knowledge that is related to their current problems. This role became an integral part of the second-round phase of this study. After being provided with standard definitions, each discussant was asked to enumerate the sources and structures for KM, both explicit and tacit. The results were coded and subsequently pooled by network, then tabulated into the second-order summary in table 7.1. This table provides an overview of each PMN's KM activities. The externally derived explicit knowledge sources for each network are first identified, followed by an account of those sources of explicit knowledge that are created by the networks themselves. The tacit knowledge that can be identified as a result of PMN processes is then documented. This is followed by an accounting of the formal efforts the fourteen networks make in managing either explicit or tacit knowledge. Finally, any knowledge created by the process that is fed back into its component organizations, or attendant problems in this process, are highlighted. The PMNs are grouped by their type of network, from information to action. What table 7.1 makes very clear is that, despite the paucity of public management literature regarding KM, each PMN is extensively engaged in these activities. In this sense they are no different than most public organizations that are heavily steeped in human capital and application of technical solutions.

It is clear that every network begins its KM process by integrating existing sources of information and databases from external sources. "We rely on our partners to be the first-line source of information. Part of why we exist is to share what each agency has to offer," related one Darby executive. The third column of table 7.1, "External Origin Information," highlights the type of existing agency-based data and in some cases the sources, an available/useable category. For most of the networks these raw knowledge inputs are composed of existing data bases, scientific studies, prior planning documents, online data collections, reports/studies from state or federal government agencies, technical bulletins and training manuals from affiliated groups, GIS-based mapping, and information systems from government agencies and nongovernmental organizations. Information sources from component members appear to be most critical for virtually every network.

There appears to be a small difference between the four types of networks, although some rely on more sources than others. It appears that the three outreach networks have to begin with one or more of their key partners to start the knowledge process in order to convert it into strategic blueprinting. For example, Small Communities requires the finance and regulatory information of EPA, Ohio Water Authority, and Ohio USDA/RD, as well as the training information from Ohio State Extension. Likewise, the 317 Group must begin with certain data gathered from FSSA-DDARS in order to function. Action networks similarly begin their processes with essential partner data, such as local government and USDOT and USEPA data for the two transportation PMNs, and agency service data for Iowa Communications. Information and development networks appear to be able to choose from an even broader variety of sources, although their actions essentially begin with similar inputs. We can conclude that networks do indeed rely on the pooling of information from partners and other sources to begin their KM processes. "We try to find studies wherever they exist—on the Internet, university reports, vendor reports, articles, databases, whatever might be useful," a Small Communities finance administrator related.

The next step is to convert that information that is most essential to those forms of explicit knowledge that are useful to the PMNs' purposes. The fourth column of table 7.1 displays the most important of such network conversions under the heading "Internal Origins of Explicit Knowledge," a "what we make" category. Clearly there are fewer entries here, but again, every one of the fourteen PMNs engages at least one type of explicit knowledge that the network itself undertakes. These include inventories of existing studies, map libraries, program evaluation and planning studies, usable fact sheets and practical guides, video presentations, summaries of prior studies, data bases of experts, strategies, shared staff-based development centers, poll results, conferences and workshops, web-based GIS services, joint mapping and joint modeling projects, electronic bulletin boards, joint studies, counting-tracking and profiling, funding assistance studies, services studies, market studies, and long-range plans.

The network's type appears to be essential here. In general, information networks use libraries and inventory, and rarely go beyond the compiling of existing information to making it widely available. The two watershed networks, for example, are limited by mission and resources residing totally in its participating organizations, where the real environmental management decisions are made. The same is true of Indiana Economic Development, which is the venue of economic development (ED) information but not ED policy. Developmental networks are better equipped to take on their own studies and to promote shared staff; they even foster their own knowledge-building activities, but only those that would support their capacity-building missions. Partnership for Rural Nebraska and Iowa Geographic are prime examples. They generate many new information sources and involve a great deal of human resource cooperative efforts, but only as means of helping their member organizations, not for strategies or decisions. In contrast, outreach and action networks do some form of converting information into the strategic information that they need to conduct their work. Examples are USDA/Nebraska's funding tracking management book, the 317 Group's INSIGHT and DART,

(text continues on page 138)

TABLE 7.1 Knowledge Management in the PMNs

Network	Type	External Origin Information	Internal Origin Explicit Knowledge	Process-Derived Tacit Knowledge	Management of Explicit and Tacit Knowledge	Emergent Knowledge or Problems for Participant Organizations
Darby	1	Darby Vision Watershed Plan (of 3 SWCD Plans), Floodplain Studies, Hellbranch Watershed Plan; Ohio EPA studies and databases, Columbia/ Franklin County Plans, GIS Mapping, EPA Study of Darby Stresses, Hydrologic Unit Assessment, Biological and Chemical Sampling of Watershed, Big Darby Creek Storm Project-OSU, Metro Parks studies	Darby library at TNC; Darby inventory of area maps; Darby Vision—inventory of studies	Consultations with local landowners by partners; workshops with local govt. and landowners; Darby book of best practices; multiple task groups, e.g., Hellbranch Watershed Forum, communities of practice; Darby Vision disseminated best practices; USDA/ SWCD best-practice demos; Operation Future (conservation-based farmer group)	Darby provides the forum for exposure, does not manage; self-managing through all adjunctive groups	None—only from other providers
Indiana Economic Development	1	Strategic planning based on cluster analysis, federal and state data studies, shift from compiling own data to accessing on-line sources, Statistics Indiana, Dept. of Commerce, Indiana (Univ.) Business Research Ctr.	Use of ED Panels, e.g., the strategic plan; special studies, e.g., tax abatement, TIF state economic report card; program evaluation studies	Captured from many project panels and advisory committees, IEDC staff mentor departmental field staff, convening of key actors for workshops, sessions to exchange best practices in ED	Indiana Economic Devel. organizes staff and facilitates plan mtgs., other study advisory committees	External sources of knowledge far exceed internal; data generated for state agencies, e.g., Commerce, Workforce, Agriculture departments

Lower Platte	I	Natural Resource District (NRD), EPA Studies, Army Corps of Engineers Studies, U.S. Geological Survey	Fact sheets and guides, public policy study; web-based GIS for watershed, video presentation on river conditions, cumulative impacts study; water/wastewater study	"Build a conversation" strategy with land owners, SWOT workshops with local officials, issue/problem-based mtgs., expert presentations at Alliance mtgs., inf. mtgs. on wells and septic systems	Alliance as broker of info. on degradation and mitigation channeled by three NRDs, work with local govt. assns.	Lower Platte is intermediary between three NRDs and state agencies
Iowa Enterprise	D	USSBA data, Iowa Dept. of Econ. Devel., Iowa Rural Devel. Council	Business succession study, database of consultants for home-based businesses	Workshops on home-based business operation; tapping into Iowa's SBDCs—how to start a business; "Business After Hours" hands-on services, e.g., how to build a website	Absence of database of Iowa's small home businesses, attempts to promote networking among peers ended in 2002	Recognition that help from other sources, consultants, chambers of commerce, and building a knowledge base is the mission of Iowa Enterprise
Indiana Rural Council	D	Material from affiliated groups, e.g., Purdue U. Extension, Indiana Agricultural Leadership Inst., Rural Communities Assist. Prog.; Dept. of Commerce; Dept. of Agriculture; Indiana Economic Devel. Council; Indiana Land Resources Council	Indiana Cooperative Devel. Center, Indiana Rural Devel. Strategy	Task groups/communities of practice: value-added agric., infrastructure, and water, leadership and community devel., housing; annual mtgs. as leadership conferences; community visitation teams	Focus on relationship building	Next phase: series of rural forums and summits

continued

TABLE 7.1 (continued)

Network	Type	External Origin Information	Internal Origin Explicit Knowledge	Process-Derived Tacit Knowledge	Management of Explicit and Tacit Knowledge	Emergent Knowledge or Problems for Participant Organizations
Partnership for Rural Nebraska	D	Neb. Dept. of Economic Devel., CARI-U of Neb., USDA/Nebraska, Rural Initiatives, Rural Devel. Commission	Rural Poll, e.g., eight on quality of life; research and factual info. extensive at Annual Inst., Nebraska Coop. Develop. Center	Rural Inst. sessions; task forces and committees as communities of practice, particularly education	Compiler of *Rural News Bits*, constant eval. of sessions, constant connection with Neb. Devel. Net. mtgs., potential to expand actions considered to be next step from exchange of practices and experiences to codified knowledge	Major conduit between scientific knowledge and rural development programs
Iowa Geographic	D	Databases/mapping of local and state govt. agencies, Iowa State U. GIS lab, Dept. of Transportation net, Dept. of Natural Resources mapping	GIS conference and assoc. workshops, web-based GIS server, Iowa GIS clearinghouse on web, color infrared mapping project	Hands-on work by state GIS coord. with local govts., manuals for hands-on GIS serv., presentations at quarterly mtgs. on tech. issues and experiences—not documented, extensive comm. system expected to be communities of practice—uneven in involvement	Interaction with other GIS users, using Iowa Comm. for mtgs. limits interaction and exchange of practices, at a crossroads where tacit knowledge component needs to be ratcheted up, involving GIS staff from other agencies is a problem	Lacks intranet capacity; need for more exchange sessions, agency experiences untapped; web has much greater potential

Small Communities	O	Ohio EPA, Ohio Water Devel. Authority, Ohio State U. Extension, Ohio Rural Community Action Program, Ohio Rural Water Assoc., USDA/RD	Funding format for local govts., bulletin board, standardized income study	Technical fact sheets (some outdated), Steering Committee notes, workshops on water management, committees (Finance, Education) and work groups as communities of practice, periodic follow-up on communities	Technology-transfer projects not captured, support for Ohio State University Extension workshops	Knowledge development untapped in most areas
USDA/Nebraska	O	Nebraska DED, Partnership for Rural Neb, Neb. Devel. Network, Neb. Value-Added Partnership, U. of Neb, USDA, Neb. SBA	Internally generated management book—tracks funding and related info, pilot project on county devel. profile	Sponsorship of many forums on what works and what doesn't, training seminars in value-added agric. and energy progs., water and wastewater comm. as community of practice	USDA-revised reporting results in a paper trail of descriptive and analytical info. on projects and progs., all decisions and administrative letters stored electronically	Freedom of Information Act limits others' access to USDA's stored knowledge—all access by special request
317 Group	O	Indiana FSSA-DDARS, Indiana U. Institute on Disability and Community, Arc of Indiana, INARF, Governor's Planning Council for Developmental Disabilities	INsight (on Medicaid Waiver/case mgmt.), DART (tracks 317's six main points), reports from Bureau of Quality Improvement Services, financial studies, waiting list studies	Arc sponsored contacts with families on how person-centered planning works; advisory group venue of constant exch. of info.; and input to state govt.; Arc comm. with consumer and advocacy groups; public forums on waiting lists; ISETPG (Indiana Statewide Education & Training Planning Grp.) prepares professionals to work in disability community, in order to improve services	Arc program not documented; feedback surveys on the program; most studies of costs, counts of community service, group size, etc., hand-compiled; scarce information on day services; no training and much process knowledge lost in process; legislative hearings/studies generate data	Not considered useful by those outside of government; focus is on the money, not the program impact

continued

TABLE 7.1 (continued)

Network	Type	External Origin Information	Internal Origin Explicit Knowledge	Process-Derived Tacit Knowledge	Management of Explicit and Tacit Knowledge	Emergent Knowledge or Problems for Participant Organizations
Iowa Communications	A	Dept. of Trans., Dept of Public Safety, DED-Workforce Devel., Dept. of Corrections, Dept. of Educ., Iowa Public TV	100% business review process, core serv. studies, capital mgmt. studies, service operations studies	Interactive process to establish service for operations problems, constant staff outreach with agencies	Needs Internet study; service feedback from agencies and users is documented	Usage reports for the agencies
Enhanced Data	A	Other state portal data, Dept. of Administration, business trends studies, agency-submitted proposals and justifications	Market studies by staff on accessIndiana contact	Not systematically analyzed—holes in adoption process, "Word of mouth" feedback, Intelnet crash courses for new agency reps., some from contract help desk	Long learning curve experienced by new state administrators; usually trial by fire; Intelnet staff have organized web-use variety; library records policies and decisions; Intelnet analyzes service requests; after-the-fact reporting of rates of adoption, fees, etc.; accessIndiana portals don't always work	Quarterly general manager's report on portal operations and revenues

Agency		Data sources	Communities of practice	Process experiences	Data requests
Kentuckiana Agency	A	USDOT, USEPA, local government units data, LOJIC (area info. consortium), USGS, State of Indiana, River City Transit	Travel demand forecasting model, project management databases, long-range plan, air pollution model, transit studies, mapping projects, origin-destination study, traffic count data	Workgroups of Technical Committee as communities of practice, valuable exchanges around the table about political and technical knowledge	Process experiences not codified, e.g., bicycle and pedestrian work shops and exchanges; data accessibility not in PDF format; hard for nonstaff to access; info. provided to two committees on demand	Numerous data requests for local govts., modeling and planning data for small governments, state planning, federal decision making
Des Moines Metro	A	USDOT, USEPA, local government unit data, Iowa DOT, Iowa Regional Councils, Federal Transit Authority	Long-range plan, travel demand model, socio-economic demand model, mapping projects, intelligent transit system model, traffic counts	Informal only, e.g., with 45 local govts.; roundtables—trails, transit, goods movement as communities of practice; info-sharing (tech) among 2 comms.; public hearings, workshops, and open info. sessions	Analysis of STP or transportation improvement, study of non-STP trails and streetscapes; mapping of various land-use plans	Local government data requests, modeling and planning data for small govts., data for other regional plans, state planning, federal decision making

Iowa Communications' 100 percent business-review and capital-management studies, Enhanced Data's market studies, or the two MPOs' travel-demand models. Indeed, the latter two PMNs rely on a series of internally generated studies that constitute the explicit knowledge base for their planning and project actions. All networks appear to convert some information that comes from partners into codified knowledge.

What about tacit or informal knowledge? Not surprisingly, this proved somewhat harder to ascertain, given the fact that it is so embedded in the senses and experiences. "A lot of what we do we don't record. There are limits on the time we can devote to this (network) activity. Only a few meeting minutes exist in Partnership for Rural Nebraska." Nevertheless, some discussants were able to generalize on the tacit knowledge experiences they had encountered within their PMN. The fifth column of table 7.1, "Process-Derived Tacit Knowledge," a "what we experience" category, summarizes these activities by network. They include direct consultations, workshops, best-practices books, internal task groups as communities of practice (self-organized groups who communicate with one another based on common work practices, interests, or aims), project panels, advisory committees, technical presentations, hands-on outreach or how-to sessions, community visitation teams, conferences and institutes, one-to-one outreach consultation/instruction, working manuals, circulated committee notes, feedback/follow-up sessions, public hearings and forums, roundtables of experts/interested persons, and informal personal exchanges.

At first glance there do not appear to be differences among the four types, but the outreach and action networks seem to require committees working as subgroups, their real communities of practice, to directly process external information and internal knowledge into their strategies or decisions. In other words, subgroup processes such as task groups, and to some extent technical information combined with informal exchanges, are essential tacit knowledge steps for their operation. Small Communities, for example, must use working groups as communities of practice to convert knowledge about water regulations, finance, and technology in order to make the adjustments necessary to plan strategies. In this way, explicit and tacit knowledge must be converted into some form of action for all seven of these networks, whereas the implicit process is less formal and demanding in the other two types of networks.

The next issue concerns the extent to which the PMNs have a formal management program that addresses either explicit or tacit knowledge. The sixth column of table 7.1, "Management of Explicit and Tacit Knowledge," a "how we handle it" category, indicates that there is less formal activity involved than in internally generated explicit or tacit knowledge. These activities include: providing a vehicle for other interests to share knowledge, facilitating study groups or special committees, facilitating work and study groups as communities of practice, promotion of peer networking, compiling information, evaluation of program sessions, facilitating shared-staff meetings, organizing joint operations, transfer of technologies, promoting workshops and training sessions, recording program and administrative decisions, conducting feedback surveys and studies of client costs, sharing information, presentations at legislative hearings, analyses of service requests, and organization and operation of mapping programs and decision models.

What is clear from the interaction with network discussants is that networks rarely make formal efforts to write up or codify the tacit knowledge they generate. With few exceptions—the 317 Group collaborative work lab, the service studies of Enhanced Data and Iowa Communications, and the water management training that is a spin-off of Small Communities—network leaders and activists spend the overwhelming amount of their time on organizing external information and creating their own source explicit knowledge. Simply put, while tacit knowledge is regularly transacted, there is not a great deal of formal effort that goes into codification. As one Lower Platte administrator related, "There is a lot of learning at the table, but it is of the informal type."

Are there differences among the four types? The informational and developmental networks focus on creating opportunities to deal with knowledge interactively, whereas the other two types of networks are geared toward ensuring that their KM programs are organized and operated in ways that support their strategies and courses of action. For these networks, KM is geared to reducing uncertainty by forging some form of agreement or working solution. They must make sure that the knowledge they work with is available for formulating a solution. As identified earlier, it appears that knowledge is not converted, but tacit and explicit knowledge are connected.

That leaves the concern of how the knowledge generated might go beyond the network's use, and be fed back into the participating organizations and/or the partner communities. The seventh and final column of table 7.1, identified as "Emergent Knowledge or Problems for Participant Organizations," a category of "who benefits by our work," contains this information. There is much less in this category than in the other facets of KM. Findings include data generated for public agencies, contact with consultants and technical persons in the field, public forums, conversion of scientific knowledge into education programs, technical exchange sessions, web postings, legislative decision making, reports useful to public agencies, fulfilling data needs of small governments, and modeling for associated plans and programs. Nevertheless, many discussants felt that in an indirect and long-run fashion, PMN activities in KM benefit their home agency. A local official related that "Kentuckiana Agency does over one-half million dollars of research that we take advantage of, and would have to otherwise purchase for our nonfederal transportation decisions."

The informational and developmental networks seem to serve as a conduit for knowledge that then filters through to their public and partner organizations.

For example, Indiana Economic Development and Iowa Geographic make ED and GIS knowledge available but neither does much to actively feed it into practice. As the opening quote for this chapter suggests, Iowa Geographic leaders feel that it lacks real intranet capacity, and that their website has considerable more potential in this regard. Some Iowa Geographic activists recognized that more exchange sessions need to be interactively fed back into agency experience sessions. Only their biannual conference touches on this to some extent. The most important conclusion for the outreach and action networks seemed to be the lost opportunities in helping agencies. This is due to a number of barriers: access restrictions, lack of utility to agencies, the internal operational nature of some reports, and network-generated knowledge that is not in an easily usable format. On the other hand, the two MPOs, Kentuckiana Agency and Des Moines Metro, do feed much of their information-based knowledge for state planning and federal funding decision-making purposes. Their local governments also rely heavily on MPO-generated knowledge. One must also factor in that network involvement levels broaden the scope of access to information bases of partner agencies, those sources already enumerated in the third column of table 7.1. Discussants repeatedly stated that their network does not duplicate existing sources and that involvement has raised awareness of numerous new databases and information sources, which they in turn have accessed and used in their own agency's knowledge-development process.

From this array of network experiences, one can easily conclude that PMNs manage the kind of knowledge that they need to accomplish their missions. Very few discussants actually considered the activities identified in table 7.1 as those of knowledge management, but when it was defined for them they agreed that it was a central function of their existence. None of the participants had a formal title like CKO or even KM specialist, perhaps because virtually all network participants were working at these functions.

Information networks tend to broker, arrange, and serve as catalysts for the disparate parties to arrange knowledge under their umbrella. Developmental networks produce and organize that knowledge, which can serve the capabilities and needs of their partners. Outreach networks also serve these needs, but additionally need to facilitate—manage—the kind of knowledge that will support the strategic actions that emerge from their deliberations. Action networks do all of these things but also acquire old-fashioned decision-making knowledge, the knowledge that supports interorganization decision.

Tacit knowledge is almost universally recognized as an important aspect of the KM process, and the operating approaches of many subgroups, which are similar to communities of practice, are prevalent. Very little effort is made, however, to codify or add to tacit knowledge by organizing it in a formal way. It will be demonstrated in the next section that different kinds of around-the-table discussions loom large but are rarely recorded. It is through the organized, explicit KM processes identified here that the PMNs convert tacit knowledge; for example, in data building and interpreting sessions, work groups on information systems and models, information exchanges, workshops and training sessions, and statewide conferences.

USING PMN-GENERATED KNOWLEDGE

Now that an overview of each PMN's KM activities has been identified, the analysis shifts to their applications. Since most of the networks engage or have engaged in anywhere from a dozen or so to several hundred KM projects, it is impossible to inventory all of them. The range is considerable: at one end, Iowa Enterprise has focused primarily on one or two studies of member needs and a business succession study, while at the other end Iowa Communications and Enhanced Data are constantly developing knowledge-based usage and market studies to aid in their decision making. As a result, the focus in this section will be on the type of KM projects that exemplify each PMN's utilization.

These examples have been compiled in table 7.2, which contains project illustrations of KM applications. Each is drawn from among those summarized in table 7.1. In other words, one concrete project is selected that fits into "Internal Origin Explicit Knowledge" from the earlier table. The purpose of table 7.2 is thus not to count, but to demonstrate by example how PMNs use the knowledge they create, and who is most responsible for using that knowledge. The third column in the table identifies the KM project that is carried out by the PMN internally, which is then followed in the fourth column by a description of the exemplary project. The all-important fifth column shows how that study or project has been utilized ("Knowledge Use"). The last two columns identify whether that use was direct or internal, or indirect or external to the PMN, along with related explanations or comments in the last column. These examples demonstrate the important role of PMNs in creating problem-oriented usable knowledge.

Although not a complete inventory, the projects listed in table 7.2 reveal a bit more about each type of network. The three informational networks and Iowa Enterprise all demonstrate how knowledge can enhance the policymaking process in an indirect fashion. Each adds in its own way to the base of knowledge about environmental degradation, or small business problems, or communication gaps in rural areas that can be and have been picked up by more direct actors: local governments, conservation districts, and state agencies. The other three developmental network examples drive home their capacity-building orientation. The best practices, networking, community development

(text continues on page 145)

TABLE 7.2 Exemplary Uses of PMN Knowledge

PMN	Type	Project/Study	Description	Knowledge Use	Direct/Indirect	Comments
Darby	I	Ohio EPA Technical Hydrologic Study	Study of environmental threats posed by development on western limits of Franklin County	Water quality management plan, external advisory group, local development restrictions	Indirect	Darby was catalyst for bringing disparate parties together
Indiana Economic Development	I	Broadband study	Supply and demand dynamics of interconnections, particularly in rural areas	Broadband conference, promotion by Dept. of Commerce, incorporation into rural strategy	Indirect	Indiana Economic Development put broadband on state government agenda
Lower Platte	I	Public policy study	Analysis of options for river mitigation in densely developed area between Lincoln and Omaha	Mitigation strategies incorporated into three conservation district plans—many project spin-offs	Indirect	Has driven Lower Platte agendas for over 10 years
Iowa Enterprise	D	Business succession study	Analysis of small businesses in rural areas when entrepreneurs retire	Incorporation into Iowa's rural economic development strategy by DED	Indirect	In cooperation with Rural Development Council

Name	Type	Activity	Description	Approach	Linkage	Notes
Indiana Rural Council	D	Community visitation teams	Rotating groups of community development specialists analyze individual community problems and help local leaders develop plans	Interactive (specialists-locals) development programs	Indirect	Also utilizes the expertise of USDA-Extension, Rural Community Action, and others as partners
Partnership for Rural Nebraska	D	Annual Rural Institute	Three-day conference of practitioners, researchers, and leaders—focused sessions and mobile workshops	Best practices, networking, expanded individual and agency perspectives and information	Indirect	Has attracted top agency heads and political leaders along with specialists
Iowa Geographic	D	Project/study assistance to local governments	Hands-on, extension-related introduction of geographic information to local governments	Expanded local ability to engage in land-use mapping and environmentally sensitive topographical mapping	Indirect	Cooperates with Iowa State Extension service
Small Communities	O	Decentralized drainage system	Search for an affordable, permit-friendly cluster septic collection system for small areas	Feasible wastewater approach for rural developments of under fifty users	Quasi-direct	A model adopted by Ohio EPA, multiple funders, agency regulatory officials
USDA/Nebraska	O	Rural housing models study	Multiagency look at rural housing resources and development of a consumer guide	Assisted multiple agency personnel in helping low-income, rural citizens access housing	Quasi-direct	USDA/Nebraska was lead agency in joint effort

continued

TABLE 7.2 (continued)

PMN	Type	Project/Study	Description	Knowledge Use	Direct/Indirect	Comments
317 Group	O	Community supports financing study	A look at Indiana's position among Midwest states on financing community living for the developmentally disabled	Support for 317 Group strategy in informing MR/DD (legislative) Commission	Quasi-direct	Contributed to increased funding
Iowa Communications	A	Annual capacity/usage studies	Patterns of educational usage	Iowa Communications video scheduling for distance education	Direct	Interactive with Dept. of Educ., higher educ. institutions
Enhanced Data	A	Market feasibility studies	Patterns and charges in other states for government web portal use	Use policies and charges for state government web portal, e.g., drivers and hunting licenses, tax return filing, food stamps	Direct	Basis of establishing agency agreements on web portal use
Kentuckiana Agency	A	Intelligent transportation system	Model incorporating traffic demand, accidents, congestion, future roads, etc.	Transportation improvement and long-range plans	Direct	Major determinant in annual work program submitted to federal government
Des Moines Metro	A	Traffic demand model	Study of traffic patterns, congestion, future demands plus history of internal funding decisions	Decision-making tool for staff, technical, and policy committees	Direct	Also used for TIP and long-range plans

plans, and local mapping abilities are all the end results of this knowledge application. It is important to note that all of these uses are indirect and in many cases extend over long periods of time. Not surprisingly, the outreach networks make an immediate impact, albeit in a quasi-direct fashion, as they forge strategies. Most importantly, their housing, wastewater, and funding-status studies can all be directly linked to a result that was a product of a PMN effort, even though other agencies or bodies actually made the decisions. Finally, the four action networks demonstrate through the examples selected how internally generated knowledge is put to direct use. Each looks at capacity/usage, marketing, or modeling to set plans, policies, or funding. In other words, knowledge is used to directly support internal network decision making.

The observations relating to network use of knowledge appear to be critical. At least from time to time, all networks appear to need to generate usable knowledge in order to amplify problems, or to meet the collaboratively derived gaps or needs. However, its use may not be direct. Some networks, particularly the informational and developmental types, do create valuable and useful knowledge even though it may not be transformed internally by the network itself. On the other hand, the other two types of networks—outreach and action—are able to point to direct uses of their knowledge to serve the most immediate of their issues. For both types, brokering of such knowledge use involves the type of learning processes that will be identified in the next section. Finally, the examples in table 7.2 suggest that knowledge use for all types of networks can be either long-term or short-term, although the indirect use for informational and developmental PMNs almost always suggests longer-term effects. The other two types of networks can and do experience longer-term knowledge use effects, but the examples identified here demonstrate shorter-usage time lines. In general, all PMNs come together to jointly create usable knowledge. We will next focus on the process of how that knowledge is produced.

MODES OF KNOWLEDGE DEVELOPMENT: PMN LEARNING STRATEGIES

As entities that are heavily involved in the exchange of information and the discovery and adaptation of knowledge, PMNs need preparation for brokered consensus (Koppenjan and Klijn 2004). This involves looking at a problem or issue in depth, conducting research into available technologies, tapping into or developing alternative data bases, and, most importantly, finding information-based solutions. The latter involves discussions of legal, technical, financial, and political feasibility (Agranoff 1986). These discussions are normally preceded by an information search that enhances the learning and knowledge-producing ability of the collaborative. In other words, these predecision modes reinforce the capacities of PMNs to engage in KM. These modes will first be described and categorized according to the field research, followed by a summary of their usage. At least six different learning/knowledge modes can be identified.

The first mode is simply group discussion following a loose format, where technical and/or legal and financial information is converted to knowledge. This process is conducted by the partners in the enterprise, a shared diversity of expertise by those brought to the table. When networks follow this mode the administrators almost always bring in their agency's relevant technical experts. Networks also do a great deal of their work in work groups (committees, task forces), which we identified as the equivalent to communities of practice. For example, Partnership for Rural Nebraska organizes its annual Rural Institute by bringing together program specialists from its federal and state government and NGO partners, along with a committee local to the rotating venue under the rubric of its Education Committee. In this way, the latest in community and economic development ideas are offered to the participants. In a similar fashion, Indiana Rural Council has deployed community visitation teams to selected small communities, employing volunteer experts in business development, town planning, public works, market analysis, environmental management, and others in order to develop action plans. The teams spend one to two days in the community; near the end of the visit they agree on conclusions and write a joint report. In other cases, the various PMN partners meet as a plenary to match technical information with potential solutions. Virtually every network employs this mode at one time or another.

A second mode involves high degrees of political negotiations when issues are sensitive and players that go beyond the network need to be utilized. For example, when Kentuckiana Agency began to research possible locations for a second bridge over the Ohio River to connect Louisville and Kentucky with the Indiana side, the data were somewhat swept aside as the mayor of Louisville and the chief executive of Jefferson County (since merged) got into a city-suburbs battle. The ultimate result was two bridges, which deferred federal money for other projects for up to twenty-five years. The 317 Group is in constant political negotiations with FSSA/DDARS administrators and state legislators over levels of service, funding rules, operating regulations, and state appropriations to support the program. If there are minor political considerations involved, network partners can utilize political decision makers to help solve a problem. As an example, Iowa Geographic was faced with a transition-related crisis when Iowa state government's new chief information officer withdrew support for its state GIS coordinator. After negotiations between the governor's office and Iowa State University Extension, the GIS coordinator position moved to Extension.

A third mode involves addressing problems through the straightforward application of technology or preestablished formats that amount to decision rules. Once a problem is discovered or a need is agreed upon, there is a pre-scribed technical or normative means of meeting the problem. The example in chapter 5 of airborne anthrax training though Iowa Communications is one example. This followed the established pattern of Iowa Communications' use of technology in partnering with government agencies.

A fourth mode is for a network to have established formulaic process pro-cedures to prepare partners for decisions. USDA/Nebraska uses a template of potential collaborators when the organization's personnel follow its coordina-tion plan. For example, its many lending activities are standardized when it partners with local banks and savings and loans, USDA rural utilities (tele-phone, electric), development districts and the State of Nebraska, Department of Economic Development. Iowa Enterprise has a set method of advising home-based and microbusinesses that include area Small Business Development Cen-ters, volunteer assistance such as SCORE, USSBA, state agencies, and private credit institutions, in that order. A more complicated formulaic process is Des Moines Metro's method of adopting individual community projects in its Transportation Improvement Plan. This protracted process described in chap-ter 3 is designed to enhance a metropolitan-wide perspective and reduce con-flict between the City of Des Moines and the suburbs. A number of networks find that this method enhances partnering and facilitates consensus.

A fifth method simply uses data-driven means of producing decision-mak-ing information. A core input into the learning and consensus process is re-search that is rooted in an existing database. Enhanced Data meetings for setting use rates for state government mailing lists always begin with a staff report that, in effect, is a market feasibility study of costs, number of poten-tial users, type of potential users such as for profit or nonprofit, expected return rates for lists, and so on. The staff report normally contains a recommended rate structure and use policy. As is the case with most transportation agencies (Metropolitan Planning Organizations) that bridge jurisdictions, Kentuckiana Agency relies on its technical support staff to compile data from multiple sources and jurisdictions including traffic counting, geographic information systems, mass transit route monitoring, maintenance and project management updates, socioeconomic data, crash data, and bicycle and pedestrian facilities. This database is plugged into a travel model, the basis of Kentuckiana Agency decision knowledge. The travel model is applied to all proposed plans and projects, and becomes the basic input for decisions made by the Kentuckiana Agency Transportation Technical Committee, and ultimately its Policy Com-mittee. A number of other networks follow this data-driven mode for some of their decisions, but none more so than the four action networks most involved in policy/programs.

A sixth and final decision-learning strategy is one that involves a predecision simulation or electronic decision-making techniques. In these cases network partners attempt to sort and sift large quantities of information, and use a form of group technique to aid in learning and agreement when they actually arrive at the decision-making stage. Lower Platte had a single experience with a charrette, a data-assisted simulation of the status of a ten-mile stretch of the Platte River. The data and process led to the partners' mock solution for remediation of this stretch. While the charrette proved to be a successful demonstration of preparing Lower Platte for making remediation decisions, it raised a great deal of anxiety and opposition among landowners and local government officials despite its status as an exercise. It has not been repeated. The 317 Group has twice used an Indiana University computerized executive laboratory to build agendas for future meetings, and issues related to updating its plans and formulating a legislative agenda. The electronic exercise combined a commissioned research project with data supplied by the State of Indiana, Family and Social Services Administration. The individual agendas of the participating agencies and NGOs were also factored in. Beyond these examples, few networks have engaged in this type of simulated activity, relying much more on data-driven, technical, or formulaic preparation.

The extent to which the PMNs employ one or more of these modes is displayed in table 7.3, which identifies network use of learning modes. These results are derived from coding this portion of the responses to the decision/course of operation questions that were originally identified in chapter 3. Discussants were asked about decision-making modes or how they reached agreement regarding the type of activity a particular PMN chooses to undertake. Clearly the PMNs have to engage in multiple modes of converting knowledge to action, and the outreach and action networks most oriented toward policy/programs appear to need virtually all of these modes. All fourteen networks regularly engage in group discussion (third column) as a mode of resolving its issues. This is not surprising, given the PMNs' need to blend so many different organizational missions, cultures, norms, and rules and regulations into some activity. Notice the reminder ([a]) that information networks do not make any type of decision, but provide a forum for issues on which others act. Nevertheless, they are venues for important discussions in their particular policy domains. By contrast, the fourth column of table 7.3 indicates that not all PMNs engage in political negotiations as a knowledge development mode, but most do from time to time. Other than the information networks and Iowa Enterprise, two of the three outreach groups do not engage in political negotiations, relying instead on prescribed and formulaic processes.

The next two types of learning modes, technical/normative and formulaic, are presented in columns five and six of table 7.3. These look at two categories where a mixed pattern occurs. Note that these modes predominate among

(text continues on page 152)

TABLE 7.3 Knowledge in Action Network Management

Network	Type	Group Discussion	Political Negotiations	Prescribed Technical or Normative	Formulaic Process	Data Driven	Behavioral Preaction Simulation
Darby	I	Action potential of watershed reports[a]		Potential mitigation; strategies/regulatory requirements[a]		Chemical and hydrologic remediation options[a]	
Indiana Economic Development	I	Regional panels and project advisory committees[a]	With governor's office and state agency heads over agenda/work[a]		For some planning studies[a]	Some, e.g., tax studies[a]	
Lower Platte	I	At all Alliance meetings to promote studies[a]		Potential mitigation; strategies/regulatory requirements[a]		Chemical and hydrologic remediation options[a]	Charrette used for demonstration, not action
Iowa Enterprise	D	Constantly, on mission and activities of Iowa Enterprise		On the mechanics of business starts and web development			
Indiana Rural Council	D	Basis of work group communities of practice	Concerning the funding for rural develop. strategy			Only for Water and Infrastructure Group	

continued

TABLE 7.3 (continued)

Network	Type	Group Discussion	Political Negotiations	Prescribed Technical or Normative	Formulaic Process	Data Driven	Behavioral Preaction Simulation
Partnership for Rural Nebraska	D	Constant staff-sharing—basis of most action	Occasionally, over funding and programs			Only results of Rural Poll	
Iowa Geographic	D	Basis of knowledge actions taken	Over funding and location of state GIS coordinator	Normally for mapping and web uses		Normally for mapping and web uses	
Small Communities	D	Basis of Steering Committee decisions		Essential position of regulatory/legal as part of all projects and tech. adaptations	Basis of virtually all finance committee recommendations	Input on users, rates, repayment data essential for finance comm. recommendations	In some training sessions
USDA/Nebraska	O	Constant interaction with partners and cofunders		For some projects	Basis of virtually all funding proposals	For many loans and grants	
317 Group	O	Constantly, with state officials	Over funding renewal and major administrative changes	For Medicaid waiver	For small-setting programs	To present program improvements	Indiana University Collaborative Work Lab before renewal for input

Iowa Communications	A	Only in major problems with an agency	Constant problem of legislation funding and authorization	Established process for services and access; programming for-mats and venues	Rate setting based in law	Usage data constantly drive service changes	
Enhanced Data	A	Basis of most rate decisions	Rarely, but has occurred	Follow market studies	Attempt to set rates by formulas pitted against agency proposals	On usage and rate setting	
Kentuckiana Agency	A	Extensively within Technical Comm-ittee, some in Policy Committee	Constantly	Particularly for TIP projects	On matters of cost sharing and project eligibility	Constant basis of two committees' decisions	Focus groups used once for bridge location decision
Des Moines Metro	A	Within technical committees	On TIP projects	Particularly for TIP projects	Project cost sharing and for project eligibility	Basis of two com-mittees' decisions	

aFormal action not taken; basis of presentation and discussion.

outreach and action networks. This is perhaps due to greater demands to use hard information, and work within prescribed regulations to develop strategies, plans, and policies. There would also appear to be greater pressure to reach agreement on a strategy or policy.

Every network but one uses data-driven modes, displayed in the next-to-last column of table 7.3. This allows them to move to their next step of reaching agreement. Again, this is not surprising given that one of the first things a multiorganization group normally does is to look at a problem through the lens of data, advance and tailor information to a problem, and examine the problem before making a decision. Joint data/information/knowledge work is a raison d'être for our PMNs.

Finally, as suggested, the last column in table 7.3 demonstrates that the use of behavioral preactivity simulation is almost absent from the networks, with only four PMNs ever reporting the undertaking of this type of mode. A count for these four reveals that each use proves to be a one-time or occasional occurrence, limited to particular issues or projects. It is clearly not a regular PMN practice.

We can conclude that, for most PMNs, discussion and data-driven learning followed by political, technical, and formulaic processes constitute the prevailing modes of converting information into usable knowledge. The six approaches define the primary ways that PMNs organize their databases into usable knowledge/information to help their agreement/decision needs and expectations. It must also be kept in mind that these are explained in this study as "pure types" for heuristic purposes; in actual situations one may prevail but some combination of the others will normally be employed as well. The six types represent different vehicles or opportunities for collaborative exchange within the collaborarchy, and have the potential to enhance learning on an interagency basis.

In short, the networks operate their KM approaches in this way: The PMNs interactively transact explicit knowledge and convert it to tacit knowledge by process. Whether verbal or data-based, the potential pool of information is derived from many different sources, most importantly from agencies that are brought together on the basis of some interdependency. Participating administrators are exposed to a great deal of information that they would not ordinarily access in their own agencies. They learn about the work of other agencies. They increase their transdisciplinary understanding, as legal, technical, financial, and political considerations interact. Both group and individual learning curves increase, as one set of information and subsequent discussions build for future actions. Indeed, in many ways the decision-preparation process makes networks into quintessential interactive information processing/knowledge-seeking bodies, another facet of being a collaborarchy.

CONCLUSION

Although there are many unknowns about the extent and nature of KM within public organizations, this research has cast some light on these activities within PMNs. As interorganizational bodies, these public officials are about "sensemaking," drawing attention to new possibilities, structuring the unknown, and grounded in "deductions from well articulated theories as it is in inductions from specific cases" (Weick 1995, 13). Sensemaking "is about the ways people generate what they interpret" (ibid., 15). The activities depicted here—ICT supports, approaches to converting data and information, and learning modes—constitute extensive benchmarks for networks in KM. It would have been surprising if the PMNs had proved devoid of such activities, inasmuch as networks are in the business of making sense out of difficult, interagency problems and pointing to potential or possible solutions.

The activities present in PMNs are not the KM activities highlighted when so-called high-flying corporations are discussed. For example, those identified in Davenport and Prusak (1998) include expert systems, artificial intelligence, case-based reasoning programs, broad knowledge repositories, concentrated knowledge domains, real-time knowledge systems, and longer-term analysis systems. These more sophisticated approaches appear to be limited to a small number of large avant-garde corporations (and perhaps public agencies), not the typical business, and clearly not to the public sector entities studied here.

In the same way as the average business or public agency, the networks under study incorporate information sources from constituent organizations, then convert their own information to that knowledge geared to their major problems/mission, which is then converted into processes that help them choose the activities they ultimately pursue. This is handled primarily through their work groups or subcommittees, who in effect become very much like communities of practice. Observations and experiences are exchanged, data are interpreted, learning experiences emerge, and tacit knowledge rises to the top. Little of this process is formally converted from explicit to tacit, but it would be incorrect to say that knowledge is not managed. The PMNs create important learning communities. As McDermott concludes:

> Since information is meaningful only to the community that uses it, the community itself needs to determine the balance of how much they need to think together, collect and organize common information, or generate standards. Since knowledge includes both information and thinking, only the community can keep that information up-to-date, rich, alive, and available to community members at just the right time, and useful. Only community members can understand what parts of it are important.

When communities determine what they need to share and what forum
will best enable them to share it, they can more readily own both the
knowledge and the forums for sharing it. (2000, 31)

Most PMN participants would agree that they constitute such communities
that place a premium on what is needed, and proceed without considering the
latest fads in KM approaches.

It is important to conclude with an important limitation. This book has been
able to tease out those few KM activities that were the most visible to discussants, based on questions and answers and a few descriptive documents relating to information sources, program sessions, or committees. For example, the
Technical Committee workgroups of Kentuckiana Agency dig deep into KM
as they blend engineering, planning, and political concentrations into traffic
counts, the Intelligent Transit model, pollution models, and others with specific improvement projects. This proceeding, where explicit and tacit knowledge essentially come together, is a core process but one difficult to capture in
a research project with a general focus. A great deal is undoubtedly lost by the
research process. However, that is what public managers do in PMNs. Clearly
a great deal of KM is less visible or lies beneath the surface, but is deeply im-
bedded in what the PMNs do. Managing knowledge is the reason that PMN
nonadministrative committees, task groups, and work groups exist.

. . . .

CHAPTER EIGHT

Do Networks Perform? Adding Value and Accounting for Costs

So why do the partners add to their "bureaucratic" time by participating in Iowa Enterprise? At times it really pushes our administrative day well into evenings, with our help sessions . . . and planning conferences and studies. But there is a gap out there of service to small and home-based business in this state that no one federal or state agency or university can fill. Together we can exchange information, learn to work with small business, and, speaking as a federal government program director, helps me do my job.

IF PERFORMANCE IS a hallmark of the new public management, do public networks perform? Since the publication of Osborne and Gaebler's *Reinventing Government* (1992), public agency form and process is not enough for either practitioners or academics, because these pillars stop short of measured results. Questions of performance extend beyond the hierarchical organization to the difficult arenas of interorganizational and intergovernmental collaborative efforts (Provan and Milward 2001; Radin 2000), since public administration takes networks seriously (O'Toole 1997). One experienced practitioner concludes, "Today's enlightened leaders in both public and private sectors understand the value chains of which they are a part, and they know that most of their pressing problems can be solved by collaborative actions with others" (Linden 2002, xvi). Pattakos and Dundon, experts on innovation, suggest that a true culture of innovation depends on efficacious collaborative activity. They indicate, however, that one of the biggest obstacles to building creative capacity is "how to capitalize on insights and ideas across the functional silos that thwart even the best intentions" (2003, 15).

The essay by Agranoff and McGuire on "Big Questions in Public Network Management Research," raised the issue of "whether public management networks produce solutions and results that otherwise would not have occurred through single, hierarchical organizations" (2001b, 318). The social change thesis provides one perspective on this, that the emerging information or knowledge era makes collaborative networking imperative (Lipnack and Stamps 1994; Clegg 1990; Kooiman 1993). Related to this is the problem change thesis, that society is now tackling more difficult problems with few apparent solutions (Harmon and Mayer 1986) and that networks inevitably emerge to bridge the resulting jurisdictional and organizational gaps. Changing intergovernmental roles (Agranoff and McGuire 2003a; O'Toole 1996) and emerging interactive technologies (Provan and Milward 1991, 1995; Harrison and Weiss 1998) also give rise to bureaucratic changes and the need to network. These explanations demonstrate that we know more about the forces that give rise to networks than about assessing their performance.

This chapter demonstrates that the question regarding performance in networks is somewhat complex when we focus on the different kinds of public values added. Thus the chapter attempts to provide an accounting of the different types of values added from the standpoint of the (1) administrator/specialist, (2) participating organization, (3) network process, and (4) network outcomes. This is followed by a discussion of the costs of networking, again as reflected by the discussants. Finally, a general accounting of the benefits is offered, which summarizes twenty-one PMN activities identified in previous chapters.

ADDING PUBLIC VALUE

The primary concern with network performance appears to center on the question of whether collaboration adds value to the public undertaking. As Moore suggests, public managers seek to "discover, define and produce public value," extending discovery of means to focus on ends, and becoming "important innovators in changing what public organizations do and how they do it" (1995, 20). In a similar vein, managers in networks must look to the value of what they are producing, to paraphrase Moore. In Bardach's pathbreaking book on interagency action, he defines collaboration "as any joint activity by two or more agencies that is intended to increase public value by their working together rather than separately" (1998, 8). From an administrative standpoint, he asserts that collaboration creates social value in the same way as its counterparts, differentiation and specialization. Collaboration results need to be assessed because any loss in efficiency due to political, institutional, and technical pressures diminishes public value (ibid., 11). We should not be impressed by the idea of collaboration per se, but only if it produces better organizational performance or lower costs than its alternatives.

Klijn suggests that, as collaborative structures, "networks facilitate interaction, decision-making, cooperation and learning, since they provide the resources to support these activities, such as recognizable interaction patterns, common rules and organizational forms, and sometimes even a common language" (2003a, 32). These are the lessons of chapters 3 through 7. Networks are also bodies that connect "public policies with their strategic and institutionalized context: the network of public, semi-public, and private actors participating in certain policy fields" (Kickert, Klijn, and Koppenjan 1997, 1). By engaging in these behaviors, different networks facilitate a variety of inter-organizational interactions (Alter and Hage 1993). Networks raise the potential for more rational decision making. Multiple actors representing different mandates not only overcome information and resource asymmetries, but create synergistic learning and problem solving that might not have been considered if only single entities had been involved (Agranoff and McGuire 2003a).

In hierarchical organizations, performance or value can be more easily attributed to effectiveness by analyzing success in achieving goals. This test has to be modified with regard to networks. Klijn and Koppenjan (2000) suggest that the goal achievement method has less credence because objectives are more autonomous and have no central coordinating actor, and each of several actors may have differing objectives. They further argue that the use of *ex ante* formulated objectives is usually untenable because actors adapt their perceptions and objectives interactively, responding to other parties and to the environment. Also, if certain parties do not participate in the interaction process, the chances are high that their interests and preferences will not be represented in the derived solution. As a result, network results need to be measured by the "*ex post* satisfying" criterion (Teisman 1992, 1995; quoted in Klijn and Koppenjan 2000), which is based on the subjective judgment of network actors. In the final analysis, actors have to determine the benefits derived along with considering the costs. Thus both substantive and process elements need to be weighed.

Since networks are exchange vehicles and learning entities, a great deal of what is accomplished emanates from the "actions of interaction" (Dundon 2002, 181). Dundon concludes that innovation process networks can enhance teamwork, reduce boundaries, and promote the innovative spirit. These non-linear processes require high degrees of flexibility to accommodate changes, tracking and reporting, decision making at the working level, and parallel processing techniques. Form and function can contribute to value. In the network approach, the ex post judgments of actors about collaborated process and collaborated outcome are used in order to determine the success or failure of policy processes (Klijn and Koppenjan 2000; McGuire 2002). As a result, heavy reliance is placed on the determinations made by the administrators involved in the PMNs, in terms of both process and outcome value adding.

As the KM processes identified in chapter 7 and the decision-making modes analyzed in chapter 3 indicate, the question regarding the value-adding features of networks centers on their ability to handle information/technology/resources through a nonhierarchical, self-organizing process, held together by evolving mutual obligation and by reaching consensus-based decisions. As demonstrated, PMNs operate on both vertical (federal, state, local) and horizontal (county, special district, nongovernmental) planes. The research tries to incorporate these concerns.

To understand value adding, one must look at process and outcome from personal, organization, and network perspectives. As the guided discussions were analyzed, it became clear that administrators were not only discussing process and outcome gains accrued for their networks, but they also mentioned the benefits that network involvement accrues to the home organization and to themselves as managers and program specialists. For these participants, the rationale for investment in the network entailed more than serving some collective, vaguely understood public purpose such as facilitated transportation or rural development, but also involved certain advantages that the network could bring to their organization's mission and functioning, and to them as professionals involved in public programs.

MANAGER AND PROFESSIONAL

Perhaps the most overlooked dimension in the literature relates to those benefits that accrue to the boundary-spanning individuals who represent organizations in networks. An exception is Craig Thomas's (2003) study of interagency collaboration in biodiversity preservation, in which he analyzes the differences between administrators and specialists. Thomas finds that program specialists/ professionals see the direct benefits of collaboration more easily. The five work groups of the Kentuckiana Agency Technical Committee, for example, provide a depth of specialized knowledge and contacts that improves the ability of program specialists to deal with their own program challenges and, in working with one another across jurisdictions, with the two states' transportation-related NGOs and with the federal government. Administrators find this more difficult. For example, the bicycle pedestrian task group has created opportunities to bridge the boundaries of normal transit modes and to discover new routes for those who prefer these means; this is conceptually easy for transportation professionals but not for elected officials.

The benefits to the manager/specialist of networking are identified in table 8.1. It presents representative comments, categorized and ranked in order of importance, of PMN activity regarding this individual dimension. It makes clear that network participants meet many of the same professional needs that they do in hierarchical organizations, such as acquiring knowledge and skills of a broad interdisciplinary nature, but the scope of this content is considerably broader. The ranking is based on the frequency of each type of comment made under each category. Comments related to enhanced scientific and technical learning and knowledge were the most frequent personal value responses, whereas those related to public service were seventh in frequency. The comments are not organized by network type because there were no real differences between them.

Of first order were responses related to scientific and technical knowledge enhancement. This key function amounts to expansion of the individual's personal potential, which broadens the range of possible potential solutions. Typical responses included those related to scientific enhancement, skill, and educational growth, and skill development. The concept of interdisciplinarity and interorganizational cultural exposure is also of high importance. Here the second-most important issue is that the network becomes a venue for exposure, exchange, and application of the various disciplinary approaches, such as legal, financial, engineering, planning, and political, to the difficult problems that these PMNs address. Peer learning and process growth are also paramount. Additionally, one learns how to work within the various organization/agency cultures. These two top priorities—scientific/technical and process enhancement—stand out among the various personal values added. They confirm the utility of networks as genuine interorganization learning venues.

Of intermediate importance is that ranked third in priority, expanding abilities to manage, particularly in public management. Representative responses identify growth in intergovernmental relations, understanding the role of NGOs with government, and increasing the ability to work with different publics. Here participants value the network as providing new and different experiences, helping the manager operate from a multiorganizational perspective, and enlarging one's perspective on public management beyond that of the home agency. A fourth intermediate priority is the potential to engage in further networking. Typical responses related to opportunities to fill gaps in contacts, new interagency opportunities, and even finding the players. In other words, exchanges during the process of networking within the PMN lead to further networking: one-to-one, among three or more partner agencies, and so on. A fifth and somewhat related priority is that of helping managers/professionals explore an array of programs and become aware of new aspects of a subject. Working through seemingly intractable problems is aided by network presentations and discussions. This not only expands the range of potential programs to link to possible solutions, but also helps the manager/professional deal with the inevitable complexity of the problem at hand.

Of lower priority, but nevertheless important were access to decision makers (sixth) and opportunities to perform a public service (seventh). The network provides multiple connections to agency heads, state legislators,

(text continues on page 163)

TABLE 8.1 Personal and Professional Value Added by PMN Participants (All Types of Networks)

Rank Order	Category/Type	Representative Comments
First	Enhanced scientific and technical learning/access to knowledge	• Integrating science for nonscientists • Depth of technical watershed knowledge • Expands to social and political processes—beyond science and technology • Link to additional expertise • Has vast educational value • Broadens professional information base • Forces one to learn about latest technology • Enhances ICT technical skills • Improved modeling/engineering skills
Second	Learning how to learn with different disciplinary and organizational cultures/interdisciplinarity	• Peer-to-peer learning • Hones collaborative skills • How to deal with multiple stakeholders • Enhanced skills in group dynamics, conflict management • Builds mutual respect and trust • Work with professional peers across agencies • Allows one to put on different lenses • Learn the people and how to work with them • Interdisciplinary interaction

Third	Expand public management abilities/improved managerial skills	• Opportunity to extend my years of public administration experience
		• Broadens program management abilities
		• Sharpened personal intergovernmental perspective
		• Exposure to a variety of federal/state rules, regulations, standards
		• Understand the nature of different publics
		• Working with the variety of NGOs and public agencies is like getting a second MPA
		• The nonprofit nature of government is made clear
		• Enhances governmental exposure
		• Become aware of public needs, services expectations
		• New perspectives on other public agencies
Fourth	Informal (dyadic, triadic, etc.) networking opportunities and spin-offs	• Exchanges with other jurisdictions' elected officials
		• Builds my personal contact/information and resource base
		• Enhanced personal contacts
		• A place to bridge the boundaries
		• Connecting with other agencies
		• Learn the people and how to work with them
		• Access to state, local decision makers

continued

TABLE 8.1 (continued)

Rank Order	Category/Type	Representative Comments
Fifth	Program awareness/new aspects of the subject	• Awareness of other programs • Depth of watershed knowledge • Reach into the depths of the water industry • Helps to see the complexity of problems • Able to see multidimensions of complex problems • Learn how to combine high-tech with government processes, e.g., budgeting
Sixth	Access to policy/program decision makers	• Helps my city connect the important piece—where the policy is made • Awareness of where the cages are rattled within code agencies and commissions • Intermediaries between federal, state, and local officials—where the real decisions are made
Seventh	Public service opportunities	• Reinforces the spirit of meaningful public service • Brings out a broader perspective of area needs to us all • See the public interest from a broader perspective

local elected officials, and NGO executives and board members, as well as important program contacts with federal and state administrators. It helps participants learn where the decisions are made. To the boundary spanner, it means that one is contributing to problem resolution in a way that goes beyond the narrow perspective of one's own agency or program. Together these seven priorities suggest that from the standpoint of network results, managers and program specialists use their involvement to expand their personal capacities to collaborate. To Bardach (1998) these are critical elements on which additional levels of capability to achieve collaborated results can accrue.

ADVANTAGES TO THE AGENCY

By contrast, benefits and results of networking to participating organizations are deeply rooted in the literature on networking. Synthesizing the baseline literature from when the age of the network became visible, a number of authors remind us of the need to network in order to expand information and access expertise from other organizations, pool and access financial and other resources, share risks and innovation investments, manage uncertainty, fulfill the need for flexibility in operation and response time, and assess other adaptive efficiencies (Alter and Hage 1993; Powell 1990; Perrow 1992). As an example, although the Indiana Economic Development Council is reluctant to take formal positions as a PMN, its research on economic trends and practices in other states accrues to the agencies most heavily invested in it, such as the Indiana Department of Family and Social Services Administration and the Indiana Small Business Development Center, providing them with expanded information and the potential to pool resources or access adaptive efficiencies. Not only does the network itself benefit from collaborative research, but the agencies themselves do as well.

The benefits of being a part of a network are illustrated in table 8.2. The table reports representative summary comments pooled by each type of PMN. They are combined by type rather than in rank order because the category of PMN does prove to make a difference. Each of the PMNs within the four types—information, development, outreach, and activity—brings many benefits to the home organization in terms of useful information and potential solutions; for those networks more involved in policy/program this last factor is essential and frequent.

Because information networks have a narrow focus, it is clear that the participating agencies mainly benefit from information pooling and opportunities for some form of coordination down the line. Notice that comments are limited to "learning," or "raising organization's knowledge," or future "opportunities" to do something. No specific activities were identified. The potential for subsequent action should not be written off as meaningless, but its indirect benefit to the home organization is clear. To a degree, even with these limitations the activities must be worth some level of investment for many administrators.

Development network participants demonstrate the value of exchange but also point to capacity-related new techniques, trends, and opportunities; discussions that can lead to partners taking on activities at some point; direct educational programming; and the spurring toward joining with new partners. Typical comments include "pooling of expertise," "calling partners to take action," and "working on similar missions." This raises the value ante considerably, not only by giving these PMNs specific own-source programs to deliver for their partners, but also in the production of knowledge usable for the network and the home agency. In other words, it adds a valued group product.

Outreach network administrators and specialists report accruing both types of the kinds of benefits previously mentioned, but they also work more closely to try to fit the various pieces into the puzzle, leverage funds among one another, get involved in policy negotiations, and indirectly channel tangible resources. Terms like "sharing of the potential funding burden," "fitting in with other federal, state programs," and "stimulating program growth" are typical. Again, something more is added to the value chain: clarified agency rules, reciprocal programming and resources, and a clearer picture of where the agency fits in. Strategies are part of the picture here, helping the agency see its lateral potential in a real-world way.

The final type, action networks, share these benefits but go considerably further through responses such as setting rates, engaging in regulatory policies, allocating funding, and establishing priorities that also lead to funding. Here typical comments are "decides on important plan components," "third-party rate and regulatory policy mechanisms," "direct customer service at low cost," and "money for projects." In other words, they do the policy and program work that accrues direct benefit to the agency partner.

Clearly PMNs bring different benefits to their partner organizations. Informational networks are limited in scope but do provide useful information, whereas developmental networks can also point to new capabilities that accrue to the home agency as well as the collective. But the real benefits to the home agency are spin-offs from outreach and action networks of a strategic or program/policy nature. The potential program/funding connections of outreach networks and the funding and policy benefits of the action networks bring important values to the participating agency.

(text continues on page 168)

TABLE 8.2   Values Added to the Home Organization/Agency Network, by Type

Network Type/Network	Types of Values Added: Representative Comments
Information (Darby, Indiana Economic Development, Lower Platte)	• Assists our agency in watershed coordination • Access to other agencies' information • Learn about funding opportunities • Enhances agency's profile to be at the table • A convening venue for like-mission agencies • Access to multiple sources of expertise • Raises organization's knowledge consciousness • Opportunity for one-to-one coordination • Easier for (dyadic) reach across agencies
Developmental (Iowa Enterprise, Indiana Rural Council, Partnership for Rural Nebraska, Iowa Geographic)	• Exposure to new ICT techniques • Important place to be exposed to new trends and operating practices • Access to broad array of information and programs • At the table with other rural interests—potential for us to act individually • This agency learns about new funding opportunities and we act on them • Helps our agency find new partners • Call on partners to take action • Pooling of multiple types of expertise • Legitimizes our program's agenda by garnering the support of others

continued

TABLE 8.2 (continued)

Network Type/Network	Types of Values Added: Representative Comments
Developmental (Iowa Enterprise, Indiana Rural Council, Partnership for Rural Nebraska, Iowa Geographic)	• Another channel for this agency's staff to work on mission-related programs • The council helped our agency launch its own new service areas • Coordination saves agency efforts • Development of areas of expertise far beyond the capacity of this agency • The council helps our program get into new areas
Outreach (Small Communities, USDA/RD, 317 Group)	• How our federal agency fits in with other federal, state programs and how coordinated solutions can be identified • Sharing of the potential funding burden with other agencies • Awareness of other agencies' programs, rules, agendas • Loaned technical people • Potential clients for our agency's program • Fund-leveraging opportunities • Stimulate program growth with partners • Input into the state policymaking process far beyond lobbying; we negotiate potential program changes with decision-makers • Indirectly leads to new resources for our agency

Action (Iowa Communications, Enhanced Data, Kentuckiana Agency, Des Moines Metro)

- Direct service customer for other public agencies at lower cost
- Rate setting based on public agency input
- The (network) relies on the agencies to demonstrate collective public value
- Set fees that generate revenue, shared with each agency
- A third-party rate and regulatory policy mechanism
- Helps our agency promote its public data-use mission
- We are part of a broader policymaking process
- Exposure to new technology
- The MPO decides on important plan components and funds projects that benefit this jurisdiction
- Provides data, information for small governments
- Enhances our planning and mapping capacities
- A place to have my government's transportation needs supported
- A venue to try for metropolitan perspectives and sometimes decisions
- Money for projects
- Another conduit for federal money; we have to be there to get a share
- A way to find and reach local officials who ultimately make transportation choices

NETWORK PROCESS

The importance of accounting for network process results was suggested earlier, particularly their ability to satisfy the organizational and professional expectations of those involved. They are both similar to and different from those of single organizations. As indicated in chapter 6, network processes are more collective than authority based in regard to organizing, decision making, and programming, but in terms of the human resource dynamics of communication, leadership, group structure, and mechanisms of reaching collaborative agreements, they are more similar to those of single organizations (Agranoff 2003). As a process, network management was said to involve a steering of interaction processes that sequences the following phases: activation, or initiating activation processes; guided mediation; finding strategic consensus; joint problem solving; and activities of maintenance, implementation, and adjustment (Kickert and Koppenjan 1997). For example, the Small Communities network in Ohio follows a similarly phased sequence as it uses participant knowledge and contributed resources to explore and develop capacities in collaborating. Its strategic blueprints are virtually always the products of a clearly established process that combines scientific/technical, legal regulatory, and financing information as it engages its multiple actors from university, consulting, government, and nongovernment sectors.

The values added by network processes as reported in representative comments are summarized in table 8.3, and again are organized by the four types of PMNs. This table demonstrates the importance of collaborative process as a lasting value of participation. It is important to bear in mind that many process responses that are attributed to information and development networks are sometimes repeated for the outreach and action networks as well, but the coding purpose here is geared to distinguishing between the types.

The benefits of information networks processes are clearly limited to raising issues and concerns, discussions about them, and identifying agendas for others to pursue. Frustration over these limitations was expressed by one discussant. Typical responses related to continuing dialogue, attention to particular issues, and influencing the agendas of other interests. The greatest value added here clearly lies in subsequent action by others. Development network discussants report somewhat more benefits, as they view their processes as related to building platforms for collaboration, creating venues or forums for the issues they work on, providing opportunities for learning and aspects of professional enhancement, and, to some degree, enhancement of federal-state relations. The process is very important for these development networks because of what they potentially launch through their educational programs and by sharing knowledge. Outreach networks appear to be able to reach beyond the

(text continues on page 172)

TABLE 8.3 Values Added by Network Processes

Network Type/Network	Representative Comments
Information (Darby, Indiana Economic Development, Lower Platte)	• Keeps the dialogue open for watershed interests • Teamwork frustrating—Darby can't do anything • Focuses attention on nonpoint source pollution • Call attention to key issues, e.g., education and workforce needs • Benefit from shared thinking • Conversations that would not otherwise be held • A place to bring together NRDs and state agencies • Have put many issues on the table for other jurisdictions, e.g., zoning, septics • A catalyst for managers to process one-on-one between Alliance meetings
Development (Iowa Enterprise, Indiana Rural Council, Partnership for Rural Nebraska, Iowa Geographic)	• A place to raise new concerns, e.g., business succession • Bureaucrats and nonbureaucrats both at the table with the same concerns • Builds real public sector/private sector collaboration • Provides a statewide forum on rural issues • When we are all at the table, we build on one another • Improved federal-state relations • A multiple agency buy-in • Nonpartisan venue to explore important policy concerns

continued

TABLE 8.3 (continued)

Network Type/Network	Representative Comments
Development (Iowa Enterprise, Indiana Rural Council, Partnership for Rural Nebraska, Iowa Geographic)	• We learn how to span the boundaries within Partnership for Rural Nebraska • Create a cooperation mindset • Meetings are a learning experience • Valuable learning among and within our communities • Tacit education because of sharing of experience • A venue to test new ideas
Outreach (Small Communities, USDA/RD, 317 Group)	• Knowledge of one another's working relationships as communities are helped • Synergistic effects from partnering on particular proposals • Make the impossible appear possible • New opportunities through joint funding arrangements • Many of our efforts, e.g., water and wastewater committee, a major process effort • Improved interaction between public and private efforts • Helps providers pay attention to some key issues, e.g., autism, cerebral palsy • Greater time management through collaboration • Agreed-on strategic data collection and sharing

Action (Iowa Communications, Enhanced Data, Kentuckiana Agency, Des Moines Metro)

- Enhances interactive service orientation
- Agency/Iowa Communications staff use interactive synergistic mode of reaching solutions
- Public-private cooperation: reaching beyond the fiber links
- Emergencies, e.g., bioterrorism, anthrax, pull together Iowa Communications, state agencies, counties at 156 sites
- Process designed to accommodate proposing agency
- As a participative group have streamlined agency processes
- Creative reflection leads to a variety of solutions that we have adopted
- Nonpartisan forum for federal, two states, local governments to express their issues and concerns
- A place for elected officials, administrators, planners, engineers to interact
- Kentuckiana Agency interactions have led to many new collaborative projects
- A public forum for the most important transportation issues
- Policy committee debates and decides on the larger issues
- While people are at the table for the money we try to shift focus to metro concerns
- Peer interaction builds important federal-state-local problems resolution atmosphere
- A good forum for mutual self-education and metro issues

interactive and capability spin-offs to synergistically gear their processes toward useful joint arrangements, such as funding blueprints and data issues, as they gear toward policy or program choices made interactively and reciprocally. Although one or two respondents did think that the process wasted a great deal of time that dyadic interaction could have avoided, a much greater sense of multiagency interaction time benefit was expressed by others, since the dialogue brings the group closer to a solution. As a result, the process pays off for most respondents.

As one might expect, real-world payoff is clearly the case for the action networks. Here process ultimately leads to very tangible outcomes—policies, standards, funding—that emanate from the multiorganizational interactive processes organized by the various forums that the network provides. Interactions that lead to problem resolution, decisions on issues, and programs are representative. As the mainstream network literature suggests, these PMNs are able to use process to deliver—within their limited interagency/interjurisdictional scope—by exploring the changes needed to address those policy problems that transcend agency and jurisdiction domain.

The networks thus become important platforms for bringing together individuals who have potential resources and a stake in certain problems, deepening and broadening the knowledge pool of technical information, and adapting it to immediate situations. To the outreach and action networks the process presents opportunities for interagency processing and problem resolution on a regular, channeled basis. Perhaps most important are other collective benefits, including those that are related to continuing interagency group processing: information flows; new information channels; potential problem-solving avenues; mutual learning, training, and development; comprehensive/strategic planning; and mutual understanding that leads to increased trust. Without the constant massaging of these elements of group dynamics or applied behavioral science directed to interagency activity (Weiner 1990), network outcomes are more difficult to achieve.

TANGIBLE OUTCOMES

This leaves the concrete outcomes of network activity, the results commonly associated with performance. As O'Toole (1997) indicates, networked solutions are needed to: (1) try to solve the most difficult policy problems that no single agency can tackle, (2) overcome the limitations on direct government intervention in order to solve real problems, (3) recognize that political imperatives usually demand broad coalitions of interests to solve problems, (4) capture second-order program effects, such as lack of employment opportunities in rural development, that generate interdependencies, and (5) cope with layers of mandates and requirements that invoke the involvement of many jurisdictions and organizations. In this respect, tangible public performance is hard to directly measure in relation to networked solutions. Behn suggests "the one-bill, one-policy, one-organization, one-accountability holdee principle doesn't work for performance" because most programs involve collaborative undertakings (2001, 77). Although the Iowa Communications Network is a state-chartered program, its legal requirements for competitive broadcast and service pricing means that it must serve many interests and functions in ways that satisfy numerous users, stakeholders, and public agencies. Although it originally provided extended education and telemedicine services, it is now heavily engaged in homeland security, economic development, information transmission and intranet provision, among other processes, all of which must be accomplished collaboratively by Iowa Communications and its public agency partner users.

Networks provide venues for collaboration that lead directly and/or indirectly to solutions. Table 8.4 displays a summary of representative comments, sorted by network type, of these tangible benefits. It illustrates the reactions of discussants when asked to identify the major tangible outcomes or real-world public values that can be easily attributed to their efforts. Many of the results reflected in table 8.3 as process results are transformed here into tangible benefits as well. Table 8.4 demonstrates that networks can produce collaborative value. The most dramatic differences between the four types emerge when separated by type.

Information networks' limitations to problem exchanges show up once again. Their results are always indirect, as they generate various types of informational knowledge that others may use. They can point to the research and data that they have made accessible, the partnerships formed as spin-offs, and new programs and grants by their member agencies. As a result, their forums always lead to something that some other entity follows up on, such as the working partnerships, actionable information/knowledge, or grants or projects of other organizations.

By contrast, development networks can point to these and more results, particularly their formally organized knowledge-building sessions, exchange of working capabilities, other forms of knowledge dissemination, and knowledge development. A development network can point to a set of community visitations, rural institutes/polls/studies, and color-infrared technologies as real successes. Their most tangible results are limited more to knowledge management than policy/program solutions, but are quite prominent in this respect.

Outreach networks have an even greater level of concrete results, through outreach contacts that lead to new funding and partnerships, policy blueprints and proposals, and jointly derived plans that ultimately lead to decisions

(text continues on page 177)

TABLE 8.4   Tangible Values Added, by Network Type

Network Type/Network	Representative Comments
Information (Darby, Indiana Economic Development, Lower Platte)	• Only indirect studies, new forums, and plans by other entities • Data access • Has led to many agency/jurisdiction partnerships, e.g., Hellbranch Run Partners • Survival is one accomplishment • Our efforts led to the state obtaining National Scenic Rivers designation • The state economic development strategies; twelve regional plans • Many studies, e.g., taxes, tax investment financing, and Welfare-to-Work • Our economic scorecards • Joint-sponsored research studies, public policy study • Down the line, new grants for our partners • Joint data sets • Many spin-off remediation projects by partners based on Alliance conclusions, e.g., regional water system
Development (Iowa Enterprise, Indiana Rural Council, Partnership for Rural Nebraska, Iowa Geographic)	• "How to find" and "where to go" assists me for microbusinesses • Conference and after-hours assistance sessions • Models of success transmitted on Iowa Communications • Shared staff and resources • Rural development plan • Cooperative Development Center (Indiana), Nebraska Cooperative Development Center

- Meetings, summits, forums
- Working partnerships, e.g., Indiana Rural Council and RCAP, Cooperative Extension, Agriculture Leadership Institute
- Community visitations
- Rural Institute
- Improved ICT capacity
- Joint didactic agency briefings
- Increased GPS capacity; server-clearinghouse of GIS
- Color-infrared mapping
- Technical presentations
- Outreach (GIS) to small governments
- Improved GIS professional practice

Outreach (Small Communities, USDA/RD, 317 Group)

- Two-thirds of communities assisted ultimately received funding
- Total contact/assistance to over 220 governments in Ohio
- Training programs
- Adapted technologies
- Special efforts, Appalachia, brownfields
- Joint program partnerships organized, e.g., value-added agriculture
- Programs organized with Partnership for Rural Nebraska, Nebraska Development Network
- Arranged numerous joint-funded projects with partnering agencies
- The 317 strategy with all parties buying in; renewed in second round
- Communication: newsletter, website, special publications
- Expanded databases, models, and finance studies
- Group plans translated into successful legislative programming with new funds

continued

TABLE 8.4   (continued)

Network Type/Network	Representative Comments
Action (Iowa Communications, Enhanced Data, Kentuckiana Agency, Des Moines Metro)	• Low-cost distance education as a result of Iowa Communications/ educational interaction • Co-located ICT services in state government and in higher education • State-owned infrastructure; 770 local sites for fiber optic cable plus • Enhanced agency income • Policies that are set for portal use • Improved public access to data, information • Approved long-range plan for metro area • Hundreds of TIP projects approved • Funding allocations • Enhanced multimodal—bicycle, pedestrian, transit, rural, handicapped—access • Allocation of money into trail development • Increased federal dollars • Regional-based traffic models • Economic development spin-offs

enacted or approved by others. Many of these results are also a direct follow-up of their knowledge management activities with these networks; for example, the guidance on small-town water system problems, laying out of joint fund/program partnerships, and the 317 Plan itself. These stand out as results garnered by these networks.

The last set of entries in table 8.4 shows that action networks really "get there," so to speak, since their work leads to knowledge-based policy adjustments, fund allocations, regulatory standards, and plans linked to action. Here is where low-cost distance education, new roads and other infrastructure, web portal use, polluted stream regeneration, and other direct results arise. These results include the dollars allocated, rates set, infrastructure developed—the results that policy-making and collaborative decision bodies are expected to make. Their work clearly leads to new initiatives that result from network decisions.

Results of a tangible nature, then, are highly dependent on PMN type. The two policy/program-oriented networks, outreach and action, can make the policy adaptations that they are able to agree on, facilitated solutions, applications to places such as a metropolitan area, reciprocal programming, enhanced governance, and program and service innovations. These outcomes represent the kind of adjustments that intergovernmental policy networks are designed to address (Agranoff and McGuire 2001b; Kickert and Koppenjan 1997; O'Toole 1997). Other outcomes, more universal to all four types, relate to the end-stages of the process itself: exchanged resources, program interfaces, joint or collaborated databases, mutually adapted technologies, and enhanced interagency knowledge infrastructures. While some of these products may fall short of policy solutions or new ways of programming (although their potential for subsequent solution should not be underestimated), they are the only outcomes that some networks can achieve, that is, those that are nonstrategic.

The value-adding balance sheet in tables 8.1 to 8.4 suggests that there is more to network production than policy adjustment. Whereas forged policy solutions may be the ultimate aim (at least for those scholars that attribute such outcomes), it appears equally important that the acts of networking also add process and product value, and help managers and professionals as well as the agencies in which they work. This exploration suggests that for the network as a whole, a series of other values can be added to those that serve policy. The variety of values that this performance analysis of networks appears to present must be investigated more deeply.

WHAT ABOUT COSTS?

Although networks provide tremendous interorganizational and intergovernmental potential they do not come without negative forces that detract from agency and management energy and outcomes, let alone collaborated results. These forms ultimately diminish public value, and thus some identification of their downsides mentioned by the administrators and specialists allows some measure of realism, for costs always have to be weighed against benefits.

They are not organized by type for two reasons. First, network cost was not a direct question in the discussion guide but emerged in the process of the responses to the previous four issues. Second, there were really no discernible differences between the four PMN types. Six categories of concern emerged from the interactive process: lost time and opportunity costs; protracted processing based on nonhierarchical, multiorganization, multicultural human-relations processes; the exercise of organizational power or the withdrawal of it; gravitation toward consensus-based risk-aversive agendas; hoarding of resources within agencies; and policy barriers that frustrate collaboration.

Time and Opportunity Lost

Under the assumption that every administrative hour spent on inter-organizational collaboration is an hour taken away from internal management, accumulated time takes its toll at some point. Collaborative decisions and managers' reports normally take more time within networks than in their hierarchical organizations. Managers who are not full-time boundary spanners estimated that from 10 to 20 percent of their time is spent working across organizations, with a large portion spent taking actions and on projects. Most of this network time is spent in formal networks and/or in interagency committees and taskforces. The formal meetings of the networks and their operating committees normally take a small proportion of this time, at most a two- to four-hour commitment monthly or quarterly. It is the project work of the networks that takes the major portion of time commitments.

For example, Small Communities in Ohio may tie up twenty to thirty hours of time—by participants from each of three funding agencies, two university technical experts, and two program directors—to help one small community solve its water problems. Twelve to fifteen of these community-level projects are undertaken in an average year. One or two of these people would ordinarily be helping the community in any case, but since no single agency can solve the problem many more are involved. A minimum of 120 person-hours can easily be devoted to a single small-town effort. This is not a unique example. Iowa Enterprise has devoted up to 200 person-hours putting together business start-up packages to help launch and maintain a single microenterprise, including the time of federal and state government administrators. Iowa Geographic may similarly devote a total of five to seven person-days by its activists to help a single local government become a multiple-source GIS user. Indiana Rural Council has a community visitation committee of ten to twelve people that devotes two donated working days to six different small towns each year. Obviously these are not insignificant expenditures of time and expertise. Although the administrators contribute their time and expertise to enhance collaborative actions and solutions, it is nevertheless time away from the home agency.

Human Relations Costs

The costs associated with the human relations processes of networks are real as well, particularly those that lead to decisions or other forms of network action. Single organizations similarly devote efforts to processes that lead to production or results, but they have the advantage of hierarchy and its concomitant authority to ultimately decide and move things along. Networks do not. Similar human relations or group processes unfold, but mutuality in decision is a paramount value. Networks are multicultural in that different agency/organization traditions and practices need to be recognized and worked through, and sometimes worked around. Respect for the "other" is not only highly valued, it is essential to ultimately move an organization representative toward agreement. Trust, an essential ingredient in network processing, takes a great deal of time and experience to build up. Consensus, the only way that agreement or decisions can be created, does not come easily. One of the most visible efforts of the Partnership for Rural Nebraska is its annual capacity-building Rural Institute. Planning this event begins before the last one has unfolded, and involves the major partners, an ongoing Education Committee, an allied network, and a local host committee. Each program element requires a complex overlay of processes and mutual agreements that combine political, technical, and pedagogical considerations. The result is generally satisfying to stakeholders but involves human relations energy (and more time costs) that far exceed that of a training program in a single organization. Exhaustive human-relations processing is part of the price that most networks pay for collaborated results (Agranoff 2003).

Risk Aversion

Decision by consensus is essential to holding partners together, but it can drive networks toward risk-aversive agendas. This concern was suggested earlier in regard to informational networks like the watershed networks Darby and Lower Platte. They have multiple, conflicting stakeholders. Darby almost fell apart in the late 1990s because of the Nature Conservancy's support of the wildlife refuge bill before the U.S. Congress. Many local government and landowner residents saw land "takings" as a next step, which required a cooling-off period. Many discussants in informational and developmental PMNs noted their continuing frustration with their network's avoidance of tough issues, or even real decisions. For example, Indiana Economic Development, which is primarily designed to provide strategic economic planning for the state, has conducted numerous externally funded studies on the problems that have led to Indiana's manufacturing jobs decline. However, its seventy-two-member, bipartisan, business-labor, state-government board has avoided key, potentially polarizing positions on making large-scale investments in education, technical training, work-force restructuring, technology enhancement, and venture capital. Indeed, while the state government made some initial policy decisions in 2003 on developing high-tech manufacturing, the Council was silent on the policy choices required to make this happen. Indiana Economic Development tends to take safer, more factual positions, such as announcing that Indiana has lost a given number of manufacturing jobs, or identifying the importance of computer literacy programs in the high schools and vocational-technical schools. One price that networks clearly pay in order to hold its partners together is keeping issues off the decision agenda that are threatening or contrary to consensus building.

Relational Power

Lurking behind consensus is the often hidden reality of power within the network. Its exercise surrounding key decisions and actions can detract from collaborative potential. While networks are often characterized as having coequal, interdependent, patterned relationships (Klijn 1997), resource differentials and dependencies suggest power differentials (Rhodes 1981). Clegg and Hardy indicate that behind the "façade of trust and the rhetoric of collaboration," power is exercised by stronger partners over weaker partners (1996, 679). It appears logical that PMNs, composed of public agencies and public officials, would experience real power in their deliberations. In the Des Moines Metro transportation agency, the clash of power between the central city of Des Moines and the western suburbs is prominent and visible. As the major population center of the metropolitan area, the core city's interests and those of the western suburbs are different and competing, overshadowing those of the small towns, suburbs, and counties east of Des Moines. Des Moines city and the western suburbs have a propensity to dominate the other partners, which is why the elaborate policy-decision procedures illustrated in appendix B have been put into place. Enhanced Data in Indiana is composed of ten state agencies and several NGO and external representatives, but discussants referred to the power of two state program heads who exerted more control over the network processes than even the state agency that generates around 90 percent of its funds. This power within Enhanced Data was generally identified as benign—it is normally employed to advance the multiple interests of accessIndiana—but unequal power nevertheless advances the interests of the powerful agencies. Raw power in many forms, such as withholding agreement, withholding resources, exercising formal objection (veto), or temporary withdrawal from a collaborated result, are decision forces that must be accounted for.

Withholding Resources

While the interdependent nature of most networks implies some form of resource sharing, the other face of action includes resource hoarding, the failure to contribute needed resources to the collaborated enterprise. Withholding of agreement on a plan or policy adjustment on behalf of a given administrator's agency is the most important example with regard to PMN decision making. These held resources in the face of recognized interdependent conditions can also include withholding of contributed time, denial of access to an agency's programs or services, refusal to make financial allocations or contributions, nonsupply of information or technology, or holding back political and organizational support. Some agencies in the Indiana Rural Council and Partnership for Rural Nebraska only provide the most limited of their expertise, personnel, funds, or access to agency services. The best example is that innovative rural development projects are only funded by three agencies, USDA/RD in the respective states and the two state economic development departments. Each time this happens, the remaining representatives of these rural networks have to dig deeper into their own resource pools, try to evoke a change of heart, find new alternative resources, or go without critical support. Holding resources makes reaching collaborated decisions and actions difficult, and in some cases impossible.

Policy Barriers

A final cost of networking for the PMNs is the deleterious effects that arise when participants run up against policy barriers. This cost is particularly acute when a network can find and agree upon a solution. While some networks do exist to approach new solutions to policy problems, or to forge ad hoc adjustments to problems through multiagency solutions (Kickert, Klijn, and Koppenjan 1997), they sometimes hit brick walls. For example, the Indiana 317 Group has encountered a policy barrier to its goal of expanding services for deinstitutionalization beyond the minimum needed to sustain clients outside of institutional settings. The state, along with all other states, is facing the U.S. Supreme Court's *Olmstead* decision, which requires state governments to provide community services for those institutionalized handicapped individuals who are clinically ready and choose to be discharged. The 317 Group is facing a huge obstacle to the facilitation of community services: allowing Medicaid to finance personal assistance as a service out of the state's discretionary Medicaid spending. Such a change would help move many prospective dischargees off waiting lists, out of institutional settings, and into the community. This core change in policy is completely out of the 317 network's hands, or that of any participating agency—including Medicaid or Developmental Disabilities. It would require legislative revision and the governor's support of Indiana's state Medicaid plan, an unlikely prospect since the General Assembly flatlined Medicaid in 2003, in effect reducing spending. The state has proposed a 5 percent increase for 2005, which, with medical inflation well over 10 percent, constitutes a further reduction.

The personal assistance issue is not a particularly unusual example of a barrier to networks' ability to engender policy accommodation. In a different way, rural development policy decisions are not made by networks like Indiana Rural Council and Partnership for Rural Nebraska because state development departments, governors' offices, and state legislatures feel they are state policymakers. More importantly, the bulk of rural development funding comes from a federal agency, the U.S. Department of Agriculture's Rural Development (USDA/RD) programs, which are over twenty in number and amount to nearly $100 million in a rural state like Nebraska. Rural development collaboratives have consequently had their policy roles circumscribed (Radin et al. 1996). These policymaking or adjustment barriers happen most often when key decisions are considered to be external to the PMN's scope of authority, or are considered internal to an agency that cannot effectuate such changes. Therefore, just as the ability to make program changes that amount to policy adjustments can facilitate the work of networks, the inability to break policy barriers can detract from their value-adding ability.

Another commonly identified cost of network involvement is that of turf or organization domain protection from line administrators (Thomas 2003; Bardach 1998). It proved to be rarely if ever articulated as a problem or cost identified by discussants in the field, perhaps because the participant administrators were all in continuing and reasonably successful networks and these concerns may have been worked through. This may also be a problem characteristic of short-lived networks, particularly those that are informal and nonchartered. It is also possible that in order to be successful, administrators in the fourteen networks have learned to work around the serious turf questions. Another reason may be that the relatively narrow agendas that most PMNs engage, even action networks, are not threatening to turf protection. Finally, it is possible that the most strident agency boundary protectors had previously opted out of these networks and have become nonparticipants or nominal members. Whatever the reasons, turf protection was rarely mentioned as a cost or negative force in networking. Nevertheless, because of its existence as a factor in other studies, it should not be written off any research agenda.

ACCOUNTING FOR THE BENEFITS

It is now appropriate to bear the costs in mind and add the benefits or public values that the networks achieve. Examination of this process also allows a preliminary look at some of the conclusions that will be addressed at the end of this study. Seven distinct public value-adding roles for the PMNs will be presented: problem identification and information exchange, identification of extant technologies, adaptation of technologies, improving knowledge infrastructures, mutual capacity building, reciprocal strategies and programming, and joint policymaking/programming. As a lead-in to these conclusions, the seven benefits or public value categories are broken into a series of major subphases, twenty-one in all, that depict just what it is that the fourteen PMNs do in order to add value. These subcategories need no explanation, as they have been identified previously.

Table 8.5 provides a summary of the seven network benefits, broken into the twenty-one tasks and ordered by the four network types. The table represents the researchers' second-order coding of the same material that was examined in tables 8.3 and 8.4 on network process and outcome values added, combined with responses to an initial question during the second round of discussions: "The (name of network) appears to be a collaborative network that is primarily involved in [information exchange/partner capacity building/ establishing interactive strategies or setting problem solution approaches/setting joint policies or establishing linked procedures]. Can you describe what you consider to be the major ways that the network/body brings the various organizations together to [restate the purpose of the network]?" The responses were varied and it thus became useful to break down the benefits into the twenty-one categories as coded. The reader will recall that the question was asked after the networks were classified. Nevertheless, discussants provided a wide range of information that identified various phases of their activity. Subsequent coding allowed for a useful snapshot of network benefits.

The check marks in table 8.5 identify that a network engaged in a particular value-adding activity; its extent or its degree of success is not measured here. Narrative information throughout the text and particularly in chapters 4 and 5 provide considerable light on this subject. Nevertheless, table 8.5 demonstrates that networks can be efficacious information-technology-knowledge-capacity and program/policy actors that cross agencies' boundaries. However, the extent to which this is accomplished is highly dependent on type.

The first conclusion is that to be an information or development network, activities are precluded at the strategy and decision end (6 and 7), but many activities on convening, issue discussing, solution identification, and those related to technology and KM are within their reach. Second, developmental networks add the important public value of capacity enhancement (5), which in

TABLE 8.5   A Summary of Network Public Values

Network [Type]	1. Problem Identification/ Information Exchange				2. Identify Extant Technologies			3. Adaptation of Technology			4. Implement Knowledge Infrastructure		
	Convene Stake-holders	Issue Discussion	Reveal Agency Actions	Identify Possible Solutions	From Other Settings	Venues for Knowledge Exchange	Technical Task force/ Committee	Locate Existing Technology	Interactively Create Adaptation	Legal, Financial Adjustment	ICT Inside	Established KM Processes	ICT Outside
Darby [I]	✓	✓	✓	✓	✓	✓					✓		✓
Indiana Economic Devel. [I]	✓	✓	✓	✓	✓	✓	✓	✓			✓	✓	✓
Lower Platte [I]	✓	✓	✓	✓	✓	✓					✓	✓	✓
Iowa Enterprise [D]	✓	✓	✓	✓	✓	✓	✓	✓			✓	✓	✓
Indiana Rural Council [D]	✓	✓	✓	✓	✓	✓	✓	✓			✓	✓	✓
Partnership for Rural Nebraska [D]	✓	✓	✓	✓	✓	✓	✓	✓			✓	✓	✓
Iowa Geographic [O]	✓	✓	✓	✓	✓	✓	✓	✓	✓	✓	✓	✓	✓
Small Communities [O]	✓	✓	✓	✓	✓	✓	✓	✓	✓	✓	✓	✓	✓
USDA/Nebraska [O]	✓	✓	✓	✓	✓	✓		✓	✓	✓	✓	✓	✓
317 Group [O]	✓	✓	✓	✓	✓	✓	✓	✓	✓	✓	✓	✓	
Iowa Communications [A]	✓		✓	✓	✓	✓	✓	✓	✓	✓	✓	✓	✓
Enhanced Data [A]	✓	✓	✓	✓	✓	✓	✓	✓	✓	✓	✓	✓	
Kentuckiana Agency [A]	✓	✓	✓	✓	✓	✓	✓	✓	✓	✓	✓	✓	✓
Des Moines Metro [A]	✓		✓	✓	✓	✓		✓	✓	✓	✓	✓	✓

TABLE 8.5 (continued)

Network [Type]	5. Capacity Building			6. Reciprocal Programming/ Joint Strategy			7. Joint Policymaking		
	Outreach	Partner Education Individual	Enhance Agency Capabilities	Knowledge-Driven Agreement	Negotiated Solutions	Regularized Interagency Transactions	Knowledge-Driven Decisions	Consensus-Oriented Decision Process	Regularized Agency Transactions
Darby [I]		√							
Indiana Economic Development [I]									
Lower Platte [I]	√								
Iowa Enterprise [D]	√	√	√						
Indiana Rural Council [D]		√	√						
Partnership for Rural Nebraska [D]	√	√	√						
Iowa Geographic [O]	√	√	√	√	√				
Small Communities [O]	√		√	√	√	√			
USDA/Nebraska [O]				√	√	√			
317 Group [O]	√	√	√	√	√	√			
Iowa Communications [A]				√	√	√	√	√	√
Enhanced Data [A]	√			√	√	√	√	√	√
Kentuckiana Agency [A]		√	√			√	√	√	√
Des Moines Metro [A]	√	√	√	√	√	√	√	√	√

many ways adds on to the other activities, particularly their KM infrastructure (4) activities. Third, the outreach and action networks cumulatively build on activity sets 1–5, but extend themselves further into policy or program domains, either informally (6) or formally (7), depending on the type of network. It means that exchange, capacity development, and KM ordinarily precede agreement to these networks. This makes the outreach and action networks the closest to the prior literature's definitions of networks, although their KM and capacity activities can be underestimated because they make strategy and decisions. Fourth, one should not underestimate the long-term or cumulative impact of activity sets 1–5. Even though they do not directly lead to agreements or solutions, they contribute valuable collaborative dialogue through collective venues, often impacting solutions down the line. Their continuation as PMNs over long periods of time indicates that some form of value must be evident, otherwise busy agency managers would eschew network commitments and work through other collaborative means.

It is tempting to provide a summary score for each PMN, but that would clearly add false quantification to a qualitative study. The fourteen PMNs are not being ranked from most to least valued, their differences are being explained. The measure of a highly valued information network would seem to be how well they perform in issue ranges 1–2, and perhaps 4, whereas the action networks would have to be analyzed from 1–7. Such assessment, however important, is beyond the scope of this study. A clear conclusion is that within the scope and limitations of each of the four types of networks, most are highly engaged in a variety of category-relevant collaborative activities that add public value according to their missions.

CONCLUSION

One study discussant, a state government department head, concluded that "it's all about bringing the people in the 'back of the room' to the front, who have skill, information, and other things it takes to come to the front and focus on the mission of rural development. Then we can produce a process and product that is of utility." Networks do play important and varied roles in creating public value if they are understood for what they do rather than for a set of abstract functions externally ascribed. Because the current research studies what the public managers themselves tell us about what they accomplish and what it means, multiple dimensions of value adding appear possible. Contemporary networks face rapidly paced social change, tackle difficult problems with no neat technical solutions (Agranoff and McGuire 2001a), and deal with wicked problems (O'Toole 1997). For most of the problems that emerged in the twentieth century a bureaucratic organization was ideal, because problems were easily defined, goals were clear, and objectives were measurable. Networks are better suited to tackle more challenging problems since they have more venues of decision and more stakeholders. "Multiple parties means multiple alternatives to suggest and consider, more information available for all to use, and a decision system that is less bound by the frailties of individual thinking" (Agranoff and McGuire 2001a, 321). The key is synergy, which rides on the stimulation of new alternatives through the commitment and interaction of the participants. If successful, networks can contribute to public performance for the administrator, his/her organization, the public process of collaboration, and for achieving collaborated results.

When the considerable costs identified can be overcome, all of these actions add value and contribute to public performance in some way. All of the PMNs face one or more of these identified costs as they face different situations at different times, but it can be well worth the effort to overcome these costs in order to achieve the values that these supraorganizational bodies aspire to, as they extend out from the traditional agencies of government and NGOs.

CHAPTER NINE

· · · · · · · · · · · ·

NETWORKS AT THE BOUNDARIES
OF THE STATE

Our work at Indiana Economic Development is highly dependent on the [state government] administration of the time, particularly the governor's office. It is their economic development agenda that determines a great deal of our work. We are successful at bringing disparate and even conflicting parties to the table, and we can produce research, even impact the agenda, but after that it is really up to the agencies. Of course, they feel happy that we are weak or nonexistent policymakers but it no doubt explains a lot about our survival.

DOES THE EMPLOYMENT of public interorganizational networks contribute to changing the boundaries of the state? This question is often raised as a central issue in an era when traditional organizational structures are flexible and permeable. Do PMNs change the public role of government agencies as they move aspects of program decision, design, and implementation laterally, through a variety of nongovernmental agencies and organizations? Some have suggested that a hollowing out of the state has emerged through such means as contracting out or other forms of nongovernmentalization (Milward, Provan, and Else 1993; Rhodes 1997), as public agencies collaborate with the NGO sector. Others have suggested that this lateral erosion of the state's functions adds to the additional effects of internationalization and decentralization, which potentially weakens the core state on all three fronts (Keating 1999). On the other hand, it could be possible that, while present and meaningful, these effects are less threatening to government than assumed, as the opening quote suggests. These are questions of prime importance in the era of the network.

Frederickson suggests that "the most important feature of contemporary public administration is the declining relationship between jurisdiction and public management" (1999, 202). Jurisdictions of all types and levels are supposedly losing their borders due to changes in telecommunications and the concept of space, along with disarticulation of the state—its incapacity to deal with complex problems. This has led to a redefinition of what is public, moving away from government to a host of institutions and organizations that are public serving (Bozeman 1987; Frederickson 1997). These forces have changed the nature of public administration itself, and to some degree affected the democratic principle of the relationship between the public's agents and the people who are governed. In effect, it is argued that networks contribute to a loss of public agency accountability. A central issue that can be examined through the lens of the PMN is that of a changing public administration under the emergent forces of network governance in the intergovernmental sphere.

This chapter explores how networks fit into and operate within the boundaries of government. We want to see empirically how PMNs fit into the scheme of government and their contribution to governance, as identified in chapter 1. The discussion begins with the persistent question of whether collaborative bodies like networks contribute to a loss of accountability. Exploration of how networks fit into the scheme of the collaborating or conductive public agency is taken up. The boundaries of the PMNs are focused on exploring how they interact over questions of policy and programs vis-à-vis public agencies. The study then examines specific boundary questions from the perspectives of their participants: the agency's quest for control, modes of operational decisions, interests of line managers, interests of program specialists, and institutional and legal domains. Potential dimensions of network success and failure in altering agency roles and powers are discussed. The concluding section reinforces the initially suggested idea that the actual impact of networks is limited. Although they may influence and affect public decisions, networks have limited ability to diminish public agency boundaries.

ACCOUNTABILITY AND NETWORKS

Unfortunately this analysis cannot directly examine the question on loss of accountability just introduced. When agencies and organizations are involved in networks like PMNs, they are said to fall somewhere between the higher authority control mechanisms of the bureaucratic organization and the representative democracy principles of delegate responsibility (Rohr 1989). These issues appear to be magnified for complex interactive settings, where multiple parties operate with limited authority and even less direct contact with top appointed executives or legislative oversight (Agranoff and McGuire 2001a). There is the possibility of some levels of "leakage of authority" in collaborative settings (Bardach and Lesser 1996, 198).

The issue of accountability when one considers networks appears to be different than many of the contractual and intergovernmental relationships depicted in the hollow-state argument, or where the boundaries are permeable because of shared operation and implementation. Despite myriad applications of principal-agent theory to contractual and extrajurisdictional activity like grants and regulatory programming, principal-support no doubt oversimplifies the multiple interests involved in policy development and program implementation, where it is nearly impossible to establish who are the principals and who are the agents. In this regard, determining principals and agents in the Indiana 317 program, the extensive restoration efforts on the Lower Platte in Nebraska, or how state and local governments employ GIS in Iowa could be meaningless. As O'Toole's depiction of networks indicates, "They do not have the formal wherewithal to compel compliance with such cooperative undertaking" (1997, 445).

Additionally, the issue of accountability would appear to be miscast in networks when there is no exigent authority to steer the activities of the network into harmony with elected officials. Agranoff and McGuire (2001b) conclude that under these conditions it may well be that the public sector's responsibility for affecting the public interest is, at best, somewhat compromised and modestly limited by the use of networks. In the absence of legally based authority, everyone appears to be somewhat in charge, thus everyone is somewhat responsible; all network participants appear to be accountable for the scope of the network's actions, but none is absolutely responsible (Weiner 1990). More important, given the limited legally constituted scope of network democratic responsibility found in this study, expectations of accountability appear irrelevant. As has been demonstrated throughout this volume, the interaction between public agency program administrators, program specialists, and NGO officials and administrators, including private interest groups, renders the making of public policy difficult or, for many networks, impossible.

Accountability in networks and other collaborative undertakings takes on a different cast. In its broadest performance-oriented sense, it is more complicated in a postbureaucratic world. As previously indicated, Behn suggests, "the one-bill, one-policy, one-organization, one-accountability holdee principle doesn't work for performance" because most programs involve collaborative undertakings (2001, 72). In addition, accountability relationships in multiorganizational (intergovernmental) networks are clearly different from those that involve two-party principal agent models in contracting (Waterman and Meier 1998) or in intergovernmental program implementation (Chubb 1985).

GOVERNMENT, GOVERNANCE, AND NETWORKS

A new overlay of governance is now superimposed on intergovernmental relations and management, as previously identified in chapter 2. There it was suggested that the welfare state and federal programming have brought on increased intergovernmentalization of policies and programs, and the corresponding need to manage across government jurisdictional boundaries (Agranoff 1986, 1990, 2001). Government refers to the formal institutions or bodies that establish the constitutional order, defend the territory, raise and distribute revenue, establish the laws, and regulate the territorial organization of the state. On the other hand, governance represents governments' attempts to guide, steer, control, or manage the wide range of new nongovernmental actors in civil society, and to identify problems, exchange information, and sometimes jointly formulate and implement policies and programs in the economy (Hirst 2000). This governance phenomenon occurs through many vehicles, one of them being a network of actors.

It has also been indicated that the growing complexity posed by governance means that networks are well suited to the information society. It was demonstrated in chapter 7 that they have the potential for enhanced knowledge creation and adaptation through the combined efforts of officials and leaders, public and private (Agranoff and McGuire 2001a). Networks exist at all levels of government and do not necessarily supplant traditional public functions, but become important elements of a community of public operations. As the study indicates, governance networks differ from corporatist models in many ways. The primary differences lie in the fact that a variety of interests, sometimes differing, are brought to the collaborative structure; and that government is not petitioned by a set of closed interests for reward, protection, or dispute settlement, but the various interests are said to investigate, design, and sometimes agree on direction *with* government (Rhodes 1997).

MANAGING AT THE BOUNDARIES

The PMNs may affect the boundaries of the state in the sense that its operating agencies and organizations exchange, plan, and program with the state. Government capacities or their strategic and policy operating cores may be adjusted. Boundary questions, then, must be examined against the role of participating agencies. In chapters 1 and 2 we maintained that network activity does not necessarily replace the need for hierarchy/organization, but emerges as an overlay for the managers who work within the organizations. It was further stated that collaborative activity is no longer some add-on, but part of the job itself. This would include PMN activity. In order to understand the place of PMN activity in relation to both hierarchy and other, nonorganized network collaborative activity, the boundaries of the networks under investigation require definition.

It is also important to note that empirically this section represents second-order conclusions grounded in the data; they are not the result of direct questions that asked administrators to weigh the time allocated to each activity or formally define their boundaries. They result from responses to questions relating to those differences between network and organization management discussed in chapter 6. As administrators and organization executives reflected on these differences, they also provided important information on the range of collaborative activities that they engage in. This range helps us to understand the place of PMNs within the scope of administrators' internal and external activities.

The range of internal/collaborative activities is diagrammatically represented in figure 9.1. This hypothetical figure attempts to explain the work of the agency in both its internal and external relations. It is designed to depict what was repeatedly relayed by discussants, that the network under study was just one of a number of networks they might be involved in, and that network involvement was just one part of collaborative management. The agency's hierarchical or core operations include its legal authority and hierarchical operations, POSDCORB or standard operations, its mission-pursuit operations, its resource inputs-outputs, and so on. Connected to this operating core are both legal- or statutory-connected relations and nonlegal collaborative relations. Among the former, represented by solid squares/rectangles, are grant, procurement, contract, and other legal ties to other governments and NGOs, formal interagency agreements with lateral agencies, direct agreement/contracts with NGOs, and legally chartered networks. The dotted circles that overlap the core agencies represent less-formal but real collaborative activity, including lateral relations with other agencies at one's level of government, connections with NGOs, transactional coordination with other governments of an informal nature, and involvement in one or more patterned networks that are either chartered (some of which have legal standing) or nonchartered. Clearly all of these noncore activities make the hypothetical agency conductive.

Figure 9.1a puts the PMNs under study in the larger context of different types of collaborative relations, and figure 9.1b juxtaposes them with the core operations of the agency. In the real world most collaborative transactions almost always cut to the core of the operations of an agency, a sort of "ab" or "ba" rather than "a" or "b." Nevertheless, one must bear in mind that many of the operations of the public agency remain "a" only because of the fact that, except for completely hollowed-out agencies, networks add to but do not replace the work of the government organization. Beyond the "a"-only activities, one will notice that network activity a.b.5 constitutes only one of several other lateral agency relationships: a.b.1, contracts and other connections with NGOs; a.b.2, interagency agreements and connections within the same government; a.b.3, informal contacts and coordination with other governments; and a.b.4, grants, contracts, or agreements with other governments. Thus the network stands as one of at least five types of lateral relationships. Frequency

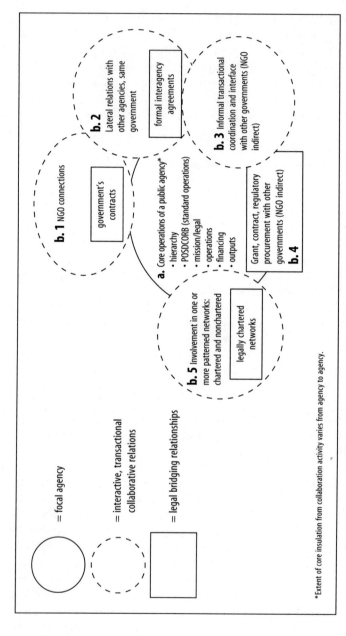

b. 1 NGO connections

government's contracts

b. 2 Lateral relations with other agencies, same government

formal interagency agreements

b. 3 Informal transactional coordination and interface with other governments (NGO indirect)

a. Core operations of a public agency*
- hierarchy
- POSDCORB (standard operations)
- mission/legal
- operations
- financing
- outputs

Grant, contract, regulatory procurement with other governments (NGO indirect) **b. 4**

b. 5 Involvement in one or more patterned networks: chartered and nonchartered

legally chartered networks

○ = focal agency

◌ = interactive, transactional collaborative relations

▭ = legal bridging relationships

*Extent of core insulation from collaboration activity varies from agency to agency.

FIGURE 9.1 Core and Lateral Relations in a Hypothetical Conductive Public Agency

of interaction between the agency and the five types is highly situational and perhaps impossible to gauge, but a number of the federal and state officials who were discussants for this study placed network involvement (a.b.5) somewhere down the list, particularly in comparison to the frequency of their work in intergovernmental grants/regulations (a.b.4), and government contracts (a.b.1) with NGOs.

The collaborative activities depicted here in a conductive public agency are complementary to the core activities of the agency. For example, the Indiana Family and Social Services Administration (FSSA) is directly responsible for administering the 317 program, particularly its state-funded component. Its DDARS division has statutory authority for organizing, staffing, budget execution, and other activities that relate to community services. The office of Medicaid finances the major federal-state part of that program. This is core or internal work for both agencies. However, 317 is carried out through NGOs by purchase care, contract, and, in some cases, grants. This is collaborative work. The two overlap in practice because so much of 317 is external to the public agency now that dollars flow to the community rather than to state institutions. FSSA maintains certain core legal, fiscal, contract, oversight, and evaluation responsibility. Its strategic operations are formulated and influenced by the 317 Group, even though the agency carries out the core program. The public agency interacts and shares data with the 317 Group, and the PMN works out potential strategies that are negotiated with the state. But the state—DDARS/FSSA—retains most of its operation as a core agency. As a result, figure 9.1 is meant to depict a public agency like FSSA/Medicaid that is involved in networks and collaborative activity as a less-hierarchical, conductive organization with an operating core that increasingly connects and coordinates through formal and informal channels in regular and patterned ways.

This conductive organization phenomenon is applied in real form in figure 9.2, where the previous figure is concretely applied to one illustrative network. On the surface it is the most bureaucratic of our fourteen PMNs, the USDA/Nebraska core and collaborative operations within Nebraska. One program in one state branch of a huge federal agency, USDA/Nebraska internally operates some twenty financing programs for individuals, communities, NGOs, and others. Its core operations (a) are by definition simultaneously statutory/regulatory-driven, routine-oriented application processing, and collaborative with its clients, but it also reaches out to partners, invoking state agencies (b.3), other federal agencies (b.2), local governments (b.4), and state associations and other NGOs (b.1). Its reach involves contractual loans, informal cooperation, blueprinted financing strategies, and involvement with a set of networks, including Partnership for Rural Nebraska. USDA thus is conductive with its operating core and sets of collaborative relationships. As it operates, USDA/Nebraska is a quintessential conductive public organization.

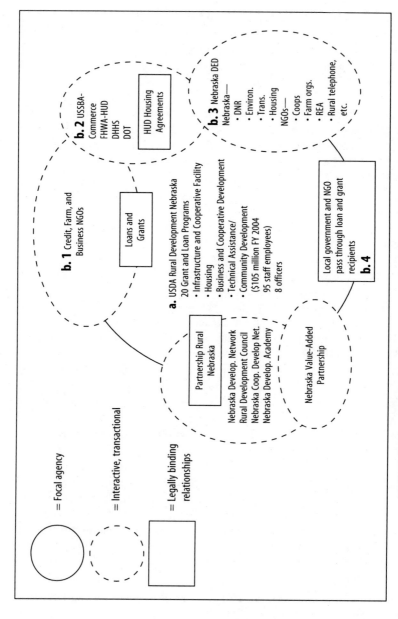

FIGURE 9.2   USDA/Nebraska as a Conductive Public Organization

The conductive agency, first introduced in chapter 6, should be thought of as a structure that remains a formal hierarchy but operates collaboratively to an increasing extent. The federal, state, and local public managers who participated in this study maintained that their agencies remained mission-driven, with many of the standard procedures, and with many or most of the hierarchical structural trappings. These remain in force for department employees, with added collaborative pressures as managers engage laterally. The collaborative linkages do not necessarily supersede the internal processes, nor are they necessarily new to the age of the network; they are simply more numerous and increasingly part of the manager's core activities.

To the agency that operates with interlocutors, the collaborative activities reach to the core on a regular basis. As in the 317 example, through the purchase of service, contracting, grants, regulatory oversight, program review, audit, and assessment, as well as facilitating cooperative programs, the manager spends a great deal of time engaging links in order to advance the core or mission-driven aspect of the agency. Whereas at one time only a few staff from an agency had liaison or official boundary-spanning roles, now many—in some agencies most—officials who do the basic work are engaged in collaborative activities.

It is important to note that transactional activity is also multidimensional. Few managers have the luxury of working only within the network, or on any other single lateral activity. Working in one of our PMNs constitutes one form of collaborative public management in one network. As figures 9.1 and 9.2 suggest, managers in agencies work both formally and informally in and out of networks, with other agencies in one's government, with NGOs, and intergovernmentally. Lateral connections come in many forms, as managers now have many options available to span their boundaries with the world of NGOs becoming more interdependent with government and governments themselves becoming highly intergovernmentalized.

Networks like the PMNs need to be put into perspective. They should be regarded along with the other forms of collaboration as entities working with agencies and helping them to do their work. The public agency remains at the core of the public program, where a considerable amount of public work remains. Rules, hierarchy, budgets, authorizations, audits, and reviews remain, as do the increasingly important collaborative tasks related to negotiating, coordinating, linking, adjusting, and joint problem solving. The public administrator in the public agency of today works within the core and at its margins.

NETWORK BOUNDARIES: PARTNERS' PERSPECTIVES

Do network activists feel that they are losing something at their agency's borders? Before the analysis moves into a network-by-network delineation, participants' general perceptions about this issue provide essential perspective. After they are asked a focused set of discussion questions relating to network impact on agency decisions/operations, agency commitment to network action, and who makes the most important policy decisions, PMN participants were asked: "Do you think networks like (name of PMN) change the legal, policy, or program roles that governments play? That is, do they push jurisdictional boundaries away from government to the nongovernmental sector or to other decision makers?" A selection of responses by each PMN is displayed in table 9.1. Observations are again organized by network type and a pooled response summary judgment of a plus (+) or minus (–) is attached to each network, indicating whether the statement supports pushing away the boundaries of the state (plus), or does not affect the boundaries (minus). The table demonstrates the highly conditional nature of networks and the role of government agencies.

For two of the three information networks, the indirect or influencing role comes out clearly, but so do real limitations posed by their inability to become involved in meaningful decisions. For the third network, Lower Platte, the jurisdictional boundaries are considered just too strong to be altered. Clearly these three networks experience the limitations posed by their missions as exchange vehicles.

Development networks also display mixed evidence. Iowa Enterprise and Indiana Rural Council are able to indirectly affect government boundaries by their knowledge-development activities, but with the reality of agency mission and turf the question of limits is also real, thus the +/– rating. For Partnership for Rural Nebraska it is clearly positive in the sense that consensus and mutually derived knowledge influence agencies. This process follows for Iowa Geographic as well, but a notable number of participants noted the real limitation that, unlike similar councils in other states, they were not able to certify GIS credentials or set operational standards. One can say that these networks feel that they do push the boundaries somewhat.

Outreach network participants clearly feel that they influence the boundaries of the state. Indeed, this group proved to be the most clear-cut in this regard. This follows naturally, since the agency program managers are sitting with one another, casting in and casting out possibilities for action over which they have control. Their deliberations constitute collective seats at a collaborative table where action may not be direct, but directly influenced. These network partners are not the final decision makers, but their blueprints are the next best thing to policy; thus they see themselves as very close to actually changing the boundaries. In this way these networks work closely with the real policy and program adjustments identified in the network literature.

(text continues on page 204)

TABLE 9.1 Boundaries of the State: Reactions of Network Participants

Network	Type	Positive/Negative	Representative Comments
Darby	I	+/−	• Our role is indirect at best, we take no action that would affect government • We can influence jurisdiction action, e.g., on land use • Only our partners can act; Darby can call attention • Through pressure and task groups that move issues along
Indiana Economic Development	I	+/−	• Strong influence on state economic development • To some extent; e.g., biocross roads, agriculture initiatives on the state agenda • The Council can woo people; as a nonstate agency can take hard positions • Only over a period of time, i.e., the water that drips has some effect • To the extent that the Council is one of many, many voices that does not make policy decisions
Lower Platte	I	−	• The districts and agencies make the decisions; the Alliance collects the data • To the extent that they can get policymakers to think outside the box • I don't think so; fear of the locals too great • Only in the sense of being more aware of problems

continued

TABLE 9.1 (continued)

Network	Type	Positive/Negative	Representative Comments
Iowa Enterprise	D	+/–	• We mostly advise and educate; have not even advocated policy • Can change public priorities, but not in a legal sense • They can in terms of raising issues, identifying values, but cannot point to any policy
Indiana Rural Council	D	+/–	• Don't think so; clarify issues but this agency has statutory mandates, guidelines, etc. • The Council likes to think it is doing that, but agency mandates seem to push us out • No, the five sectors can influence policy, the agencies make them • It has in some cases, in the sense we try to push the boundaries in Washington, Indianapolis • Have not seen that happen; we respect others' identities and roles
Partnership for Rural Nebraska	D	+	• Once you realize you are no longer the expert on everything, together we can shape the boundaries • In the sense that melded voices have some influence
Iowa Geographic	D	–	• They have the potential; if leaders take on the issues and get agencies to change direction • Partnership for Rural Nebraska and other networks help to reach beyond the standard operating procedures and take broader perspectives

			• Only in the sense we create more useful information by breaking down the walls, avoiding turf, and thinking outside of normal operations
			• Iowa Geographic really could do that if it set standards and policies but we don't; we expend software and educate people
			• Don't, but we could if we got legislative support to set GIS standards, regulate as some other state councils have
			• Not now, but would if the council was a policy-implementing body
Small Communities	O	+	• Instinctively yes, by filling the void of small community assistance where no one else is willing to step in
			• Small Communities helps government define its roles
			• In an informal way we are influential and our boundaries do expand in that way
			• They can as our partners, as we work program-to-program we have a policy influence of sorts
USDA/Nebraska	O	+	• Our program must work with other partners; we impact one another
			• We always deal at the boundaries; what has changed is that with (networks) working together has brought out into the open more
			• Yes, in the sense that collaboration is enhanced and the ultimate decision makers have more knowledge
317 Group	O	+	• Indeed, 317 has given the developmental disability advocates a seat at the policy table
			• Definitely, shifting some power to places outside of government, mostly because we were able to reach agreement

continued

TABLE 9.1 (continued)

Network	Type	Positive/Negative	Representative Comments
317 Group			• Yes, because the group became involved in everything from legislative proposals to rules and guidelines • The adjustment and agreement process led to success—for 317 the boundaries are permeable
Enhanced Data	A	+/−	• Within its restricted scope of rules and regulations • In the sense that it is still my (agency) decision but I care about what they think • Only within legislatively established boundaries • We negotiate with the agencies so much I don't think we affect their boundaries • Has the capacity to do that but hasn't really
Iowa Communications	A	+/−	• Because of the interaction we think differently; has led to code changes • In the sense that we are in constant interaction with certified users • As one of the largest users, the Iowa Communications policy definitely impacts our programs and personnel • There are real limits to this because of the Iowa Communications commission and legislative controls

Kentuckiana Agency	A	+/−

- In the sense of setting priorities and influencing program directions
- We work within the rules; people protect their boundaries
- They do, pushing government in directions that the collective body decides on, chipping away at affecting decisions
- Public involvement means that we are the influenced
- Not in the sense that jurisdictions are too important and powerful in the U.S.

Des Moines Metro	A	+/−

- MPO constrained by federal rules and tasks
- Our plans and priorities all come out of the local governments; MPO can temper their decisions
- Yes, look at land use for example, the MPO as a group affects these issues greatly
- No, the Policy Committee is the sum of its parts too often
- Not this MPO—others do—but we respect jurisdiction interests too much
- Probably true, this department has been changed a great deal, for example on the location of interstate interchanges to satisfy business interests

Why, then, the relatively mixed pattern of the action networks? It clearly appears to be a product of their limited decision scope and their tendency toward pleasing partners and reaching consensus. Enhanced Data feels that they do change agency policy, but only after extended discussions with their state agencies. Moreover, their scope of activity is narrowly proscribed to setting portal use rates and portal policies. In the larger scheme of things, these are not important functional responsibilities. In the case of Iowa Communications, the constant services and programming give and take does push into the agencies' domain a bit, but as a data and broadcast carrier these support activities are hardly at the core of user-agency operations. Its biggest government user, the Department of Education and K–12 schools, reports that they feel virtually no impact on their core educational responsibilities. Regarding the two MPOs, the mixed response comes from the fact that federal rules and regulations, coupled with all-important jurisdictional interests, make it difficult to push federal, state, and local domains in any significant way. On the other hand, as it selects projects for funding and formulates long-range plans the MPO can try to forge metropolitan perspectives and create secondary impacts like land use. This pushes back the boundaries of participating local governments somewhat. In sum, despite their legal powers, the partners in action networks report being more circumscribed than the partners in outreach networks. In general, the administrators active in the PMNs do not see their activity leading to significant pushing back of government's boundaries. They see influences and new mind sets, vehicles for impacting through enhanced knowledge, and feel their programs are affected to a great extent by collective interagency agreement.

THE PMN AND THE AGENCY BOUNDARY

Where does the agency leave off and the network's role begin? That is an important question to consider with regard to relative boundaries, now that the PMNs have been put into the scheme of the public agency's conductive activities. It is important to assess how each one's domain compares with that of the agencies that combine to form the network. The literature states that network responsibility is weak compared to that of the agencies; an entire scheme of lateral relations was hypothetically mapped out, and actually mapped out for one agency. In the many lateral relationships, the collaborative connection is legal and contractual. The possibility of a principal-agent is possible in these situations, but it has been argued that such connections rarely exist for networks. The ties identified in chapter 6—developed trust, agreed purpose, technical dependency—contribute in lieu of a contractual relationship. There is, however, some line between agency and network that may be established, as an equivalent to the contractual or principal-agent relationship.

This issue of boundaries varies considerably by the type of network, ranging from an indirect or nonexistent impact on agency activity, to very direct but negotiated agreement. As a first step toward assessing relative domain, table 9.2 explores the domain of agency versus network in terms of program impact. It displays four domain dimensions of network/agency boundaries: (1) the extent of PMN policy/program influence, (2) the extent of the domain of partner agencies/organizations, (3) the scope, if any, of PMN partner policy/program involvement, and (4) agency/organization recourse if the network makes a decision contrary to an agency's interests. The entries in this table represent blended, second-order level responses, based on first-order coding of each discussant's responses, first case-by-case and then combined by case. The coding was in response to a question regarding agency boundaries versus network boundaries: "When it comes to (name of the PMN) and its agencies, who makes the most important policy decisions?" Because there is great variance by type, each dimension will be analyzed by PMN category.

The third column in table 9.2 looks at the extent of the PMN's direct involvement in questions of policy and/or program. It is very clear that the informational and developmental networks have virtually no direct involvement in these matters. The information networks' role is to provide an exchange of research and ideas; they do not become involved in policy/program in a direct way. The same is true for developmental networks, although they do become involved in the voluntary education and training that is often adapted by partner agencies.

This is not the case for the other two types of networks. Outreach networks have important indirect policy/program involvement through their strategic orchestration, as well as through financing and assistance of local governments, and/or client programming. For example, part of the 317 Group's blueprinting role is more direct, since they have very close influence over implementing the 317 law. All four action networks play direct roles in policy and programming, although in all four cases it is also a defined or limited role: for Iowa Communications, handling rate changes and general operation of a telecommunications conduit for public agency business that is outside of Iowa Communications control; for Enhanced Data a role that is even more limited to agency-proposed accessIndiana use standards and rates; and for the two MPOs, overseeing allocation of some federal transportation funding, and planning on the metro-level only, which leaves the remainder of transportation financing, planning, and programming to local jurisdictions. Thus the extent of direct involvement varies by type from none to some; for the latter the overall picture suggests a somewhat narrow net policy involvement.

TABLE 9.2 Boundaries of PMN and Agency Authority

PMN	Type	Extent of Direct Network Policy/Program Involvement	Partner Agency/Organization Domain	Scope of PMN Partner Policy/Program Influence	Agency/Organization Recourse
Darby	I	None—exclusive research information	Complete	Indirect	Nonaction/none needed; complete agency program control
Indiana Economic Development	I	None—Plans and studies have no implied power	Complete	Indirect	Nonaction; complete agency program control
Lower Platte	I	None—exclusive research, information	Complete	Indirect	Nonaction; complete agency program control
Iowa Enterprise	D	None—Research development of capabilities	Complete	Mostly indirect, occasional	Nonaction
Indiana Rural Council	D	None—Research and organization capabilities	Complete (except small grants)	Mostly indirect, occasional	Mostly nonaction/little to none needed
Partnership for Rural Nebraska	D	None—Information and education	Complete	Mostly indirect, occasional	Mostly nonaction
Iowa Geographic	D	None—Education, research, and systems development	Virtually complete (except joint software)	Mostly indirect, occasional	Mostly nonaction
Small Communities	O	Indirect through strategic blueprinting	Officially complete, operationally interactively permeable	Indirect influence but regular	Action based on tacit agreement, or nonaction

USDA/Nebraska	O	Indirect through strategic blueprinting	Officially complete, operationally inter-actively permeable	Indirect influence but regular	Action based on tacit agreement, or nonaction
317 Group	O	Indirect through strategic blueprinting; direct by 317 Law	Officially complete, operationally inter-actively permeable	Influence indirect for those outside of government; direct for agency people	Action based on agreement or non-action
Iowa Communications	A	Direct by statute and administrative code	Shared with agency clients in the public sector	Complete over operation of network; rest shared or interactive	Control over program content, audience, and modes of delivery
Enhanced Data	A	Legal power over rates and operation of access-Indiana	All other matters relating to agency operation	Limited by statute to enumerated responsibilities	Agencies informally negotiate and adjust until consensus is reached
Kentuckiana Agency	A	Metropolitan-level plans and programs under federal law and IG agreement	All other matters of jurisdiction transportation, transit, and infrastructure	Limited to long-range plan and transportation improvement federal funds	Jurisdictions are free to self-finance any program not in long-range plan/TIP; participation in Technical and Policy Committees
Des Moines Metro	A	Metropolitan-level plans and programs under federal law and IG agreement	All other matters of jurisdiction transportation, transit, and infrastructure	Limited to long-range plan and TIP federal funds	Jurisdictions are free to self-finance any program not in long-range plan/TIP; participation in Technical and Policy Committees

This raises the other side of the question, how extensive is the agency's domain vis-à-vis the PMN? Again, this varies from complete to quite extensive. As one might expect from a quick reading of column 4 of table 9.2, it varies by type. With two minor exceptions, the policy/program domain of the home agency/organization is complete with regard to informational and developmental networks. The only difference is that Indiana Rural Council has domain, through two spin-off committees, over awarding and implementing two small grant programs, and Iowa Geographic has some joint domain with agencies over some of the GIS software it has collaboratively produced.

The outreach networks are different in that legally or officially they have no domain, but operationally and interactively they are able to permeate agency policy/program domains, which they regularly do. Small Communities, for example, cannot compel an agency to cooperate, but its discussion process normally leads to high levels of agency agreement in response to their interactive discourses. The same is true of the other outreach networks. Agencies involved in the four action networks all share some policy/program domain with their agencies, but in each case there are real limits: Iowa Communications' agencies control all nontransmission concerns; in Enhanced Data the agencies control all matters except rate and state web usage decisions; and the MPOs control all nonmetro transportation projects. In the broader scheme of issues, when it comes to network involvement the agencies generally retain all or huge measures of policy or program domain in these PMNs.

This does not mean that the networks do not influence policy or program. A substantial number of discussants made a distinction between direct policy involvement and encroachment on agency domain, and that of the PMN's indirect influence on program or policy. This dimension was made clear by most discussants. The fifth column of table 9.2 presents an overall assessment of PMN program/policy influence. The three informational networks do have some indirect influence in that they either produce or exchange studies that agencies can and do use to make program modifications. Indiana Economic Development, for example, has put issues like high-tech manufacturing and broadband communication on the agenda of Indiana's Department of Commerce.

The developmental networks also have indirect influence on policy or program, and on when an educational program or research effect leads to an agency's program change. Iowa Geographic, for example, has indirectly influenced the adoption of GIS planning technology through the many local governments that have decided to adopt it. Indiana Rural Council's work in rural housing has led to program changes adopted by the Indiana Housing Finance Authority. Partnership for Rural Nebraska has studied and raised the issue of small business retention that has indirectly affected the program approaches of Nebraska DED and USDA/Nebraska.

The outreach network efforts have more substantial and regular policy influence, albeit not directly. As they outline and reach agreement on interagency strategies, they are tacitly agreeing to agency involvement in a collaborative undertaking. For example, when Small Communities Finance Committee members agree that a community should follow a course of action, they are indirectly committing their agency to support a part of the program, should the community be eligible and follow through on an application for funds. Likewise, the 317 Group has regularly and indirectly influenced FSSA/DDARS programming, for example, their efforts to persuade the state agency to include emergency services for those on the service waiting list, a goal achieved after seven years of effort.

The action networks have more direct influence but with the exception of Iowa Communications, which has near-complete transmission/operation control, it is bounded. The MPOs and Enhanced Data are clearly limited by statute and by politics. Over their own limited PMN domains, however, they do exert considerable influence. Kentuckiana Agency, for example, has important influence on metropolitan issues like light rail, interurban transit, freeway extensions and improvements, interjurisdictional bridges, routing of state and federal highways. All of the networks have some policy/program influence, albeit considerably weightier for outreach and action networks, and more direct but circumscribed for action networks.

The final column in table 9.2 looks at what an agency/organization may do regarding a PMN decision, program, or agreement with which they cannot agree. This action would normally occur because the decision is contrary to their interests or because of statutory prohibitions. Because informational and developmental networks do not really take actions that affect the agency's policy/program domains, this is not a real concern. Nonaction is the normal mode when these PMNs exchange or create knowledge, which is usable or actionable at each agency's option. Darby partners' research projects and mediation demonstrations do influence agency/organization practices such as watershed planning in the SWCDs, but not because any agency is part of some agreement to act. In information networks partners do not have to take any recursive action should they disagree, or actions that are detrimental to their interests.

That is not true with regard to outreach networks, where action by agencies is normally taken by tacit agreement. The agency in the outreach network is not compelled to act by joint action (in this case, the nonaction alternative), but because they have informally agreed to the action, recourse is normally not at issue in response to network action. If there is strong opposition the network will often back off of their agreement, but this is rare. It is likely to work like these examples: Because USDA/Nebraska has informally agreed to partner with Nebraska DED, the Nebraska Department of Environmental Quality, and a private lender to help a small community water system, it does not have to take action in response to a network agreement. The community acts. If the community does not comply, each agency will take appropriate action. Likewise, if the 317 Group meets with FSSA/DDARS over a 317 quality-improvement program, the agency puts it into place after agreement is reached. If the provider community objects, DDARS normally backs down, delays, and comes back with a revised proposal. Once a final agreement is reached, all NGOs must comply or drop out of the program, but since consensus is mutually agreed on by the parties, there is rarely need for recourse.

The action networks' component agencies/organizations have extensive recourse abilities. For Iowa Communications, all program content, audience, and modes of delivery are ultimately theirs to transmit or not, although this decision is rarely invoked. The agencies in Enhanced Data informally negotiate proposals and adjust them until members agree to go along with the agency-drafted proposal. The partner jurisdictions in the two MPOs have two modes of recourse: first, they have representation in the two important committees where they can be heard and trade-offs can be and are made; second, if a local project is not included in the long-range plan or awarded TIP federal funds, the jurisdiction is free to go ahead with the project using local financing. While local officials would prefer to use federal funds, they can and do use internal funds. One planning director said, "We got that freeway interchange in the MPO plan and received federal funding, but because it was so vital for business development in that area, we would have financed it anyway out of city funds."

On balance, agencies have retained a great deal of their autonomy in the face of networks. They have maintained it in a very unbalanced way. For agencies in some networks it is not an issue to be concerned with, and for others autonomy is quite limited. Influence over policy or program is exclusively or mostly indirect; or in the case of action networks limited by law, the agreement process, or both. Finally, all agencies have ways of directly or indirectly protecting their domains in the light of any course of action agreed on by the network. O'Toole (1997) appears correct in stating that networks do not have the formal capabilities to compel compliance, which limits their scope considerably in regard to altering jurisdictional boundaries.

PARTICIPANTS' PERSPECTIVES ON NETWORK CONTROL BY PARTICIPATING AGENCIES

When so many public organizations are involved in collaborative ventures, do they give up their final say regarding their home agency's control over resources, programs, or policies? Gray and Ariss (1985) conclude that organizations involved in networks have a diminished ability to control outcomes unilaterally.

Peters (1996) has concluded that coordinative reforms such as the employment of networks may lead to squandering by government of its capacity to present policy solutions. In particular, attempts at coordination may shift agency control outward, with little attention to the problems and concerns of the home organization. These issues of control emerged from the research for this book, as administrators discussed their agency's role in the network, how it differs from agency management, and their agency's leadership role in networks.

One clear finding is that most networks work around and between issues of agency control. As alluded to earlier, it is not easy to relinquish the authority of jurisdiction. Some representative responses include: "Our alliance is set up so that the three initiating conservation districts (special districts) really control. We state agencies try to help them implement their decisions." "There is a power issue here. A few managers control, by protecting their needs." "Our agenda is clearly not the same as most of the others and we don't want it changed, so we stay away." "Some partners can't be influenced because they sign the agreement and disappear." "There is little control in this body, because the feds are hard to 'crack.' We are not mandated to cooperate, just expected to . . . there is little control over the agencies that belong." One agency official concluded, "I speak up for our interests but don't seek control over others." The point is that network activity represents important coordination and cooperative efforts, but it also generates recognition of agency mission and respect for the boundaries of the other organizations. This respect or trust factor (Agranoff and McGuire 2001b; Fountain 1994) means that the collective must constantly accommodate concerns of the partner agency. One clear dimension of trust is the sense that a facilitating force in the network involves recognizing the interests and wishes of partners.

Control is also a function of the type of networks involved. Information networks must tread most carefully on this issue, since they merely exchange information and contain disparate and often conflicting stakeholders who hold dearly to their interests. Anything that smacks of control can potentially backfire. Developmental networks fall somewhat in the same category, but their capacity-building efforts must ensure that they do not duplicate any prior claim of individual agencies. For example, the Partnership for Rural Nebraska could not engage its signatories in economic development planning and formal training until one of its core organizations merged with Partnership for Rural Nebraska. Outreach networks do interactively develop coordinated strategies that involve some agency concession of control over resources and operating policies, but table 9.1 indicates that they are voluntarily yielded in the face of a particular problem at hand. The administrative dispensation (implementation) of the jointly agreed-on virtual strategy, funding, or service remains within the home agency. Only action networks make the kind of decisions that affect agency control, and only to a very limited extent.

How do networks achieve mutual agreement in the face of so many barriers to control? The process of multiagency discussion of problems of mutual concern means that one must "fight the firewalls agencies put up . . . we try to change the behavior of agencies." As one agency head in a developmental network observed, it is "a matter of leveraging, marketing, and partnering, even though they have control." Another federal administrator in the same network said, "Our interest is in creating a sandbox that all organizations and public agencies with an interest in rural development can play in. We want all of our partners to earn a T-shirt that says, 'Plays Well With Others.'" The process appears to be a matter of working at the margins of core agency control.

Modes of Operational Agreements

A logical question to ask is whether collective agreements by networks change or in some way attenuate the way government agencies reach their policy and program decisions. Provan and Milward (1995) conclude that effective networks are those with centralized integration and nonfragmented core decisions. Network consolidation and integration are very difficult, almost rare tasks. We have already recognized in chapters 3 and 8 that very few of the networks studied actually make the kinds of decisions that public agencies do. For most of this work the language has therefore been conditional: they are referred to as agreements and/or decisions. Chisholm explains that "where formal arrangements are absent, insufficient, or inappropriate for providing requisite coordination, informal adaptations develop to satisfy that need" (1989, 17). He also concludes that such ad hoc arrangements permit the continued existence of formally autonomous organizations while gaining such advantages as reliability, flexibility, and representativeness. It is within this framework that most networks reach agreement.

It has been indicated that public agencies seldom lose their decision domain because decisions or agreements are generally made by consensus. Virtually every network, including the action networks, strives for consensus. One Enhanced Data state official described it this way: "Proposals are made by participating agencies, the staff researches the proposal and does a market feasibility study, the report is submitted electronically before the meeting, at the meeting discussion is held and questions are asked. If there are too many questions we table the issue until more research can be undertaken. In between meetings phone calls and one-on-one discussions ensue, the issue is brought back to the table, and if there are a lot of head nods in the yes direction we consider it to be approval." Such brokering of agreement is the norm in situations where extended decisions such as network programs, strategies, or joint policies are undertaken. "We let consensus rise to the top," said one federal program head.

The key to the network agreement process is to bring out agency position and try to engender sufficient adjustment to get joint approval. As mentioned, networks are primarily composed of two types of public employees: line managers/program heads and program administrators/specialists. The former group usually comes to the table with delegated authority. Program people usually have less authority, and it is more problematic for them to make accommodations on the spot, so to speak. In either case the group tries to get the agency to go along and help serve the overall mission of the network. In agencies where jurisdictions are represented (city, state, county), their participants' positions appear to be consistently respected. They have a form of legitimized authority behind their position. Because there is an absence of any overall legal authority in most networks, an agency cannot be compelled to go along with a given decision. While a network can presumably allow an abstention, that violates the principle of working toward consensus and respect for agency autonomy. It can also diminish trust. "Normally we duck the tough issues. Often there is no choice. We don't want to drive them away. So we do what we have to to keep them at the table. That means a less ideal decision, or no decision."

Even when an action network is making real win-lose policy decisions that affect the concerns of individual jurisdictions, jurisdictions and their politics must still be respected. The protracted Des Moines Metro decision process (appendix B) was designed to "maximize the winners and soften the blow to the losers." Iowa Communications depends on a customer base of public agencies. It cannot alienate its users, who are free to seek private, competitive carriers. Clearly networks try to avoid voting or anything that minimizes consensus. Networks operate in a way that legislative bodies do not, a nonparliamentary way, nor is their process anything like a hierarchical decision.

Network consensus-building processes are ways to compensate for the difficulties that threaten cohesion, or imperfections in formal processes like the parliamentary procedures so often used in voluntary organizations (Bardach 1998; Jennings and Krane 1994). Just as there is no hierarchical authority over public agencies in networks, there is little formal PMN organization beyond the stated officers and bylaws that resemble that of an NGO. Many PMNs do not even become this formalized. They tend to be convened and maintained by the nonmandated but committed efforts of network champions, promoters, and activists (Agranoff 2003). They require a form of "groupware," group development that reaches mutual understanding and transcends hierarchy-based communication/interaction that allows multiple cultures, procedures, and divisions of labor to come together (Agranoff and McGuire 2001b; Clegg and Hardy 1996). These consensus-driven concerns apply most strongly to action networks, but to the degree that other types of networks reach forms of agreement they are also relevant.

Line Managers in Networks

It is well understood that agency autonomy is protected by turf, the domain of problems, opportunities, and actions over which it exercises legitimate authority. To Bardach it is "probably the most fundamental of all elements of bureaucratic infrastructure" (1998, 178). Moreover, Bardach maintains that even when there is no danger of agencies losing turf, they may avoid collaboration in order to protect their autonomy. Thomas (2003) suggests that managers' search for agency protection in interagency cooperation is due to three factors: (1) their belief that they know best, and therefore they should decide how to carry out tasks, develop programs, and achieve agency missions; (2) the desire to be in control over the events surrounding them; and (3) the fact that, since people place a great value on loss aversion, managers' willingness to make forays into new territory is bounded by their desire to protect the turf they maintain.

The preceding discussion of control and operating decisions reveals that managers' desire to protect their autonomy is real, but it is not the whole story. The network is not so much a vehicle for getting public agencies to change their core functions, but a way to get "other jurisdictions to act in a way that enhances the overall mission of this body." One state agency head related, "We all have our own rules. The network formalizes the informal contacts that are going on anyway. As long as we can keep the information flow on the table to a nonthreatening style, other managers will cooperate." Another action network manager related that "the agency comes first. They might modify others' proposals but they do not oppose! The key to [name of network] is to try to get each agency to bend just a little to further a unified but not standard e-government process." Another state program head noted that network involvement is key in moving agencies beyond their turf. "My job is to develop and drive policy among different agencies, even those that do not report to the governor. It takes every trick possible to get them to move, sometimes even high-level politics. Sometimes it works and sometimes I recognize it is time to give up."

In some cases the collaborative problem is not so much overcoming turf protection, but getting line managers to become interested in the mission and operation of the network. As mentioned in chapter 6, many discussants related that their agency head was generally supportive of the aims of the network [under examination], but delegated the authority to make accommodations to program managers, who had license to speak for the agency.

In the light of the relatively minor adjustments made by most networks and the marginal decisions and threats to agency independence, networks do not appear to be overly turf-threatening to agency heads and program managers. Indeed, their very marginality may be the reason why turf battles among managers are few, and top administrators almost always give tacit or completely delegated support. The stakes are low, but undoubtedly higher than university departmental politics. Bardach concludes that "agencies will therefore not attempt to eschew autonomy-threatening relationships but to recast relationships in their least threatening form" (1998, 181). In most of the networks studied, particularly the informational, developmental, and outreach types, most potential turf battles are removed by elimination of collaborative decisions that threaten core or agency mission/mandates. The same is true with regard to major policy adjustments. Networks put a premium on the voluntary action of the individual agency. Whereas this is less the case for action networks, even there turf concerns are circumscribed by their limited scope of decision and by protracted procedures that respect agency domain. It is also possible, as Thomas (2003) concludes, that line managers working together in a process that allows them to assert their independence may ultimately lead to enhancement of subsequent cooperation. It is clearly part of the long-term trust-building process.

PROGRAM SPECIALISTS IN NETWORKS

In contrast to agency heads and line-program managers, professionals and other program specialists belong to communities that more naturally cut across agency boundaries. The role of the professional is different from that of line managers. Their work is knowledge based and geared toward solving problems. Rather than the collective challenges of the agency's boundaries, these participants tend to belong to epistemic communities and act on shared beliefs. One example is those developmental disabilities professionals who work alongside public agency and NGO association administrators in the 317 Group. Like professionals in the other networks, they see the need for a common policy enterprise or common practices associated with a set of problems to which they can direct their professional competency (Haas 1992). As a result, Thomas (2003) found that professionals are more likely than line managers to see the need for interagency accommodations through networks.

Program specialists do form a solid portion of the core in most of the networks studied, particularly that portion identified earlier as the technical core. Examples are the interdisciplinary technical committees of the MPOs, or the environmental specialists within Darby and Lower Platte. In some of the information and development networks they constitute the base of operations. For example, virtually all of the research work and agency connections that lead to potential development strategies in the Indiana Economic Development are engaged by staff and technical consultants. The administrators, elected officials, and organization heads play very minor roles in the information exchange work of the Council. Likewise, the momentum for keeping the Iowa Enterprise, Iowa

Geographic, and Partnership for Rural Nebraska going largely stems from program specialists within agencies, because most of these three networks' activity is not policy driven but involves the exchange and enhancement of technical
information and the discovery of extant technologies.

Such exchanges rely on and enhance epistemic communities within network
settings. Small Communities participants say they "focus on the technical issues and funding details, not the big program stuff." Another discussant described the mission of their network as "to bring all of the technical people to
the table, the operating staff, to exchange information and help small towns."
Another said, "I am here to learn about technology and the potential of technology transfer." A specialist in another network said, "We need to know what
other related agencies are doing, and how their projects might fit with what
we are doing. The community is solidified by long-term involvement and overlapping commitments." A 317 Group administrator observed, "In the field of
disabilities, we have been working with one another for lots of time, even
though some wear different hats over time." This was echoed by a liaison person in a Nebraska state agency, who stated, "We don't only meet regarding the
Lower Platte Alliance, but I see many of these officials from other agencies at
dozens of other committee and task force projects. In the twenty-some years I
have been in environmental programs, the same two dozen or so show up
everywhere. You not only get to know them but what their agency stands for."
In Enhanced Data one person said that relationships are built from the bot-
tom up, as "webmasters from different agencies share information and connect over projects, forming an informal work group."

Iowa Communications' three-level process of technical expertise exchange
outlined in chapter 5 is illustrative. The first level of operations and policy
expertise is exchanged through Iowa Communications' advisory committees
or councils identified in chapter 6—Telemedicine, Telecommunications,
Library, and so on. At another level are the interactions between the program
and the operational people, such as the director of education for Iowa Public
Broadcasting or the chief information officer for the Iowa Departments of
Public Health and Transportation, and Iowa Communications operations management and division heads. At yet another level, operations technology is
transmitted when Iowa Communications operating staff (some of whom are
contract employees) interact with Iowa state agency information executives and
agency technical staff. In virtually every PMN, formal work groups and technical cores similarly provide opportunities for program people to focus on
details and work out problems of an operational nature.

These issues of program operation and technical information are core functions for networks, as they bridge knowledge gaps between the silos of the agencies. Out of their deliberations come suggestions for agency adjustments and

proposals for redirection of agency resources; a plea for agency-level policy change occasionally emanates from the deliberations as well. For all but action networks, however, program specialists are not in a good position to engender high-level agency accommodation, let alone public policy change.

Knowledge transactions among specialists do play important roles in opening up the possibilities for collaboration. Thomas's study of ecosystem management demonstrates how expanding ecological knowledge "opened the technical core of agencies to environmental uncertainties" (2003, 53). Ecological knowledge led to interdependence, the building of community, and the pursuit of alternative outcomes. In a similar way, it has been demonstrated that the core work of most networks is technical work and knowledge development. Knowledge then points to the possibility of solutions, some of which call on changes in agency policy. These changes ordinarily leave the domain of specialists and involve administrators. As they are filtered up through line management, any accommodation is likely to face the previously identified gauntlets of agency autonomy.

LEGAL MANDATES OF AGENCIES

Getting an agency to make any form of policy accommodation, let alone a change in policy, poses additional obstacles to networks' ability to change the boundaries of government. For example, a huge Medicaid expansion of home services for waiting-list clients is a policy barrier for the 317 Group, as mentioned in regard to a cost of networking in chapter 8. By the same token, both the Nebraska Rural Development Commission and the Nebraska Development Network have been affected by state budget reductions, which has led to the former's merger into Nebraska DED and the latter into Partnership for Rural Nebraska. It is not unusual for key decisions external to some agency's scope of authority to present a barrier to networks' ability to engender policy accommodation. Networks do not change that.

One state regulatory agency manager involved in Darby related that even with statutory authority there are limits to engendering action. "We regulate the riparian boundaries. That is our charge. For most of the land in the watershed, local governments control the land use. We don't tell them what to do, only what we do." One federal Small Communities official noted that, despite the network, "the funders have their own controls, based on their rules . . . we can't change that." In the USDA/Nebraska network a fund manager said, "We have rigid funding guidelines which we maintain despite our involvement in the collective." In the same network, another official stated, "The operating understanding is that the statutory role and limits come before the concerns of the group [network]." An Indiana Rural Council official related, "no matter how much each generation of partner representatives becomes less hardened and more willing to change, at some point we have to see that the 'silos' are real."

Legal limits thus serve to maintain the domains of public agencies in the operation of networks. In information networks they are virtually impossible to penetrate, and would lie outside of the networks' missions. For developmental networks, capacities can be enhanced to some degree by assaulting those legal obstacles that inhibit collaborative effort, but it remains a matter of each agency's ability and/or willingness to change voluntarily. Developmental networks can encourage but not easily persuade agencies to adjust their legal protections. Outreach networks go a step further by pointing out strategies, or they can indicate avenues of legal accommodation. Because the agency is part of the strategymaking body, it may push some adjustments through, although the legal hurdle as in the Indiana Medicaid example may ultimately be insurmountable. Action networks are different because they do make policy adjustments of some type, but any decisions made remain within existing legal frameworks. TEA-21 transportation networks like Des Moines Metro and Kentuckiana Agency can accomplish many things in their long-range plans and funding priorities, so long as they conform to state and U.S. legal codes. Obviously networks are much better at exchanging and adopting technologies, and making administrative and operating changes, than they are at changing the law or most regulations. In terms of pushing the boundaries of the agency's legal core, they present little threat to agency authority.

CONCLUSION

In a leading book on the theory of public agency networks, policy networks are defined as bodies that connect public policies with their strategic and institutionalized context among the multisector actors involved in a given policy domain (Kickert, Klijn, and Koppenjan 1997). Although recognizing that power within networks is real, the governmental organizations are no longer depicted as the central steering actors in policy processes, and management activities assume a different, nontraditional, role (Klijn 1997). Rhodes suggests that policy networks do matter. Such intermediation limits political participation, defines the roles of actors, sets policy agendas, shapes the behavior of actors, protects the privilege of certain interests, and substitutes private government for public accountability. Networks contribute to the increased differentiation of polities. "Interdependence confounds centralization. More control is executed, but over less. Services continue to be delivered, but by networks of organizations which resist central direction. There are plenty of governments which government cannot steer" (Rhodes 1997, 3). Hirst suggests that networks have served as important transformative devices "on the ruins of the more centralized and hierarchical corporatist representation of the period up to the 1970s" (2000, 18–19).

Perhaps the networks under analysis are of a different type. PMNs in this study do not formulate national public policies, and focus only marginally and peripherally on major questions of their implementation. It is clear that these largely intergovernmental administrative networks are different. Only some of them have capacities for direct public policy alignment; many do not even have the ability to steer policy processes at the implementation stage. They rarely become a form of private government, they have difficulty in overcoming central agency direction, and they provide little evidence that they threaten agency autonomy. Moreover, the agencies steer the fourteen networks at least as much if not more than they steer agencies.

Bearing in mind that not all networks are alike, the study findings suggest that networks' ability to influence the public agency domain is real but quite limited in scope. As the productivity findings suggest, accommodations are made, decisions are influenced, strategies are altered, resources are directed, intensive groups exert undue influence, and public responsibility is indirectly shared. However, most of these are indirect and often long-term efforts that appear to marginally penetrate the operating cores of participating agencies. Moreover, the network is but one among a number of forms of collaborative management.

As is the case in the intergovernmental arena, each public agency is a bounded jurisdiction; it maintains day-to-day operational control over any potential network moves that involve its programs. Managers can normally choose to become involved in a network and/or they can choose another collaborative route, such as a contract or a dyadic working agreement. Line managers do not ordinarily seek to control any public agency in the network but their own. While the turf-protecting ability of line managers should never be discounted, they seek marginal adjustments in the network to foster solutions for difficult problems. Program specialists, the most active in the PMNs, want technological knowledge and interdependency awareness rather than control of others' programs. In short, it appears that too much emphasis may have been placed on the ability of networks to control government.

In an era of governance networks, the role of the state may be changed at its margins but very little at its core. Hirst (2000) reminds us that only government can pull together the various strands because it continues to distribute powers and responsibilities, remains the focus of political identity, and is the main institution of democratic legitimacy; as such, other entities view its decisions and commitments as reliable. Sharpe once concluded that "assessing the distribution of power between actors in any situation is a monstrously difficult exercise" (1986, 177). He argues that, in any kind of intergovernmental and interorganizational situation, it is even more difficult because many factors that must be accounted for strengthen government, such as legal mandates, fiscal capacity, exclusive executants, program monopoly, operational expertise, information monopolies, and even organizational slack. "Not to put too fine a point on it, *government is not just another organization*" (ibid., 177; italics his).

When pitted against the set of very real but less than polity-changing values added by networks, the power of government suggests that network impact on the power of the agency is limited and hardly system changing. Networks and the network era constitute notable overlays to the bureaucracies and the bureaucratic era. Management by network and network management have therefore become equally important endeavors, but under current conditions the network will neither replace the bureaucratic organization nor is it likely to displace its long-run power.

CHAPTER TEN

. . . .

MANAGING IN PUBLIC NETWORKS

None of us—our programs—has all of the authority, resources or know-how to solve the problems that any one of us has in our missions. That's why we band together and try to find solutions that work. It almost always means learning about issues and discussing what might work. That is the essence of metro transportation planning at Kentuckiana Agency.

SOLVING PUBLIC PROBLEMS in the current era requires intensive amounts of human capital. Much of today's public work is enmeshed in the symbolic-analytic challenge of applying particular types of data, information, and knowledge to complex situations. This is the work of contemporary public management. In order to mobilize the necessary human capital and other resources, the boundaries of the traditional bureau or agency must be crossed, within governments, intergovernmentally, and with NGOs. One important means of boundary crossing is through the collaborative networks of multiple-organizational involvement that we have been studying here.

This volume uses adapted grounded theory to explore the nature of these PMNs: what they are, what they do, how they operate, how human capital is transformed into knowledge, what public value they create, and how they affect the agencies of the state. If public managerial knowledge and practice is to be advanced and promoted, it is not enough to indicate the significance of the network for the manager. The field must delve beyond highlighting the importance of networks, it must also undertake serious empirical examination of these emergent phenomena using both quantitative (Agranoff and McGuire 2001b; O'Toole and Meier 2004) and qualitative (Koppenjan and Klijn 2004; Thomas 2003) methodologies. The present volume is designed to contribute to the qualitative tradition.

This concluding chapter brings together the previously identified findings and raises the network knowledge ante. The first section summarizes the major findings by identifying the seven key functions of PMNs that were identified by type in chapter 8 and in table 8.5. The following section then takes these findings and answers the eight research questions identified at the beginning of this book, particularly in regard to how networks and organizations are different and are similar. A modest research agenda suggested by the current study is put forward as the next steps for advancing network management. The book concludes with a discussion of how the future must continue to focus on advancing public management network theory.

WHAT NETWORKS DO

What makes networks useful? To summarize, a focused look at the kinds of public actions that PMNs undertake provides the foundation of understanding network collaborative contributions. Seven roles appear most relevant: problem identification and information exchange, identification of extant technologies, enhancement/development of emerging technologies, improving knowledge infrastructures, mutual capacity building, reciprocal strategies and programming, and joint policymaking/programming.

Problem Identification and Information Exchange

This is a common function of all the networks studied and the primary function of information networks. It is rare that a single government or agency has a monopoly on potential problem solutions, or the resources or programs to deal with them. Some problems such as nonpoint source pollution involve a wide range of actors—environmental activists, public agency managers, and specialists, along with farmers and ranchers. The information function in networks is core to its operations because multiple parties must be convened to explore the various dimensions of a problem, to become aware of the technology used to deal with each facet of a problem, and to ultimately learn the various agencies' plans to take action with regard to these technical solutions.

The key to the network information process is bringing in those stakeholders that are necessary to approach an issue. In the case of watershed management, a network like Darby has to involve farmers, state/provincial and federal environmental/natural resource/agriculture commerce agencies, local governments, developers, conservation districts, advocacy groups, and many more. Darby inevitably engenders exchanges among many opposing interests, but its aim is to get the parties to the table so all can be heard and a broad perspective on degradation and mitigation is fostered. All Darby Creek solutions appear considerably more politically and technically formidable than the original conveners ever imagined, but they are realistic. Darby leaders relate one conclusion that became clear in virtually all networks: not everyone will agree on the solution.

The next phase involves some type of formal and informal exchange of information, and broad discussion of the extent of various problems. As organizations begin to interact, they develop measures of mutual respect and, hopefully, mutual obligation or trust. Organization activities with regard to a problem(s) are put on the table. These discussions also reveal where each agency's programs and plans lie, along with potential and actual resources that could be dedicated to a problem. In Lower Platte, for example, one conservation district presented its five-year flood control and wetland development program, and the state environmental agency revealed new federal regulations regarding wastewater treatment and its new state plan. These exchanges provide important resources for network actors in terms of information useful to their role as a representative or boundary spanner for the home agency, and as part of a network pool of information. In the case of Lower Platte, it includes information exchanges among three substate conservation districts, six state agencies, and four federal agencies.

Even if a network stops short of joint strategy development or joint action potential, problem solutions can be presented in all four types of networks. First, the network can pool the information and decide that the problem has been insufficiently researched. Second, it can look more deeply into the problem. For example, conservation networks can explore the advantages/disadvantages of different kinds of nitrite-based fertilizers and their use, application amounts, time of application, and so on. Networks can also take the next step of seeing how other areas have tried to solve similar problems. An inventory of potential solutions can be taken, and network meetings and workshops can be used to learn more about the most feasible solutions. Darby has undertaken all of these means. Third, as Lower Platte has done several times, the stakeholders can be educated about how to implement a given solution, and how any potential action will intersect with other stakeholders' actions. The hope here is that the relevant network participants will voluntarily take action.

Is all of this nonaction activity worth the effort? Many of those involved in networks say that in this complex world the learning and information experiences gained are useful to the home organization, and that it raises the policy dialogue on both problems and solutions to a more realistic level. It ratchets up the potential for agency-based action. Others, who want collaborative program adjustment or joint action, are clearly frustrated by the protracting of solutions that could be solved in direct political/governmental arenas. Nevertheless, virtually all networks perform the exchange function, but some may not be able to go much further.

Identification of Extant Technologies

This function moves information one step up the line because it focuses on workable problem solutions that have resulted from other collaborative processes. How can a group of stakeholders or organizations work together to tackle a problem? Rural development provides a good example. Not only is it information based, but it has no government organization home and most program approaches are collaborative (Agranoff and McGuire 2001a; Radin et al. 1996). The rural development networks, Indiana Rural Council and Partnership for Rural Nebraska, need to know how problems of community enhancement, business attraction, or infrastructure provision are being solved elsewhere. Such program and technical information constitutes the transactional DNA of these interorganizational relationships. Most of the other networks studied performed many aspects of this function.

How is extant technology discovered and revealed? This flow of information is generated within the technical expertise reach of network participants, or it is sought outside of the network, such as from researchers and vendors. There are actually many different vehicles: roundtable presentations, attendance at regional and national conferences, speakers invited to network meetings, web postings, and email transmissions. A number of networks have technology committees devoted to finding and bringing the latest developments to the entire network. The technical committees of the transportation networks are essential for finding feasibility information that is cycled into decisions. A number of the networks studied have full-time technical staff (contracted staff, in some cases) who are subject-matter specialists primarily responsible for finding and presenting solutions. For example, Enhanced Data/accessIndiana relies on a technical staff of contractors who explore information-system approaches in other states and perform market studies for Enhanced Data network administrators. This flow of technical knowledge is part of the ongoing operations of most networks. The Iowa Communications multilevel policy, technical, and service exchange depicted in chapter 5 exemplifies this pricess. As needs are exchanged and programs adjusted, valuable telecom expertise is accessed and exchanged. Whether formal or informal, technical knowledge is accessed and enhanced by transactional contacts within the network. While this function is less of a core activity in information networks it does occur to some degree, at least among some actors within the network. The developmental, outreach, and action networks cannot exist without it.

Adaptation/Development of Emergent Technologies

This next function is an obvious extension of the previous one. There are situations in the life of a network where an extant technology is not feasible. Moreover, the network cannot make the necessary incremental adjustments to make it fit the situation at hand. These are situations where analytical thinking must be supplemented with "more creativity and vision, more mental flexibility, and more *intuition*" in order to meet the challenges of information societies in an increasingly chaotic and complex world (Franz and Pattakos 1996, 638; author emphasis). In effect, the network must collaboratively transfer or create a technical solution that is adapted from existing research and technology.

In past years Small Communities has pioneered the development and financing of wastewater reuse processes. The network has studied how a small village could establish cluster permits to install, operate, and comply with U.S. EPA regulations for a set of nearby settlements and villages. Small Communities' Technology Committee had already looked at existing technology and developed its own model system for constructing such a creative system. It was an extended process of research and development by a group of network hydrologists and engineers. The network's Finance Committee was then charged with exploring the costs and financing potential for such a system, and to report back to the Small Communities Steering Committee. State environmental officials were charged with consulting with U.S. EPA regarding the process of obtaining operational permits for cluster systems. Now that the entire process has been put together—construction, financing, permitting—the project is being piloted in a cluster with a designated village as the center of the operating entity. If the pilot project works, the cluster system will eventually become part of the Small Communities Curriculum Committee's training materials and workshops.

This network process is not unusual, particularly for outreach and action networks where funding and program adjustments are made regularly. While there are many underutilized extant technologies that can be directly transferred, there are always some that do not fit. In this case, the cluster problem was initially brought to its Technology Committee by a particular village, and Small Communities recognized that this was not an isolated problem. Could this problem have been solved by a single organization? Probably not, since no single person or agency would have all of the necessary engineering, legal, or financial expertise, not to mention those working on the politics or sequencing and processing of the project. These are important and increasingly frequent challenges for networks: taking existing knowledge and extending it to solve some new challenge where collaboration is clearly the best vehicle.

Improving Knowledge Infrastructure and Management

Since networks exist to expand and transact information among disparate agency/organization actors and apply it to problems, their capability of moving knowledge is critical. Networks do not have the same hierarchical transmission channels as organizations with their legal and moral authority, nor do participants frequently meet on a face-to-face basis. Network actors are infrequently in direct working contact with one another and/or with the clients or populations they are trying to assist. As a result, ICT transmission vehicles like email, websites, and electronic bulletin boards are important supplements to postal mail and telephone. The need for information exchange among heavily scheduled administrators and program managers in different organizations places increased pressures on adaptation of ICT communication approaches.

The work of Iowa Geographic is illustrative. As a group that shares data, explores standards, and facilitates GIS user cooperation, this seems to naturally follow. As indicated, its board and its committees meet through the Iowa Communication Network's interactive narrowcasting facilities. Iowa Geographic's state GIS coordinator is trying to expand existing GIS usage from twenty-five counties to all ninety-nine. Iowa Geographic also operates a web-based GIS clearing house with around twenty-five KM functions. Although an argument could be made that a GIS network would be an exception because its business is information, that is not the case at all. Not all PMNs are as directly involved in expanding and managing knowledge as Iowa Geographic, but most of the networks look for new ways to transform information into usable knowledge. For example, the rural development networks are very conscious that many of the people they are trying to serve live in remote locations, and try to ascertain the extent of lack of accessibility, including generational and income barriers, to the Internet. As a result, they work harder to extend electronic communication to the informal outreach networks that serve rural people: county extension, college university rural institutes, community colleges, high schools, state agency offices at the county level, chambers of commerce, and other voluntary associations. They also work on transmitting tacit knowledge. By the same token, the two transportation MPOs base their decisions on highly developed databases, information sets, models, and other forms of tacit and explicit knowledge.

Capacity Building

This commonly used term has disparate meanings in the public management literature. One widely accepted definition is the ability to anticipate and influence change; make informed and intelligent policy decisions; attract, absorb, and manage resources; and evaluate current activities in order to guide future action (Honadle 1981). Networks are heavily engaged in this type of activity, as the previous examples of the Iowa state GIS coordinator and GPS enhancement suggest. Partnership for Rural Nebraska's multiple programs are also exemplary. In regard to networks, capacity building means developing and transmitting the knowledge architecture for its subsequent solution-based activity and its adaptation by its partners and clients, a form of knowledge management. This is the core function of developmental networks, but it is also clearly an integral function of outreach and action networks and, to some limited degree, of information networks.

Most of the strategic networks try to enhance knowledge, thus developing partner capacities. They are interested not only in the transmission of knowledge, but also in its creation and utilization by its participants, collectively and within their organizations. The latter requires capability. Annual meetings, technology seminars, technical assistance, cross-training on a cross-organization basis are so important to networks in this regard. Participating organizations need to do more than acquire knowledge; they want to be able to use knowledge. Implementing knowledge into internal action requires a level of capability that is fostered by three of the four types of networks.

Reciprocal Programming/Joint Strategies

Only a small number of the PMNs prove to be involved in joint decisions that lead to policy actions, but some develop collaborative strategies for actions that are carried out within individual agencies and programs. This type of networking is commonly found among interagency human-services funding, and services bodies at the metropolitan or interlocal level (Agranoff 1986). As collaborative bodies, networks involve a variety of agencies and programs when addressing problems, and chart out agreed courses of action that are implemented elsewhere, normally by the major partners. These strategic/programmatic approaches can be institutionalized or blueprinted, such as with a common interagency funding application form, or be tailored to a particular situation, such as attracting a business. They can be ad hoc such as when a network helps a particular community access central business district improvement funds, or they can be policy-oriented such as the actions of the 317 Group's multiagency/organization plan for maintaining the developmentally disabled outside of large institutions. Reciprocal programming for strategy making can thus be either a formal or an informal activity for some networks.

Prime examples of these workings are the network activities of the USDA/ Nebraska. It is officially a state office of a federal agency. In fiscal year 2003, USDA/Nebraska funded about $85 million in rural nonfarm programs in the state, including some twenty different grant and loan programs in utilities services and infrastructure, housing, business development, and cooperatives. It informally leverages these funds on a regular basis with a host of financial partners from other federal, state, and nongovernmental organizations. Other informal networking by USDA/Nebraska includes local economic development corporations; private lending institutions; village mayors, clerks, librarians, and fire officials; community foundations; area agencies on aging; and social services agencies. In a formal sense, USDA/Nebraska is a major partner that regularly participates in the activities of Partnership for Rural Nebraska and the Nebraska Development Network (merged in 2004). It also participates more informally with several planning efforts of the Nebraska Department of

Economic Development (Community Development Block Grant), U.S. Small Business Administration, substate development districts, and county-level development associations.

A similar formalized blueprint approach is the work of the Water Environmental Wastewater Action Committee (WEWAC), a group of funders similar in mission to the Finance Committee of Small Communities. It meets monthly at USDA/Nebraska offices in Lincoln to apply their commonly established approach and preapplication for funding of water projects for small towns. After WEWAC meets and agrees it will fund each component of a program, the funding agencies deal with each city applicant through their standard agency procedures. The process avoids overlapping and duplicate applications and, most importantly, gives the applicants a realistic course of action that allows for necessary multiple-source funding. In this process, the network collaborates to help communities apply a preestablished interorganizational strategy, fit the individual applicant into the collective's framework, and make any necessary adjustments along the line. The applicant then goes through the multiple application process of each agency to actually receive funding.

These ad hoc strategic approaches constitute very important collaborative work. They fall just short of the types of decisions and policies that are usually ascribed to governance networks, but are important outputs because the joint effort pools valuable knowledge and manages it by making strategic (collective and case-based) adjustments, and implements programs interactively, albeit individually. While these actions are most typical of outreach networks, they can also be secondary functions of action networks. At least informally they can sometimes be spin-offs of developmental and, on rare occasions, information networks (such as the Hellbranch partnership spin-off from Darby). Generally speaking, incompatibility of government agency regulations and procedures prevents the actors in these networks from moving to the next step of joint decisions, but reciprocal programming and joint strategies are in many ways only one step removed, albeit an important one. Given built-in agency limitations along with lack of legal and/or funding authorization, these strategic blueprints may be the most that some networks can accomplish.

Joint Policymaking/Programming

While this function is one most associated with networks in the literature, a limited number of networks in this study actually undertake such actions as a collaborative body. Of the fourteen networks studied, only four PMNs actually vote on or enact policies that affect all of the component agencies/government organizations, and in each case they are legally chartered (two federal, two state) to take such actions. Even with delegated authority, action networks as collaboratives are quite different from representative assemblies, where formal votes are taken, majority rules, and political considerations are paramount. They are also different from rigid hierarchies, where someone is ultimately the legally responsible decision maker. In action networks heavy doses of research and technical knowledge enter into the proceedings and decisions, deliberations are as likely to be as technical as they are political, and voting is more of an enablement formality after a negotiated agreement is reached.

The Des Moines Metro decision process presented in chapter 3 is a good example. It has a Transportation Policy Committee and a Technical Committee to adopt its long-range transportation plan and to allocate federal-state transportation (highways, mass transit) project funds for the local area. This is where joint policies come into play, as the needs and feasibility study are examined by the Technical Committee with MPO and local government staff assistance, deliberated on and accommodated, and sent to the Policy Committee. Then, as a network council composed of local government officials (both elected and appointed), they are supposed to both represent their jurisdiction's interest as well as decide for the good of the metropolitan area. In practice the MPO decides more like a network than a legislative decision body, as it takes those measures to enhance a metropolitan perspective.

Most action networks have to find a way to respect component members yet adopt the necessary collaboration-supportive technical and quasi- (or pseudo-) parliamentary moves that allow them to blend knowledge with joint policy/activity. After extended network discussion Enhanced Data constantly sends agency proposals back until an agreement can be reached. Action networks come together as representatives of different government, quasi-government, and nongovernmental organizations, with all of their attendant aims, rules, and procedures. They represent different needs, organizational cultures, and political interests. They must make decisions but they do not have hierarchical authority. Instead, the kind of action they take is based on negotiated adjustment while applying extant knowledge, as the partners simultaneously go through a learning process. These are very different decision processes that are closer to those of conductive public organizations than of rigid hierarchies.

ARE NETWORKS DIFFERENT FROM ORGANIZATIONS?

This analysis has suggested that in many ways networks and conductive organizations are similar. Nevertheless, this exploration represents only the surface of network operations. The issue of differences could be an ongoing research issue for some time. Clearly PMNs are nonhierarchical authority bodies, but appear to be more like organizations than most observers assume. They also display notable differences.

With the exception of the need to pool managers and specialists from different organizations with different resources, missions, and cultures, PMNs are organized in much the same way as today's open, boundary-spanning organizations. All are structured like organizations, whether chartered or non-chartered, with some formal identity, informal power structures, officers, committees, and work groups. Those that have the authority to take public action are legally chartered like public organizations. Most, however, do not possess such legal authorization, and are voluntarily self-organized. This may be the reason why they resemble nonprofit organizations more than bureaucracies in structure. The typical partner in the network operates with delegated program and/or professional authority from the home organization, and normally speaks for that organization. This differs little from the intra-organizational boundary spanner. Finally, turf issues of partner organizations emerged rather infrequently, and thus few of the networks really tested the domains of home organizations.

Are networks managed differently than organizations? Yes, in the sense that a collective management is needed in order for these multiagency/organization entities to acquire tangible resources and human capital, support functions, and set agendas. It can only be accomplished by pooling these resources from many home agencies. The hierarchical manager becomes a mere equal partner in the network structure. Moreover, in the absence of formal-legal hierarchy, trust of an interorganizational nature, derived by smooth collaborative processes, is a key ingredient or a functional substitute. On the other hand, a new network POSDCORB did not appear. Quite to the contrary, the PMNs recreate organizational structure, planning, coordinating, reporting, and budgeting similar to that of public sector organizations.

Decision making in networks, by contrast, is necessarily different. About half of the networks studied here are not directly involved in public decisions in the problem areas they address. If they have any influence, it is indirect and long-term. The other half do have considerable influence over a narrow range of public issues, although for some it is circumscribed by agency regulations and procedures. Within network processes, knowledge is an important ingredient in decision making. Reaching consensus on agendas that are themselves driven by consensus is key within the network. Respect for partners and respect for knowledge are paramount. Votes are taken only after agreement is informally reached, not to reach agreement. In the same way, officers, committee chairs, and work group members are not assigned, but are fit in after discussion and weighing of human and other relevant resources against knowledge. While the consensus orientation may appear to be different from that of organizations, many knowledge-oriented conductive organizations undoubtedly employ similar decision-making modes, or at least are not without a substantial consensus orientation.

The way that expertise is mobilized in networks is different on the surface from that of organizations. PMNs are prime examples of how many different interests, specializations, and disciplines can be brought to the table to attack problems that themselves cross the same boundaries. The network does appear to have an edge over a single organization in multiexpertise mobilization, but there are also risks. For example, so many participants can be brought to the table that their interest-based expertise can cancel out that of the other stakeholders. The other big risk, already identified, is the lack of authority to act collectively. On the other hand, a single organization may not have internal access to the needed expertise, so it must seek it outside of its boundaries. Although the network is not the only way to acquire it (consultant contract, dyadic contact, and so on), it is an efficient way to pool expertise and access. It should be noted that at some point the public agency may deem certain expertise to be so important that it is brought in-house or directly contracted. The network is a good way but clearly not the only way to access expertise.

Both networks and organizations are in the KM business. In this way they appear alike. The network, however, provides a parallel cross-agency, problem-oriented vehicle to pool and create explicit and tacit knowledge through its core information/knowledge functions. Rather than being geared to the needs of the agency or program, the PMNs attempt to foster knowledge that relates to issues like watershed degradation, rural poverty, business succession, or metropolitan transportation without taking any single organization's needs into consideration. Networks and organizations are alike in that the techniques they use to organize and manage knowledge—databases, intranets, discussion groups, mentoring—are the same as those used by conductive organizations.

Networks accomplish their purposes mainly by working in the trenches collaboratively. It is their committees, work groups, and taskforces, composed of core activists and many other recruited experts from multiple organizations, that do the real discovery and design work. These small groups look at problems, seek technical information, apply and adapt knowledge, and propose network activities/programs to the larger core PMN groups. In this way the work of networks resembles the work of many intraorganizational, cross-departmental task forces and work groups that are common in conductive organizations. It is the cross-agency domain of the problems they work on, rather than the way they work on problems, that distinguishes networks.

In the area of performance, networks can add considerable value that the single organization cannot. Given the type of problems that PMNs attack, and given the real limitations on their ability to take formal action, they meet a reasonable set of aims. PMNs add value to the professional/manager, home agency, network process, and network outcome on a limited number of issues within the scope of the network. Most of this could not have been achieved by any of the component agencies acting alone. On the other hand, it is important to bear in mind that single public organizations do regularly add collaborative public value through other means, such as dyadic engagement, contracts, grants, working agreements, regulatory functions, and so on.

The case was made in chapter 9 that, along with other forms of collaboration, networks do influence the way governments act, and its agents/managers do change roles when they are involved in the network. Nevertheless, they push governments' boundaries only to a limited degree. Since government agencies retain their roles, the network only changes the way the world is looked at, not necessarily the world itself, in that collaborative management is clearly a normal way of conducting the public agency's business.

RESEARCH CONCERNS

Since this book is among the few systematic studies of the inside of networks, there is considerably more to be learned about these bodies. The late management guru Peter Drucker suggests that knowledge-based human capital growth has meant that "in the society of organizations no single integrating force . . . pulls individual organizations in society and community into coalition" (2001, 319). The key, he concludes, is how government can be organized to meet this need. Research into networks that operate in the public sector must devote more attention to this issue. This research suggests a modest agenda of related steps toward the understanding of networks.

Knowledge Conversion

How knowledge is transformed into action is clearly at the core of network discovery and solution processes. In addition to the various forums for deciding or choosing activity, chapter 7 identified six different predecision modes or learning strategies that administrators engage: group discussion, political negotiations, technical/normative proscription, formulaic process, data-driven strategies, and predecision simulation. These emanated from the field study and by no means complete the universe of explorations. More needs to be discovered on how explicit and tacit knowledge is converted to network solutions, programs, joint undertakings, and, for some, decisions. As Tsoukas maintains, "Knowledge management is then primarily the dynamic process of turning an unreflective practice into a reflective one by elucidating the rules guiding the activities of the practice, by helping give a particular shape to collective understandings, and by facilitating the emergence of heuristic knowledge" (2005, 136–37).

Network Management

This research is one step in the quest for a network POSDCORB equivalent. We have found many similarities to organizations. Chapter 6, an initial inside look at some of the hierarchy equivalents, identified elements of network power, communication and coordination mechanisms, planning and programming tools, and internal divisions of labor. We also reported some reflections from the managers themselves. As a result, it became possible to characterize these organized PMNs as collaborarchies that operate somewhat like voluntary NGOs, and somewhat like conductive organizations. However, only the surface has been scratched, as these managerial processes grounded in the fourteen PMNs have merely suggested which structures and operations are present. More detailed research on a broader range of networks and network functions is required to further reveal network management process.

Information and Communication Technology Use

The study of the role of ICT in networks is in its infant stages. Empirical study revealed little use of electronic groupware, or group-simulated behavioral decision techniques, or even many formal nonelectronic applications of applied behavioral approaches to network resolution or action. It did reveal extensive use of electronic communication for network interaction, structuring, brokering, and facilitating interaction. At the same time, face-to-face communication was not diminished by the overlay of ICT. Clearly more research is necessary on the role of Internet communication in the work process of forging the network's agreements that in turn lead to value adding.

There is more at stake in collaborative management as the open-source movement accelerates, making ICT software, databases, and working models more freely available. Contrary to some economists' earlier expectations, ICT has not become as widely protected as predicted. Repeated cooperation among software users leads to reciprocity and trust. Many want to share their technical work cooperatively to help solve problems, enhance their prestige, or increase their professional opportunities. Benkler (2004) argues that sharing is increasing beyond that of information via the Internet to the tools of technology, such as computing power and bandwidth. It is only a matter of time before peer-to-peer sharing accelerates this open-source trend. Social sharing represents a third mode of organizing economic production, alongside markets and the state. If these predictions come true and sharing extends beyond information technology, ICT may become an even more important platform for networks to launch their searches for knowledge.

Value Adding

The research reported here will hopefully contribute to the notion that network decisions add value in different ways in the public sector to the professionals and managers, to participating agencies, to interagency processes, and to the larger problems of public policy. The link between interactive network decisions and public value is encapsulated by Stone and associates (1999) in their social production model, where the power of new possibilities created through collaboration is paramount. In terms of choosing alternatives or making decisions among disparate parties in networks, preferences are not hard and fast. Loosely joined collections of parties have the ability to constitute new possibilities, often through fresh configurations. "As a concept, social production is simply a way of enabling people to see a larger range of possibilities" (ibid., 355). This is an arena where the process door is just being opened; for example, the work of Imperial (2004) on estuary network management.

Network Differentiation and Agreement Modes

The typology of networks employed in this study is, to a very great extent, based on the types of activities they engage and in their agreements/nonagreements. This turned out to be remarkably similar to an earlier typology employed by Alter and Hage (1993). In this study networks were distinguished by their propensity to exchange information, build capacity, blueprint strategies, and make policy and program adjustments. One resulting conclusion is that networks undertake different types of roles. Consequently, the type of public values they may add is different, as are their internal processes. Further research on network decision making does not necessarily have to adopt this typology, but must recognize that networks are differentiated in structure, purpose, activities, and results.

The extended courses of action, decision, or agreement processes of PMNs and beyond merely open the door. It appears from this research that formulating network agreement involves a protracted process that requires the best efforts of stakeholder identification, mobilization, and agreement processes. PMN actors must factor process dynamics into strategic or joint-agreement/action-based abilities. Unlike strategymaking in single organizations, which can capitalize on hierarchy, similar culture, standard operating procedures, and a relatively well-understood division of labor, network activity multiplies the potential forces for agreement. Many routines that are familiar in single organizations, such as in nonprofit NGOs, are not easily repeatable. One, for example, appears to be parliamentary procedure, an approach the author never once encountered during field observation. Other than for minor housekeeping, executive decision or executive committee decision does not exist. Some form of consensus seeking by interaction, discussion, and learning by all parties appears imperative. In this sense, those routines and exercises that seek out the big picture that are unique to networks require greater understanding. Forces of consensus must blend into some form of mutual agreement after researching and visualizing some larger picture.

Networks, Not the Network

The multiple-organization complexity faced by the manager is real but little understood. Academics examine networks and other lateral phenomena in a singular fashion. Practitioners do not enjoy such luxuries. For example, the reality of the manager sitting in city government is that of multiple and overlapping formal and informal networks. Few of them are likely to be chartered. Consider the vertical field of this public manager: it may include one or more regional agencies, one or more state agencies, or one or more federal government agencies. Their horizontal field is even more crowded, including county government, townships, nongovernmental organizations, and, in a policy field like economic development, financial institutions, developers, businesses, public-private partnerships, and more. As a result, many ostensibly intergovernmental studies have examined a network or a series of overlapping networks in distinct intergovernmental settings (Agranoff and McGuire 2003b). If one applies a mental multiplier beyond economic development to human services, transportation, community development, and environmental policy, we understand the breadth of multiorganizational networks that exist in the various policy domains.

To compound the confusion, the silos of policy domain overlap in the real world. For example, economic development and environmental policy networks intersect at many points. This says much more than that networks are important and public administration must come to grips with how they are managed, it also says that we must learn how to study how real complexity is understood and managed (Mitroff and Linstone 1993).

Networks and Governments

One research question regarding questions of accountability relates to the ultimate venues of those agreements and policy decisions made within networks versus governmental bodies. Chapter 9 provides at best a preliminary or suggestive answer. Have the boundaries of government changed as a result of networks? Some authors have suggested "no" or "barely," as they caution that government retains essential powers over decision and traditional normative and service roles. The important next, research-oriented step appears to be to examine just how and how much such network-generated complexity impacts what we have traditionally known as government. Do complexes of networks extend agreement/decision processes outward to non-governmental organizations?

TO THE FUTURE

PMN analysis will be on the research agenda of public management for some time. The large-data-set empirical studies on the important impact of public managers operating in networks offer useful constructs and point to the prominence of networking (Meier and O'Toole 2001, 2002; O'Toole and Meier 2004). Indeed, the development of a core POSDCORB equivalent depends highly on more "large N" studies like these. Similarly, the multiple-case-study analysis of Bardach (1998) and the multicity-network, interlocal study of Agranoff and McGuire (2003a) reveal a set of managerial tasks within intergovernmental networks as well as the complex web of multinetwork management of public officials. Cigler (2001), Milward and Provan (1998), and Mandell (1990, 1999, 2001) have conducted what may be called midrange empirical research on the relationships between selected structural variables and results in networks.

Empirical research on networks also requires greater depth; that is, study with conjoined contextual knowledge. This volume tries to demonstrate that principle, as it combines narrative and analytical dimensions. More work that looks within networks is required. The early theoretical works on public management (Weber 1947; Gulick and Urwick 1937), on bureaucratic structures (Barnard 1938; Simon 1947), and on public administration operations (Key Jr. 1937; Gaus and Wolcott 1940) all provided inside looks at the operations and public values created by these large-scale organizations. Although not all were based on qualitative data gathering, all were grounded in the reality of organizational functioning. Similarly, network analysis in public management must follow this grounding tradition if operational premises and theory are to be built. In addition to the current volume, one can point to the recent work of Koppenjan and Klijn (2004), where they use the single case of zinc pollution to analyze how policy networks converge, manage knowledge disputes, face uncertainty, and managerially steer a course of action. In the tradition of earlier case-study, qualitative works on interagency coordination such as Chisholm (1989) and Bardach (1998), the Klijn and Koppenjan volume additionally demonstrates the contribution of qualitative analysis to network theory construction by looking inside.

As the demands for knowledge in an organization-based society increase, it is hard to imagine that the need for interconnections like those of the network will not also increase. Castells reaches this conclusion in his study on the importance of the social transition of knowledge: "Because of the convergence of historical evolution and technological change we have entered a purely cultural pattern of social interaction and social organization. This is why information is the key ingredient in our social organization and why flows of messages and images between networks constitute the basic thread of our social structure" (1996, 477). The network, including the PMN, is here to stay along with other devices of lateral or interorganizational interaction. They are part of the collaborative overlay now placed on groups, organizations, bureaucracies, and other bounded entities.

Public managers and NGO executives in settings like those of the fourteen PMNs studied here will have similar challenges of converting information into usable knowledge. In so doing, networks like Darby, Partnership for Rural Nebraska, Small Communities, and Kentuckiana Agency provide model venues through which collaborative transactions occur. The network thus becomes a contemporary object of managerial study and practice. As a result, considerably more needs to be known about their management—what they do and how it is done.

The education of today's public and NGO manager is incomplete unless they are exposed to the myriad lateral connections that are now part of the job. The likelihood increases daily that he or she will be involved in one or more cross-organization networks. Therefore an understanding of how these networks operate is key. Best practices in networking will someday become as important a part of the public manager's repertoire as that of organizational management. At the same time, organizational management will not go away. Public management cannot discard the single organization, but as Lipnack and Stamps (1994) suggest, the network becomes an overlay on previously developed group, hierarchy, and bureaucracy means of organizing. Do not throw those organization studies and texts away! They are still operative. However, they now operate within the complex of connections—as conductive organizations.

APPENDIX A   A Detailed Look at the Fourteen PMNs

Name of Network	Description and Purpose	Type	Enabling Authority	Primary Agencies
1. accessIndiana Enhanced Data Access Review Committee (**Enhanced Data**)	Portal to Indiana State government information; Enhanced Data regulates accessIndiana, supported by a contractor for web development, sets policies for accessIndiana reviews, modifies and approves audit agency agreements, encourages public and private use, and establishes fees for enhanced access to public records.	Action	State Government	Indiana State Library; Indiana Departments of Administration, Bureau of Motor Vehicles, Secretary of State, Indiana Commission on Public Records, Indiana Commission for Higher Education; Chair, Indiana Intelnet Commission, Division of Information Technology; Office of Attorney General; State Budget Agency; and six citizen/ NGO/media representatives.
2. Des Moines Area Metropolitan Planning Organization (**Des Moines Metro**)	Responsible for transportation planning for metropolitan area under §450 of Title 23 of U.S. Code (TEA-21) through its Transportation Technical Committees.	Action	Intergovernmental Agreement	Thirteen cities, three county government members, and two associate cities. Advisory participants include Iowa Department of Transportation, U.S. Federal Highway Administration, U.S. Federal Transit Authority, Des Moines Metropolitan Transportation Authority, and Des Moines International Airport.

continued

Name of Network	Description and Purpose	Type	Enabling Authority	Primary Agencies
3. Indiana Economic Develop. Council (**Indiana Economic Develop.**)	Created by the Indiana General Assembly to serve as a research and ideas consultant for economic development strategic planning of statewide public-private organizations.	Informational	Not-for-profit 501c(3)	Seventy-two-member board of directors from state government, universities, private sector, business and labor interest groups, and NGOs. Chaired by the governor. Lt. Governor is chief executive officer of the Council (Note: in Indiana the lieutenant governor is head of the Department of Commerce and is Commissioner of Agriculture).
4. Indiana Rural Develop. Council (**Indiana Rural Council**)	IRDC provides a forum to address rural issues, seeks community input to identify problems, establishes partnerships to find solutions, enables partners to take action, and educates the public on rural issues.	Developmental	Intergovernmental Agreement/ Not-for-profit 501c(3)	U.S. Department of Housing and Urban Develop., U.S. Small Business Administration, U.S. Department of Agriculture/Rural Develop., Indiana Commissioner of Agriculture, Department of Health/Rural Health, Indiana Department of Commerce, four local-government elected officials, eight state legislative and U.S. congressional staff appointees, and four for-profit appointees.

5. Iowa Communications Network (**Iowa Communications**)	A statewide, state-administered, fiber optics network that enables authorized users such as hospitals, state and federal govt., public defense armories, libraries, schools, and higher education to communicate via high-quality, full-motion video; data; high-speed Internet communications; and phones.	Action	State Government	Iowa Telecommunications and Technology Commission, Iowa Public Television, Iowa Department of Corrections, Iowa universities and colleges, Iowa Department of Transportation, U.S. Veteran's Administration, U.S. Social Security Administration, public schools, public libraries, and others.
6. Iowa Enterprise Network (**Iowa Enterprise**)	Iowa Enterprise supports home-based and microenterprises, and provides mutual assistance and information through conferences, workshops, and web links.	Developmental	Not-for-profit 501c(3)	U.S. Small Business Administration, Iowa Department of Economic Develop., Iowa Rural Develop. Council, Iowa Area Develop. Group, Small Business Develop. Center–Des Moines, U.S. Department of Agriculture/Rural Develop., Iowa Department of Cultural Affairs, and micro-business owners.

continued

Name of Network	Description and Purpose	Type	Enabling Authority	Primary Agencies
7. Iowa Geographic Information Council (**Iowa Geographic**)	Clearinghouse for coordinated geographic information systems, data sharing, exploring standards, and facilitating cooperation among Iowans who use GIS.	Developmental	State Government	Twenty-five-member board includes representatives from university/ private college, state government, planning organizations, county governments, local governments, federal government, private businesses, and community colleges.
8. Lower Platte River Corridor Alliance (**Lower Platte**)	The Alliance fosters the development and implementation of locally drawn strategies, actions, and practices to protect and restore the rivers' sources; fosters increased understanding of the Platte River's resources; supports local efforts to achieve comprehensive and coordinated land use; promotes cooperation among local, state, and federal organizations, private and public, to meet the needs of the many varied interests of the corridor.	Informational	Intergovernmental Agreement	Lower Platte South, Lower Platte North and Papio—Missouri Natural Resources Districts, Nebraska Departments of: Natural Resources, Health and Human Services, Environmental Quality, Nebraska State Military Department, and University of Nebraska Conservation and Survey Division. Ex-officio links with U.S. Environmental Protection Agency, U.S. Geological Survey, U.S. Army Corps of Engineers, and U.S. National Park Service.

Partnership/Group	Description	Type	Structure	Participants
9. Partnership for Rural Nebraska (**Partnership for Rural Nebraska**)	A cooperative commitment to address rural opportunities and challenges identified by rural Nebraskans; to work together to meet those challenges, and provide resources and expertise to enhance development opportunities.	Developmental	Intergovernmental Agreement	State of Nebraska: Departments of Agriculture, Economic Develop., Environmental Quality, Health and Human Services System, and the Rural Develop. Commission; federal government: USDA/RD, and Natural Resources Conservation Services; The University of Nebraska; Nebraska Develop. Network.
10. Small Communities Environmental Infrastructure Group (**Small Communities**)	Coordinated efforts to assist small governments in Ohio in their development, improvement, and maintenance of their water and wastewater systems.	Outreach	Nonformal group	State of Ohio Water Develop. Authority, Ohio Environmental Protection Agency, Ohio Department of Natural Resources, U.S. Federal-State Extension Service/Ohio State University, U.S. Department of Agriculture/Rural Develop., U.S. Department of Commerce, Economic Develop. Administration, private lending representatives, university rural centers, nongovernmental organizations, and regional development districts.

continued

Name of Network	Description and Purpose	Type	Enabling Authority	Primary Agencies
11. The Darby Partnership (**Darby**)	Facilitated by The Nature Conservancy of Ohio, its federal, state, and local agencies, environmental groups and watershed citizens share information and resources to address stresses to the streams and serve as a think tank for conservation efforts in the watershed.	Informational	Nonformal group	U.S. Department of Agriculture, Natural Resources Conservation Service, Ohio Department of Natural Resources, Ohio Environmental Protection Agency, U.S. Geological Survey, six county soil and water conservation districts, City of Columbus, Columbus and Franklin County Metro Parks, Mid-Ohio Regional Planning Commission, The Nature Conservancy, The Darby Creek Association, and several NGOs.
12. United States Department of Agriculture/Rural Develop. Nebraska Outreach Programs (**USDA/Nebraska**)	USDA/RD in Nebraska uses outreach to leverage other programs' funds to augment its funding, as well as assisting rural cooperatives, value-adding businesses, small municipal water systems, public facilities, and housing for small communities.	Outreach	Federal Government	USDA/RD, Partnership for Rural Nebraska, Nebraska Department of Economic Develop., Nebraska Rural Develop. Commission, Nebraska Develop. Network, University of Nebraska–Extension, Develop. districts, Nebraska colleges, and county and city governments.

		Action	Intergovernmental Agreement	
13. Kentuckiana Regional Planning and Development Agency (**Kentuckiana Agency**)	Responsible for transportation planning for two-state Louisville metropolitan area under $450 of Title 23 of U.S. Code (TEA-21) through its Transportation Policy and Technical Coordinating Committees.			Two Indiana county governments, three Kentucky county governments, city government elected officials, Indiana and Kentucky State Transportation agencies, Transit Authority of River City, Regional Airport Authority, Federal Highway Administration, Federal Transit Administration.
		Outreach	Nonformal	
14. Indiana 317 Task-force/Group (**317 Group**)	Developing a strategy to implement state/federal noninstitutional services for the disabled based on personal choice.			Public members representing NGOs, State Departments (Family and Social Services, Transportation, Commerce, Housing Finance Authority), State Budget Agency, university, and provider trade associations.

APPENDIX B

. . . .

THE SEQUENCE OF CODING FOR THE TYPOLOGY

THE RESEARCH SEQUENCE in the study follows a general pattern close to those of Eisenhart (1989) and Carney (1990), with the exception that full-case write-ups were not conducted in this variable-oriented study. Phase I and Phase II analyses were considered two attempts to gather data on a highly related set of research questions. Other than an initial question in Phase II asking for an update, there was no attempt to measure change over time. Because case write-ups were not utilized, the analysis moves quickly from various coding steps to cross-case analysis. The later stages of theoretical analysis were completed after the conclusion of the second round of fieldwork.

Analysis began in the field as each site was visited individually as a case, and discussion issues were framed within the context of each network. Site-based impressions were recorded through memos after each field visit. Emerging conceptual memos were periodically produced and placed in a general file. For each network a case portfolio was developed that included documents, completed discussion guides, observation notes, and supporting material. This allowed for recovery of case-level data and later writing of supporting vignettes.

An initial set of codes was established based on the categories set out in the discussion guide. Questions whose relevance did not materialize were eliminated. More frequently, some questions were collapsed into others. Others were broken out, based on subquestions or breadth of response. For example, the question on "what makes management in networks different" was naturally split into similarities/differences and then into different aspects of management, such as organizing and coordinating. In the case of the decision-making questions, a natural split occurred between the differences among networks and the reported sequences of decision.

Each case file was then read and discussion responses (and to a lesser degree other information) were cross-identified by a discussant/document identifying code for each preliminary item. This was followed by a second reading for potential code, and the coding scheme was refined and organized. The material was reread and coded, category by category, across the 150 discussants.

Case-based vignettes were also identified with a few substantive and discussant-identifying labels. For example, one decision-making sequence was labeled "Des Moines Metro-2/CONVOL," which referred to the convoluted decision process employed by the Des Moines transportation agency most coherently explained by discussant number two from Des Moines Metro. The coding and labeling allowed for the construction of patterns and sequences. This kind of patterning also allowed confirmation of different styles of network participants: champions, sustainers, contributors, and signatories (nominal members). Another useful pattern refers to the life cycle of each network. This patterning allowed for preliminary displays of the data; checklist matrices to see which of the networks fit into each category; and working typologies, such as the four types of networks.

The process by which the fourfold typology in chapter 3 was developed is illustrative of the way grounded theory emerges from qualitative data. The first step was to read all of the discussants' responses to the decision-making question listed in the chapter. The first reading was through the entire set of responses, across the cases. Possible coding categories were jotted down. A second reading was case by case. By the end of the second reading, a potential start list of codes (table B.1 column a) had been generated. The next, case-by-case pass led to actual coding. As coding proceeded it became clear that the original start list of twelve categories could be collapsed into nine, due to lack of responses and because of some highly related responses. After several hours of working on this most difficult part of the process, the nine categories intuitively appeared to fit some sort of progression, ranging from nondecisional exchange of information to the type of policy/program decisions that the literature claims networks make. After all of the data was coded and individual responses were categorized within each network, a progression was attempted, as displayed in table B.1 column b. It appeared that there might be a continuum of sorts.

The continuum possibility was probed by summarizing the coded data, by network, into sorted categories. Table 3.1 in chapter 3 is an attempt to fill in or find blank cells that reflect a combined response for the nine types of actions/decisions listed in table B.1 of this Appendix. Recall that networks in table 3.1 are displayed in alphabetical order. Each cell's entry contains a summary description of a key event that characterizes a network action. An entry means that the network regularly takes such an action at that level, ranked from 1 to 9. This kind of second-order matrix allows the analyst to get a focused look at how multiple cases are arrayed. It thus provides a first glimpse of some ordering, not to mention strong implications for potential substantive explanations. In this case it clearly confirmed our hunch from listening to responses in the field that not all networks make policy decisions. They do something, however, and the "something" began to emerge by studying table 3.1 in chapter 3.

Reflection confirmed our previous speculation that a typology or categorization fits the data. Responses from two or three networks in the field were

TABLE B.1   List of Codes—Decision Question

(a) Unordered Listing—Start List	(b) Ordered Listing/Relabel/Code
Policy adjustment	Network information exchange
Review of plans/plan approval	Agendas/network work plans
Exchange information/share ideas	Scientific reports/studies
New technology/scientific information	Forums/member enhancement/assistance
Technology transfer combined with new technology	Web link/information systems development
Member development/staff training	Strategic blueprint/fund leveraging
Group decision-making development (dropped, only relevant in two instances)	Plan review
Funding strategies/advice on action steps	Mutual policy/program adjustment
Exchange of resources (combined with funding strategies)	Network policymaking
Websites/e-operations/electronic contacts/info. systems	
Meetings/annual conferences/plans/ programs	
Program adjustment/mutual action	

similar, and table 3.1 showed empty spaces and full spaces in a potential pattern. Thus table 3.1 was transformed into the cluster summary shown here in table B.2, noting key or characterizing actions/decisions, and listing the numerical range of efforts of the three highest or core actions on the now-imposed 1–9 scale. This alphabetical list of networks demonstrated low (1–3), medium (5–7), and high (7–9) scores. Clearly those with low scores primarily exchanged information, and those with high scores were involved in policy and program planning. An intermediate but higher middle-range group appeared to be those that performed strategic assistance for other organizations. This left another category, the lower middle-range intermediate group. The numbers were not a perfect fit because networks like Partnership for Rural Nebraska, Indiana Rural Council, Iowa Geographic, and perhaps Iowa Enterprise did more than exchange information but less than strategy engagement. It appeared that they

TABLE B.2 Cluster of Key Actions by Network Worksheet

Network	Key Actions	Network	Key Actions
Darby	Meetings; partner reports; info. exchange (1–3)[a]	Indiana Rural Council	Meeting briefings; task group plans; water and power vision task groups; annual meeting (1–2, 4)
Des Moines Metro	Meetings; reports; info. system; plan review; policy adj.; fund policy (7–9)	Kentuckiana Agency	Monthly tech. and policy meetings; special reports; databases; TIP plan; fund approval (7–9)
Enhanced Data	Info. exchange; web links; plan review; web policy (7–9)	Lower Platte	State of river report; work plan; web based GIS (2–3, 5)
Iowa Communications	User contacts; strategic plan; tech assistance; plan review; use policy; operations policy (7–9)	Partnership for Rural Nebraska	Annual institute; rural poll; education agenda; joint training; electronic rural news (3–5)
Indiana Economic Development	Econ. conditions; research projects (1–3)	Small Communities	Research technology transfer training; strategic assistance; finance comm.; informal plan review (5–7)
Iowa Enterprise	Workshops; assistance plans; topic forums; web links (2, 4–5)	USDA/Nebraska	Informal info.; annual plan; USDA web links; strategic and fund leveraging; plan review (5–7)
Iowa Geographic	Conference; work plan; new applications; web links (3–5)	317 Group	Special meetings; info. exchange; legislature initiatives; impact studies; future sessions; web links; case management; legislature audit (5–7)

[a] Range of highest three or core activities on 1–9 scale from the vignette in chapter 3.

TABLE B.3 Numerical Ordering of Fourteen
Networks into Categorization

Range	Network	Designation
1–3	Darby	Informational
1–3	Indiana Economic Development	Informational
2–3, 5	Lower Platte	Informational
2, 4–5	Iowa Enterprise	Developmental
1–2, 5	Indiana Rural Council	Developmental
3–5	Partnership for Rural Nebraska	Developmental
3–5	Iowa Geographic	Developmental
5–7	Small Communities	Outreach
5–7	USDA/Nebraska	Outreach
5–7	317 Group	Outreach
7–9	Iowa Communications	Action
7–9	Enhanced Data	Action
7–9	Kentuckiana Agency	Action
7–9	Des Moines Metro	Action

were involved in helping their organization members become better at what they do, and were doing some partnering. Since four networks fell into this category, the need for a fourth, development-related category became evident.

The ultimate four-fold classification displayed in numerical range in table B.3 shows the action/decision progression ranging from 1–3 to 7–9. Hours of reading the responses, coding, and handling the data led to several periods of reflection regarding their labeling. It is important to point out that no single respondent used those labels in a direct or identifying way. Nevertheless, certain responses such as "We don't make decisions, we exchange information," "This body is responsible for metropolitan plan development and fund allocations," "Small Communities does not make funding allocations or decisions, our Finance Committee guides small towns to find a way to solve their water problems," or "The Partnership assists its component organizations in becoming better at rural development" were obviously suggestive. In the end, it was the researchers' imposed characterization, labeling, and definition that provided a label for each set that best fit the data together.

In this way, the adapted grounded theory follows the canons of inductive methodologists like Strauss and Corbin (1998) and Marshall and Rossman (1995), and organizes data in a way similar to Miles and Huberman (1994). It clearly requires many hours of analysis and reanalysis, and a great deal of insight and conceptualization. As a systematic way to organize, analyze, and present verbal data, the work can prove rewarding.

REFERENCES

Agranoff, Robert. 1986. *Intergovernmental Management: Human Services Problem Solving in Six Metropolitan Areas*. Albany: State University of New York Press.

———. 1990. Managing Federalism through Human Services Intergovernmental Bodies. *Publius: The Journal of Federalism* 20:1–22.

———. 2001. Managing within the Matrix: Does Collaborative Federalism Exist? *Publius: The Journal of Federalism* 31 (Summer): 31–56.

———. 2003. *Leveraging Networks: A Guide for Public Managers Working across Organizations*. Arlington, VA: IBM Endowment for the Business of Government.

Agranoff, Robert, and Michael McGuire. 1998. Multinetwork Management: Collaboration and the Hollow State in Local Economic Policy. *Journal of Public Administration Research and Theory* 8:67–91.

———. 2001a. American Federalism and the Search for Models of Management. *Public Administration Review* 61(6): 671–81.

———. 2001b. Big Questions in Public Network Management Research. *Journal of Public Administration Research and Theory* 11 (July): 295–326.

———. 2003a. *Collaborative Public Management: New Strategies for Local Governments*. Washington, DC: Georgetown University Press.

———. 2003b. Inside the Matrix: Integrating the Paradigms of Intergovernmental and Network Management. *International Journal of Public Administration* 26 (12): 1401–22.

Agranoff, Robert, and Beryl A. Radin. 1991. The Comparative Case Study Approach in Public Administration. In *Research in Public Administration*, vol. 1, ed. James L. Perry. Greenwich, CT: JAI Press.

Allen, Thomas. 1984. *Managing the Flow of Technology*. Cambridge, MA: MIT Press.

Alter, Catherine, and Jerald Hage. 1993. *Organizations Working Together*. Newbury Park, CA: SAGE.

Ashford, Douglas E. 1986. *The Emergence of Welfare States*. Oxford, UK: Basil Blackwell.

Austin, James E. 2000. *The Collaboration Challenge*. San Francisco: Jossey-Bass.

Barber, Benjamin. 1983. *The Logic and Limits of Trust*. New Brunswick, NJ: Rutgers University Press.

Bardach, Eugene. 1998. *Getting Agencies to Work Together*. Washington, DC: Brookings Institution Press.

Bardach, Eugene, and Cara Lesser. 1996. Accountability in Human Services Collaboratives: For What? For Whom? *Journal of Public Administration Research and Theory* 6 (3): 197–224.

Barnard, Chester. 1938. *The Functions of the Executive*. Cambridge, MA: Harvard University Press.

Behn, Robert D. 2001. *Rethinking Democratic Accountability*. Washington, DC: Brookings Institution Press.

Benkler, Yochai. 2004. Sharing Nicely: On Shareable Goods and the Emergence of Sharing as a Modality in Economic Production. *Yale Law Journal* (November).

Berry, F. S., R. S. Brower, S. O. Choi, W. Xinfang Goa, Jang HeeSoun, Kwon Myungjung, and J. Word. 2004. Three Traditions of Network Research: What the Public Management Research Agenda Can Learn from Other Research Communities. *Public Administration Review* 64 (5): 539–52.

Bozeman, Barry. 1987. *All Organizations are Public: Bridging Public and Private Organizational Theory*. San Francisco: Jossey-Bass.

Braddock, David, and Richard Hemp. 2004. *Developmental Disabilities Services Finding: 2004 Progress Report*. Indianapolis, IN. Report prepared for the Indiana Association of Rehabilitation Facilities, Arc of Indiana, Indiana Governor's Planning Council for People with Disabilities, and Indiana Institute on Disability and Community.

Burt, Ronald S. 1980. Models of Network Structure. *American Review of Sociology* 6 (1): 79–141.

———. 1992. *Structural Holes: The Social Structure of Competition*. Cambridge, MA: Harvard University Press.

———. 2001. Bandwidth and Echo: Trust, Information and Gossip in Social Networks. In *Networks and Markets*, eds. James E. Rauch and Alessandra Casella. New York: Russell Sage Foundation.

Campbell, Andrew, and Michael Gould. 1999. *The Collaborative Enterprise*. Reading, MA: Perseus Books.

Carney, T. F. 1990. *Collaborative Inquiry Methodology*. Windsor, ON: University of Windsor, Division of Instructional Development.

Carrington, Peter J., John Scott, and Stanley Wasserman, eds. 2005. *Models and Methods in Social Network Analysis*. Cambridge: Cambridge University Press.

Castells, Manuel. 1996. *The Rise of the Network Society*. Oxford, UK: Blackwell.

Chisholm, Donald. 1989. *Coordination without Hierarchy: Informal Structures in Multiorganizational Systems*. Berkeley: University of California Press.

Chrislip, David D., and Carl E. Larson. 1994. *Collaborative Leadership*. San Francisco: Jossey-Bass.

Chubb, John E. 1985. The Politicial Economy of Federalism. *American Political Science Review* 79 (December): 994–1015.

Church, Thomas W., and Robert Nakamura. 1993. *Cleaning Up the Mess: Implementation Strategies in Superfund*. Washington, DC: Brookings Institution Press.

Cigler, Beverly. 2001. Multiorganization, Multisector and Multicommunity Organization: Setting the Research Agenda. In *Getting Results through Collaboration*, ed. Myrna Mandell. Westport, CT: Quorum Books.

Clegg, Stewart R. 1990. *Modern Organizations: Organization Studies in the Postmodern World*. London: SAGE.

Clegg, Stewart R., and Cynthia Hardy. 1996. Conclusions: Representation. In *Handbook of Studies*, eds. Stewart R. Clegg, Cynthia Hardy, and Walter R. Nord. London: SAGE.

Collier, David, Jason Seawright, and Henry E. Brady. 2003. Qualitative versus Quantitative: What Might This Distinction Mean? *Qualitative Methods Newsletter* 1 (2): 4–8.

Cross, Rob, Andrew Parker, Laurence Prusak, and Stephen P. Borgatti. 2003. Knowing What We Know: Supporting Knowledge Creation and Sharing in Social Networks. In *Networks in the Knowledge Economy*, eds. Rob Cross, Andrew Parker, and Lisa Sasson. New York: Oxford University Press.

Davenport, Thomas H., and Laurence Prusak. 1998. *Working Knowledge: How Organizations Manage What They Know*. Boston, MA: Harvard Business School Press.

Dexter, Lewis A. 1970. *Elite and Specialized Interviewing*. Evanston, IL: Northwestern University Press.

Drucker, Peter F. 1974. *Management: Tasks, Responsibilities, Practices*. New York: Harper and Row.

———. 1995. *Managing in a Time of Great Change*. New York: Truman Talley Books.

———. 2001. *The Essential Drucker: Selections from the Management Works of Peter F. Drucker*. New York: Harper Collins.

Dundon, Elaine. 2002. *The Seeds of Innovation: Cultivating the Synergy That Fosters Innovation*. New York: AMACOM.

Economist. 2005. Management and IT: The Cart Pulling the Horse. *Economist* (April 9): 53.

Eisenhardt, Kathleen M. 1989. Building Theories from Case Study Research. *Academy of Management Review* 14 (4): 532–50.

Feldman, Martha S. 1989. *Order without Design: Information Production and Policy-Making*. Stanford, CA: Stanford University Press.

———. 1995. *Strategies for Interpreting Qualitative Data*. Thousand Oaks, CA: SAGE.

Ferguson, Ronald F., and Sara E. Stoutland. 1999. Reconceiving the Community Development Field. In *Urban Problems and Community Development*, Ronald F. Ferguson and William T. Dickens. Washington, DC: Brookings.

Finnemore, Martha, and Kathryn Sikkink. 2001. Taking Stock: The Constructivist Research Program in International Relations and Comparative Politics. *Annual Review of Political Science*. Vol. 4. Palo Alto, CA: Annual Reviews.

Flora, Peter, and Arnold Heidenheimer. 1981. *The Development of Welfare States in Europe and America*. New Brunswick, NJ: Transaction Books.

Fountain, Jane E. 1994. Trust as a Basis for Interorganizational Form. Paper presented at conference of Network Analysis and Innovations in Public Programs, University of Wisconsin-Madison.

Franz, Roger, and Alex N. Pattakos. 1996. Economic Growth and Evolution: The Intuitive Connection. In *Intuition at Work*, eds. Roger Franz and Alex N. Pattakos. San Francisco: New Leaders Press.

Frederickson, David G., and H. George Frederickson. 2006. *Measuring the Performance of the Hollow State*. Washington, DC: Georgetown University Press.

Frederickson, H. George. 1997. *The Spirit of Public Administration*. San Francisco: Jossey-Bass.

———. 1999. The Repositioning of American Public Administration. *PS: Political Science and Politics* 32 (4): 701–11.

Galaskiewicz, Joseph, and Akbar Zaheer. 1999. Networks of Competitive Advantage. *Research in the Sociology of Organizations* 16 (1): 237–61.

Gaus, John M., and Leon O. Wolcott. 1940. *Public Administration and the United States Department of Agriculture*. Chicago: Public Administration Service.

Geertz, Clifford. 1973. Thick Description: Toward an Interpretive Theory of Culture. In *The Interpretation of Cultures*, ed. Clifford Geertz. New York: Basic Books.

Glaser, Barney, and Anselm Strauss. 1967. *The Discovery of Grounded Theory*. Chicago: Aldine.

Goggin, Malcolm L. 1986. The "Two Few Cases/Too Many Variables" Problem in Implementation Research. *Western Political Quarterly* 39 (3): 329–47.

Granovetter, Mark S. 1973. The Strength of Weak Ties. *American Journal of Sociology* 78:1360–80.

Gray, Barbara. 1989. *Collaborating: Finding Common Ground for Multiparty Problems*. San Francisco: Jossey-Bass.

Gray, Barbara, and Sonny S. Ariss. 1985. Politics and Strategic Change across Organizational Life Cycles. *Academy of Management Review* 10 (4): 707–23.

Groff, Theodore, R., and Thomas P. Jones. 2003. *Introduction to Knowledge Management*. Amsterdam: Butterworth Heineman.

Guba, Egon G., and Yvonna S. Lincoln. 1981. *Effective Evaluation*. San Francisco: Jossey-Bass.

Gulick, Luther, and Lyndall F. Urwick, eds. 1937. *Papers on the Science of Administration*. New York: Institute of Public Administration.

Hanf, Kenneth, Benny Hjern, and David O. Porter. 1978. Local Networks of Manpower Training in the Federal Republic of Germany and Sweden. In *Interorganizational Policy Making: Limits to Coordination and Central Control*, eds. Kenneth Hanf and Fritz W. Scharpf. London: SAGE Publications.

Harmon, Michael M., and Richard L. Mayer. 1986. *Organization Theory for Public Administration*. Glenview, IL: Scott, Foresman.

Harrison, Bennet, and Marcus Weiss. 1998. *Workforce Development Networks*. Thousand Oaks, CA: SAGE.

Haas, Peter M. 1992. Introduction: Epistemic Communities and International Policy Coordination. *International Organization* 46 (1): 1–35.

Hirst, Paul. 2000. Democracy and Governance. In *Debating Governance*, ed. Jon Pierre. Oxford: Oxford University Press.

Honadle, Beth Walter. 1981. A Capacity-Building Framework: A Search for Concept and Purpose. *Public Administration Review* 41:575–80.

Imperial, Mark. 2004. *Collaboration and Performance Management in Network Settings: Lessons from Three Watershed Governance Efforts*. Washington, DC: IBM Center for the Business of Government.

INARF. 2003. "317 Plan Gets Good Marks from MR/DD Commission." *INARF On-Line* August 29, Indianapolis (www.inarf.org).

Innes, Judith E., and David E. Booher. 1999. Consensus Building and Complex Adaptive Systems: A Framework for Evaluating Collaborative Planning. *Journal of the American Planning Association* 65 (Autumn): 412–23.

Jennings, Edward T., and Jo Ann Ewalt. 1998. Interorganizational Coordination, Administrative Consolidation, and Policy Performance. *Public Administration Review* 58 (July-August): 341–48.

Jennings, Edward T., and Dale Krane. 1994. Coordination and Welfare Reform: The Quest for the Philosopher's Stone. *Public Administration Review* 54 (4): 341–48.

Keating, Michael. 1999. "Regions and International Affairs: Motives, Opportunities and Strategies." *Regional and Federal Studies* 9:1 (Spring): 1–16.

Kelle, Udo, ed. 1995. *Computer-Aided Qualitative Data Analysis.* London: SAGE.

Key, Jr., V. O. 1937. *The Administration of Federal Grants to the States.* Chicago: Public Administration Service.

Kickert, Walter J. M., Erik-Hans Klijn, and Joop F. M. Koppenjan. 1997. Introduction: A Management Perspective on Policy Networks. In *Managing Complex Networks,* eds. Walter J. M. Kickert, Erik-Hans Klijn, and Joop F. M. Koppenjan. London: SAGE.

Kickert, Walter J. M., and Joop F. M. Koppenjan. 1997. Public Management and Network Management: An Overview. In *Managing Complex Networks,* eds. Walter J. M. Kickert, Erik-Hans Klijn, and Joop F. M. Koppenjan. London: SAGE.

KIPDA. 2004. *2005 Work Plan.* Louisville, KY: Kentuckiana Planning and Development Agency.

Klijn, Erik-Hans. 1996. Analyzing and Managing Policy Processes in Complex Networks. *Administration and Society* 28:90–119.

———. 1997. Policy Networks: An Overview. In *Managing Complex Networks,* eds. Walter J. M. Kickert, Hans-Erik Klijn, and Joop F. M. Koppenjan. London: SAGE.

———. 2003a. Networks and Governance: A Perspective on Public Policy and Public Administration. In *Governing Networks,* ed. Ari Salminen. Amsterdam: IUS Press.

———. 2003b. Governing Networks in the Hollow State: Contracting Out, Process Management, or a Combination of the Two? *Public Management Review* 4 (2): 149–65.

Klijn, Erik-Hans, and Joop F. M. Koppenjan. 2000. Public Management and Policy Networks: Foundations of a Network Approach to Governance. *Public Management* 2 (2): 135–58.

———. 2006. Institutional Design: Changing Institutional Features of Networks. *Public Management Review* 8 (1): 141–60.

Kooiman, Jan. 1993. *Modern Governance: New Government-Society Interactions.* London: SAGE.

———. 2003. *Governing as Governance.* London: SAGE.

Koppenjan, Joop F. M., and Erik H. Klijn. 2004. *Managing Uncertainties in Networks.* London: Routledge.

Korfmacher, Katrina Smith. 2000. What's the Point of Partnering? A Case Study of Ecosystem Management in the Darby Creek Watershed. *American Behavioral Scientist* 44 (4): 547–63.

Laumann, Edward O., L. Galaskiewicz, and P. V. Marsden. 1978. Community Structure as Interorganizational Linkages. *Annual Review of Sociology* 4:455–84.

Linden, Russell M. 2002. *Working across Boundaries: Making Collaboration Work in Government and Nonprofit Organizations.* San Francisco: Jossey-Bass.

Lipnack, Jessica, and Jeffrey Stamps. 1994. *The Age of the Network.* New York: John Wiley and Sons.

Loughlin, John. 2000. Regional Autonomy and State Paradigm Shifts. *Regional and Federal Studies* 10 (Summer): 10–34.

Mandell, Myrna P. 1990. Network Management: Strategic Behavior in the Public Sector. In *Strategies for Managing Intergovernmental Policies and Networks*, eds. Robert W. Gage and Myrna P. Mandell. New York: Praeger.

———. 1999. Community Collaborations: Working through Network Structures. *Policy Studies Review* 16 (1): 42–64.

———. 2001. The Impact of Network Structures on Community-Building Efforts: The Los Angeles Round Table for Children Community Studies. In *Getting Results through Collaboration: Networks and Network Structures for Public Policy and Management*, ed. Myrna P. Mandell. Westport, CT: Quorum Books.

Mandell, M. P., and Todd A. Steelman. 2003. Understanding What Can Be Accomplished through Interorganizational Innovations: The Importance of Typologies, Content and Management Strategies. *Public Management Review* 5 (2): 197–224.

Manskopf, Dick. 2000. Darby Partnership.www.bigdarby.org/aHome.htm.

Marshall, Catherine, and Gretchen B. Rossman. 1995. *Designing Qualitative Research*. Thousand Oaks, CA: SAGE.

Maxwell, Joseph A. 1996. *Qualitative Research Design*. Thousand Oaks, CA: SAGE.

McDermott, Richard. 2000. Why Information Technology Inspired but Cannot Deliver Knowledge Management. In *Knowledge and Communities*, eds. Eric L. Lesser, Michael A. Fontaine, and Jason A. Slusher. Boston, MA: Butterworth-Heinemann.

McGuire, Michael. 1999. The "More Means More" Assumption: Congruence vs. Contingency in Local Economic Development Research. *Economic Development Quarterly* 13 (2): 157–71.

———. 2000. Collaborative Policy Making and Administration: The Operational Demands of Local Economic Development. *Economic Development Quarterly* 14:276–91.

———. 2002. Managing Networks: Propositions on What Managers Do and Why They Do It. *Public Administration Review* 62 (5): 426–33.

McMaster, Michael D. 1995. *The Intelligence Advantage: Organizing for Complexity*. London: Knowledge Based Development, Ltd.

Meier, Kenneth J., and Laurence J. O'Toole Jr. 2001. Managerial Strategies and Behavior in Networks: A Model with Evidence from U.S. Public Education. *Journal of Public Administration Research and Theory* 11 (3): 271–93.

———. 2002. Public Management and Organizational Performance. *Journal of Policy Analysis and Management* 23 (1): 31–47.

Metcalfe, Robert. 1996. *The Internet after the Fad*. http://americanhistory.si.edu/csr/comphist/montic/.

Miles, Matthew B., and A. Michael Huberman. 1994. *Qualitative Data Analysis*. 2nd ed. Thousand Oaks, CA: SAGE.

Milward, H. Brinton, and Keith G. Provan. 1998. Principles for Controlling Agents: The Political Economy of Network Structure. *Journal of Public Administration Research and Theory* 8 (2): 203–21.

Milward, H. Brinton, Keith G. Provan, and Barbara A. Else. 1993. What Does the "Hollow State" Look Like? In *Public Management: The State of the Art*, ed. Barry Bozeman. San Francisco: Jossey-Bass.

Mitroff, Ian I., and Harold A. Linstone. 1993. *The Unbounded Mind*. New York: Oxford.

Mohrman, Susan Albers, Ramkrishnan U. Tenkasi, and Allan M. Mohrman Jr. 2003. The Role of Networks in Fundamental Organizational Change: A Grounded Analysis. *Journal of Applied Behavioral Science* 39, no. 3 (September): 301–23.

Moore, Mark H. 1995. *Creating Public Value: Strategic Management in Government.* Cambridge, MA: Harvard University Press.

Nohria, Nitin. 1992. Information and Search in the Creation of New Business Ventures: The Case of the 128 Venture Group. In *Networks and Organizations: Structure, Form, and Action,* eds. Nitin Nohria and Robert Eccles. Boston, MA: Harvard Business School Press.

Ohio Water Development Authority (OWDA). 2002. *Annual Report.* Columbus, OH: Author.

Olshfski, Dorothy, and Lung Teng Hu. 2004. Seeking Knowledge Management in the U.S. Paper presented at Annual Meeting of the American Political Science Association, Chicago, IL.

Osborne, David, and Ted Gaebler. 1992. *Reinventing Government.* Reading, MA: Addison-Wesley.

O'Toole, Laurence J., Jr. 1996. "Hollowing the Infrastructure: Revolving Loan Programs and Network Dynamics in the American States." *Journal of Public Administration Research Theory* 6:225–42.

———. 1997. Treating Networks Seriously: Practical and Research-Based Agendas in Public Administration. *Public Administration Review* 57 (1): 45–52.

O'Toole, Laurence J., Jr., and Kenneth J. Meier. 1996. Hollowing the Infrastructure: Revolving Loan Programs and Network Dynamics in the American States. *Journal of Public Administration Research Theory* 6:225–42.

———. 2004. Public Management in Intergovernmental Networks: Matching Structural Networks and Managerial Networking. *Journal of Public Administration Research and Theory* 14 (4): 469–94.

Pasternack, Bruce A., and Albert Viscio. 1998. *The Centerless Corporation.* New York: Simon and Schuster.

Pattakos, Alex N. 2004. *Prisoners of Our Thoughts: The Work of Victor Frankel.* San Francisco: Barret-Kholer.

Pattakos, Alex N., and Elaine Dundon. 2003. Cultivating Innovation in Government: Oxymoron or Core Competency? *Canadian Government Executive* 10 (3): 14–16.

Patton, Michael Quinn. 2002. *Qualitative Research and Evaluation Methods.* 3rd ed. Thousand Oaks, CA: SAGE.

Pennings, Johannes M. 1981. Strategically Interdependent Organizations. In *Handbook of Organization Design,* eds. Paul Nystrom and William O. Starbuck. New York: Oxford.

Perrow, Charles. 1992. Small Firm Networks. In *Networks and Organizations: Structure, Form, and Action,* eds. Nitin Nohria and Robert G. Eccles. Boston, MA: Harvard Business School Press.

Peters, B. Guy. 1996. *The Future of Governing: Four Emerging Models.* Lawrence: University Press of Kansas.

———. 2000. Globalization, Institutions and Governance. In *Governance in the Twenty-First Century: Revitalizing the Public Service,* eds. B. Guy Peters and Donald J. Savoie. Montreal and Kingston: McGill-Queen's University Press.

Polanyi, Michael. 1962. *Personal Knowledge.* Chicago, IL: University of Chicago Press.

Polanyi, Michael, and Herbert Prosch. 1975. *Meaning.* Chicago: University of Chicago Press.

Powell, Walter W. 1990. Neither Market nor Hierarchy: Network Forms of Organization. In *Research in Organizational Behavior,* eds. Barry Staw and Larry L. Cummings. Greenwich, CT: JAI Press.

Provan, Keith, and H. Brinton Milward. 1991. Institutional-Level Norms and Organizational Involvement in a Service-Implementation Network. *Journal of Public Administration Research and Theory* 1 (4): 391–417.

———. 1995. A Preliminary Theory of Interorganizational Effectiveness: A Comparative Study of Four Community Mental Health Systems. *Administrative Science Quarterly* 40 (1): 1–33.

———. 2001. Do Networks Really Work? A Framework for Evaluating Public Sector Organizational Networks. *Public Administration Review* 61 (4): 414–23.

Radin, Beryl. 2000. Intergovernmental Relationships and the Federal Performance Movement. *Publius: The Journal of Federalism* 30 (Winter/Spring): 143–58.

Radin, Beryl A., Robert Agranoff, Ann O'M. Bowman, Gregory C. Buntz, Steven J. Ott, Barbara S. Romzek, and Robert H. Wilson. 1996. *New Governance for Rural America: Creating Intergovernmental Partnerships.* Lawrence: University Press of Kansas.

Radin, Beryl A., and Willis D. Hawley. 1988. *The Politics of Federal Reorganization: Creating the U.S. Department of Education.* New York: Permagon.

Rauch, James E., and Gary G. Hamilton. 2001. Networks and Markets: Concepts for Bridging Disciplines. In *Networks and Markets,* eds. James E. Rauch and Alessandra Casella. New York: Russell Sage Foundation.

Reich, Robert B. 1991. *The Work of Nations.* New York: Alfred A. Knopf.

Rhodes, R. A. W. 1981. *Control and Power in Central-Local Relations.* Aldershot, UK: Gower.

———. 1997. *Understanding Governance: Policy Networks, Governance, Reflexivity and Accountability.* Buckingham, UK: Open University Press.

Rohr, John A. 1989. *Ethics for Bureaucrats: An Essay on Law and Virtue.* 2nd ed. New York: Marcel Dekker.

Sabel, Charles F. 1992. Studied Trust: Building New Forms of Cooperation in a Volatile Economy. In *Industrial Districts and Local Economic Regeneration,* eds. Werner Sengenberger and Frank Pyke. Geneva: International Institute for Labor Studies.

Saint-Onge, H., and C. Armstrong. 2004. *The Conductive Organization.* Amsterdam: Elsevier.

Salamon, Lester M. 1995. *Partners in Public Service.* Baltimore, MD: Johns Hopkins University Press.

Senge, Peter M. 1990. *The Fifth Discipline: The Art and Practice of the Learning Organization.* New York: Doubleday.

Sharpe, Laurence J. 1986. Intergovernmental Policy-Making: The Limits of Subnational Autonomy. In *Guidance, Control, and Evaluation in the Public Sector,* eds. Franz-Xaver Kaufman, Glandomenico Majone, and Vincent Ostrom. Berlin: Walter de Gruyter.

Sherman, Howard, and Ron Shultz. 1998. *Open Boundaries: Creating Business Innovation through Complexity*. Reading, MA: Perseus Books.

Simon, Herbert A. 1947. *Administrative Behavior*. New York: Free Press.

Smith, Hendrick. 1995. *Rethinking America: Innovative Strategies and Partnerships in Business and Education*. New York: Avon Books.

Smith, Steven Rathgeb, and Michael Lipsky. 1993. *Nonprofits for Hire: The Welfare State in the Age of Contracting*. Cambridge, MA: Harvard University Press.

Stewart, Thomas A. 2001. *The Wealth of Knowledge: Intellectual Capital and the Twenty-First Century Organization*. New York: Doubleday.

Stone, Clarence. 1989. *Regime Politics*. Lawrence: University Press of Kansas.

Stone, Clarence, Kathryn Doherty, Cheryl Jones, and Timothy Ross. 1999. Schools and Disadvantaged Neighborhoods: The Community Development Challenge. In *Urban Problems and Community Development*, eds. Ronald F. Ferguson and William T. Dickens. Washington, DC: Brookings Institution Press.

Strauss, Anselm, and Juliet Corbin. 1998. *Basics of Qualitative Research: Techniques and Procedures for Developing Grounded Theory*. Thousand Oaks, CA: SAGE.

Thomas, Craig W. 2003. *Bureaucratic Landscapes: Interagency Cooperation and the Preservation of Biodiversity*. Cambridge, MA: MIT Press.

Tsoukas, Haridimos. 2005. *Complex Knowledge*. Oxford: Oxford University Press.

Vogel, Ronald K., and Norman Nezelkewicz. 2002. Metropolitan Planning Organizations and the New Regionalism: The Case of Louisville. *Publius: The Journal of Federalism* 32 (1): 107–30.

Waterman, Richard W., and Kenneth J. Meier. 1998. Principal Agent Models: An Expansion. *Journal of Public Administration Research and Theory* 8 (2): 173–202.

Weber, Max. 1947. *Theory of Social and Economic Organization*. Trans. Alan Henderson and Jake Parsons. Glencoe, IL: The Free Press.

Weick, Karl E. 1995. *Sensemaking in Organizations*. Thousand Oaks, CA: SAGE.

Weiner, Myron E. 1990. *Human Services Management*. 2nd ed. Belmont, CA: Wadsworth.

Wendt, Alexander. 1999. *Social Theory of International Relations*. Cambridge: Cambridge University Press.

White, Harrison C. 1992. *Identity and Control: A Structural Theory of Social Action*. Princeton, NJ: Princeton University Press.

Williams, Walter, Richard P. Elmore, and Richard P. Nathan. 1981. *Studying Implementation*. New York: Academic Press.

Wilson, James Q. 1975. The Rise of the Bureaucratic State. *The Public Interest*. 41 (Fall): 77–103.

Windhoff-Héntier, Andriene. 1992. The Internationalization of Domestic Policy: A Motor of Decentralization. Paper prepared for European Consortium for Political Research Joint Sessions, Limerick, Ireland.

Wolcott, Harry F. 1994. *Transforming Qualitative Data*. Thousand Oaks, CA: SAGE.

Wolf, Thomas. 1999. *Managing a Nonprofit Organization in the Twenty-First Century*. New York: Simon and Schuster.

Wondolleck, Julia M., and Steven L. Jaffee. 2000. *Making Collaboration Work: Lessons from Innovation in Natural Resource Management*. Washington, DC: Island Press.

Wright, Deil S. 1988. *Understanding Intergovernmental Relations*. 3rd ed. Belmont, CA: Wadsworth.

Wright, Deil S., and Chung-Lae Cho. 2000. State Administration and Intergovernmental Interdependency: Do National Impacts on State Agencies Contribute to Organizational Turbulence? In *Handbook of State Government Administration*, ed. John J. Gargan. New York: Marcel Dekker.

Wright, Deil S., and Dale Krane. 1998. Intergovernmental Management (IGM). In *International Encyclopedia of Public Policy and Administration*, ed. Jay M. Shafritz. Boulder, CO: Westview.

Yildiz, Mete. 2004. Peeking into the Black Box of E-government Policy-Making: The Case of Turkey. PhD diss., Indiana University-Bloomington.

Yuchtman, E., and Stanley E. Seashore. 1967. A System Resource Approach to Organizational Effectiveness. *American Sociological Review* 32:891–903.

INDEX

Note: Page numbers followed by *t* or *f* indicate tables and figures in the text.

enabling authority and stated rules/
procedures, 13t, 89, 90t, 240; as
information network, 13t; internal/
external communication and
promotion, 102t; knowledge management, 131, 132t, 140, 142t, 149t;
network boundaries, 199t, 206t, 208;
network organization (internal
arrangement and grouping), 112t;
organization affiliation, 16t; partner-
ships/coalitions, 55–56; primary
agencies, 13t, 240; strategic and
planning approaches (strategic tools/
programming), 107, 108t; technology
("broadband project"), 56, 65; types
of actions/decisions made, 46t; values
added, 163, 165t, 169t, 174t, 184–85t
Indiana Rural Council, 13t, 63–64; costs
of networking, 178–79, 181, 182;
description and purpose, 13t, 63–64,
240; as development network, 13t;
elements of network power and
operating authority, 95, 97t, 100;
enabling authority and stated rules/
procedures, 13t, 89, 90t, 240; internal/
external communication and
promotion, 102t, 104; knowledge
management, 133t, 143t, 146, 149t;
network boundaries, 198, 200t, 206t,
208, 218; network organization
(internal arrangement and grouping),
113t, 117, 118; organization affiliation, 16t; primary agencies, 13t, 240;
strategic and planning approaches
(strategic tools/programming), 108t,
110; trust and network cohesion, 122;
types of actions/decisions made, 46t;
values added, 165–66t, 169–70t, 174–
75t, 184–85t, 224
information networks, 10, 10t, 51–57,
64, 65; and authority (network power
and operating authority), 96–99t; and
authority (nonhierarchical), 90–91t,
92; and boundaries of the state/
network, 198, 199t, 205, 206t, 208–10,
211, 218; decision making, 44;

knowledge management, 131, 132–
33t, 138–40, 141–45, 142–44t, 149t;
managerial process, 96–99t, 108–9t;
problem identification and information exchange, 223; speculation on
their avoidance if policy/program or
action-related strategic blueprinting,
65; strategy planning and implementation (strategic tools/programming),
108–9t; trust and the network
structure, 120–21; value adding/
performance issues, 163–64, 165t,
168, 169t, 173, 174t, 183–86, 184–85t.
See also Darby Partnership; Indiana
Economic Development; Lower Platte
Innes, Judith E., 27
interdisciplinarity, 159, 160t
intergovernmental management (IGM),
24, 25
intergovernmental relations (IGR), 24
internal technical influence, and power
in networks, 94–95, 96–99t
intuitional analysis, 38
Iowa Communications, 13t, 78–80, 81; as
action network, 13t; 79–80; criticisms,
80; description and purpose, 13t, 78–
80, 241; elements of network power
and operating authority, 94, 95, 97t;
enabling authority and stated rules/
procedures, 13t, 89, 91t, 92, 241;
internal/external communication and
promotion, 103t, 104; knowledge
management, 136t, 138, 139, 141, 144t,
147, 151t, 226; network boundaries,
202t, 204, 205, 207t, 208, 209, 210,
213, 216; network organization
(internal arrangement and grouping),
115t, 117; organization affiliation, 16t;
primary agencies, 13t, 241; strategic
and planning approaches (strategic
tools/programming), 109t, 110; types
of actions/decisions made, 45t; values
added, 167t, 171t, 173, 176t, 184–85t,
224, 226
Iowa Enterprise, 13t, 64; costs of
networking, 178; description and

network boundaries, 195, 196f, 198, 200t, 206t, 208, 211, 216, 217; network organization (internal arrangement and grouping), 113t, 117, 118; ongoing activities, 58–60; organization affiliation, 17t; partners and primary agencies, 14t, 57–58, 59, 65, 243; strategic and planning approaches (strategic tools/program-ming), 107, 108t; trust and network cohesion, 122; types of actions/decisions made, 47t; values added, 165–66t, 169–70t, 174–75t, 184–85t, 224, 226, 227

Pattakos, Alex N., 155

performance and PMNs: question of whether networks perform, 155–56; social change thesis/problem change thesis, 156. *See also* value adding and network performance

Peters, B. Guy, 5, 211

plan reviews (as PMN action/decision), 45–47t

PMN research concerns (general), 23–33, 232–36; boundaries of govern-ment, 235–36; contextual studies and qualitative data gathering, 236; forces behind the emergence of networks, 23–24; future, 236–37; implementa-tion issues, 33; information and communication technology use, 233; knowledge management/conversion, 29, 232, 236–37; measuring network performance, 30–31; moving into an explanatory framework, 48–49; network cohesion tools, 27–29; network differentiation and agree-ment modes, 234–35; network management, 233; and problem of highly visible programs in most research, 12; the processes of decision making, 26–27; public management research tradition, 25; question of whether network management is different, 26; studies of collaborative management, 9; understanding cross-

organization networks, 237; value adding (and social production model), 234

PMN research (methodology of the present study), 35–50, 247–51; activists/public managers studied, 40–41; case study write-ups, 42, 247; concept formation phase, 39–40, 247; conceptualizing and classifying, 41–42; data gathering, 39–41, 247–48; demonstrating findings/deriving the typology, 43–49, 247–51; deriving the decision question, 43–44, 247–49; document analysis, 40, 251; early field notes and immediate observations in the field, 42, 247; emergence of hypotheses/theoretical statements (and replication logic), 42; first phase (mixed methods), 40, 247; focus on decision-making roles, 36, 43–49; grounded theory approach, 35–39, 41–43, 49–50, 248, 251; nine-level matrix of PMN actions/decisions, 43–48, 45–47t; on-site guided discus-sions, 40; operational sequence of analytical development, 42–43, 247–51; selecting networks/searching for cases, 40, 247; site visits and observa-tion at meetings/conferences, 40, 247; systematic case data analysis mode, 37; theory building, 42. *See also* grounded theory

PMN research (present study), 1–22, 247–51; addressing managers' perspectives, 2; chartered/non-chartered networks, 7–8; defining "cooperation" and collaborative processes, 2–3; defining "networks," 2–3, 7; differences among networks, 1–2, 3–4, 10; eight research questions, 11; features of the PMNs under study, 31; focus of the present study, 9; issue of representativeness, 18; networks and the collaborative enterprise, 1–3; networks' core participants, 12–18, 13–15t; networks' organization